Peter Baines spent twenty-two years with the New South Wales Police leading teams in response to acts of terrorism and natural disasters on a scale not previously seen.

As part of the leadership team that responded to Bali after the bombings in 2002 and then the tsunami of 26 December 2004 in South-East Asia, Peter headed up multiple rotations into Thailand to help in the identification process of those who died.

He was deeply touched by the number of children left orphaned by the disaster and was inspired to set up an organisation that could make a difference. In late 2005, Hands Across the Water was formed.

Peter has received various awards including Australian of the Year New South Wales Finalist for 2010. He was the first New South Wales Police Officer to be awarded the Humanitarian Overseas Service Medal.

He now speaks and advises many corporate organisations, both nationally and internationally, about leadership and corporate social responsibility.

www.handsacrossthewater.org.au
peter@peterbaines.com.au

Part of the proceeds of the sale of this book will go to
Hands Across the Water.

HANDS ACROSS THE WATER

Peter Baines

MACMILLAN

Pan Macmillan Australia

First published 2011 in Macmillan by Pan Macmillan Australia Pty Limited
1 Market Street, Sydney

National Library of Australia
Cataloguing-in-Publication data:

Author: Baines, Peter.
Hands across the water / Peter Baines.

ISBN: 9781742610566 (pbk.)

Baines, Peter.
Hands Across the Water.
Police – Australia – Biography.
Philanthropists – Australia – Biography.
Indian Ocean Tsunami, 2004 – Thailand.
Search and rescue operations – Employees – Health and hygiene.
Orphans – Thailand.
Charities – Australia.
Disaster relief – Thailand.
Tsunami damage – Thailand.
Natural disasters – Social aspects – Thailand.
Natural disasters – Economic aspects – Thailand.

361.763092

Typeset in 11.5/16.5pt Sabon by Post Pre-press Group, Australia
Cover design: Deborah Parry Graphics
Cover photographs courtesy of Will Horner
Printed in Australia by McPherson's Printing Group

Papers used by Pan Macmillan Australia Pty Ltd are natural, recyclable
products made from wood grown in sustainable forests. The
manufacturing processes conform to the environmental regulations of
the country of origin.

To my three kids, Lachlan, Kelsey and Jack, and to Nicole Perry.

Contents

Chapter 1

The Opening

The group that piled into the bus with our Thai driver was in high spirits, as excited as children on Christmas Eve. We were on our way to the orphanage, two and a half hours' drive away from our hotel on the southern tip of Phuket. We were about to see the results of all the hard work we'd put in over the past twelve months. For Gill Williams and myself there was the excitement and anticipation, but there was more too. We shared something the others couldn't.

Gill was the leader of the Thames Valley Police Dive Unit and had spent several months in Thailand following the 2004 Boxing Day tsunami as part of the UK response team. I had met Gilly during my final rotation there in 2005, when she worked as the Body Release Officer at the Disaster Victim Identification site. Gilly is a special person whose heart is matched in size only by the huge smile that fills her entire face. Within hours of meeting her, my team and I had adopted her as an Australian. What set her apart from the rest of us, though, was her posh accent and lily-white skin. I didn't know it then, but I would develop a bond with her as close as a brother or sister.

The rhythmic humming of the bus's engine brought the chatter of the group to a peaceful silence. Travelling with us were Ian, Gill's husband, a couple of their friends from the UK who had joined the fundraising work, and Nicole, my wife. As we left behind the traffic of Phuket and passed over the Sarasong Bridge onto the mainland, there was time for reflection. I was back in Thailand for the first time since my last rotation leading the Australian forensic team in the identification of those who had lost their lives in the tsunami.

In the twelve months since I'd last driven these roads, there had been a great deal of change for me on a personal level, and a complete transformation of the area of Khao Lak, where the orphanage was located. One of the most obvious differences was how green everything was. In the tsunami-affected area the water travelled two kilometres inland and was stopped only by an escarpment. When it hit the escarpment it tore away tonnes and tonnes of soil, which were then deposited in the low-lying areas as the water settled and eventually receded. I was now seeing grass and small trees in place of what had previously been a brown sandy landscape.

It was a surreal experience to turn off the main road and look to my left and see the two-storey orphanage building. It quite literally took my breath away. It stood tall and proud and exuded a sense of strength. It was so different from anything in the surrounding community. It was *Baan Tharn Namchai*, the Home of the Stream of Love, and this was the first time I had set eyes on it.

Gilly and I looked at each other, and without saying a word we spoke thousands. We had shared a journey few could understand, and this was one of the happiest moments on that journey.

Emotions were flooding through me. There was sadness for those who had lost so much. The thousands of people in this southern area of Thailand who had lived a simple coastal life surrounded by family and the waters of the Andaman Sea. Work, if you could call it that, had meant spending their days fishing in the warm clear waters, then spending their evenings with family and friends from their community. No wonder they are such a happy race of people. But life as they knew it was irrevocably changed on that fateful day of 26 December 2004. For those who survived, nothing would ever be the same again. How could it be? Some had lost their entire family; most had lost a loved one, or their home, or their livelihood. Some had lost all three.

I felt sadness for the international tourists who had come to visit Thailand, the land of smiles; for many of them, a smile would take a long time to return. Many left Thailand without their families intact, and sadly many left in a body bag.

There was also a sense of pride and achievement, and a feeling that I had contributed to something pretty special.

Stepping out of the bus I found myself in a sea of smiling young faces. Most of the children had no idea who we were and why so much fuss was being made about a busload of *farang* (white foreigners). None of the thirty-two children spoke any English beyond 'hello', which was about the extent of my Thai, but their smiles and giggles were enough for me to know that Baan Tharn Namchai was a home filled with love.

I felt goose bumps run up my arms. Seeing the building, the kids, the staff, I wondered how I could ever repay this community for all the gifts they had given me, for this rich, warm feeling I was experiencing right now.

Khru Prateep and Khun Rotjana, their hands clasped together in the traditional Thai welcome, walked towards us with happy smiles and eyes filled with deep and honest appreciation.

Khru Prateep is the founder of the Duang Prateep Foundation (DPF), which started working with the poor of the Khlong Toei slums in Bangkok in 1978. She is a tiny lady in stature, but the richness of her soul and her sense of service for others is beyond that of anyone I have met. DPF was the organisation that had responded in the aftermath of the tsunami and was now leading the humanitarian response in this particular area of Thailand.

Khun Rotjana was among the first to leave Bangkok with DPF and travel south to the tsunami-affected area. She immediately set up home for the orphans, becoming a mother to thirty-two additional children.

Getting out of the mini-van and being greeted by Khru Prateep and Khun Rotjana, right there, right then, things changed for me.

Thailand no longer represented the tsunami, it represented Hands Across the Water.

Chapter 2

My Addiction

My addiction started like most other people's.
I was offered that first taste, and in a life-changing moment of excitement and weakness I succumbed. I knew it was going to be no good for me, but I told myself that I'd be fine, that I was stronger than most. I could handle it.

I had seen many others who had fallen by the wayside, their lives ruined by the drug, but I was going to be different.

Why?

Because I knew how to handle it.

Taking that first 'hit' was like something I had never experienced before. I became a ten-foot-tall mountain of muscle, ready for anything and absolutely bulletproof. This drug could propel me through an eighteen-hour day without rest, and keep me going for twenty days straight on one meal a day.

I knew that most of my colleagues were riding high on the drug too. It was like a secret club we all belonged to. We were invincible, unstoppable in our quest.

Then suddenly things changed.

They took the drug away from me. All my colleagues disappeared and I was left to fend for myself again.

I was back home to normal life. My rotation was over. But I was hanging out for more. Seriously, I needed that adrenalin-fuelled lifestyle. I thought I could handle it, but maybe I was wrong. Maybe it would all start to turn ugly, just as they always said it would.

But I didn't care. All I needed was one more hit.

You see, my drug was crisis management.

I recognise now that my dependency on it was a result of continually being confronted by situations that required immediate and often difficult action plans. These situations might be brought about by terrorism, accidents or Mother Nature behaving at her worst.

In the face of injury, death, destruction and grief, I had to quickly recognise what work needed to be done, and how to overcome the seemingly insurmountable challenges that present themselves in these times of crisis.

Once you've worked effectively in these kinds of intense, heightened situations, it's difficult to settle back into ordinary day-to-day work. And once you've been in those situations a few times, it's virtually impossible. It becomes like an addiction; you crave the challenge, the adrenalin, the urgency. Nothing on a smaller scale comes close to matching what you feel in those times.

Although I wasn't aware of it then, it was probably these types of scenarios that attracted me to the New South Wales Police Force in the first place. And in what would prove to be a strange twist it was these adrenalin-fuelled crisis responses that would see me resign from the NSW Police. Not because I couldn't cope with them any more, or because they had worn me out, but because I couldn't face spending the remainder of my career hoping that I would get a chance to respond to something that would top what we had experienced in Thailand.

The impact of these crisis situations was quite profound on all aspects of my life.

I was a nineteen-year-old rookie straight from the Academy when a call came over the police radio requesting we respond to a violent domestic situation. The urgency of a job that is broadcast over the police radio is signified by the sounding of one, two or three beeps which precedes any information. It is done to grab the attention of those listening with one ear to the radio and one ear to a conversation in the station or your partner as you drive on patrol. One beep was never anything to get too excited about – it was sometimes broadcasting a memo '. . . keep a look out for . . .', that type of thing – two beeps meant it was as serious as it gets and three beeps was a signal one, which meant a police officer required immediate and urgent assistance.

In the station at Merrylands, there was one beep over the radio which was quickly followed by a second, and then the radio operator began with 'Twenty six one, twenty six one, report of a violent domestic occurring now . . .' and this was followed by the address. The two beeps gave us an automatic licence to drive fast. Running out the back of the Merrylands Police Station and jumping into a car with my buddy was an awesome first-time experience. My heart was pounding so hard I swear it could have burst right out of my chest, my breathing was fast and shallow and my hands were sweaty. With lights flashing and siren blaring, the passing scenery was a blur. The best part was the knowledge that we weren't going to be caught by the cops. We were the cops!

Turning off the siren as we arrived at the house, things became more intense. The noise of the siren was replaced with the sound of yelling, screaming and crying coming from inside the house. Pushing open the front door my body was certainly in fight or flight mode, but flight wasn't an option. Cowering in the corner of the lounge room was a badly beaten and bleeding woman who at the

husband had sustained a prolonged and violent attack.
their two young children held one another in fear at
the top of the stairs.

The sound of the handcuffs locking around the husband's
wrists and the feel of the cold metal on my hands was reassuring,
not only to the victim of this all too common crime, but also to me
that I had the chance to make a difference in this job.

Although there was the odd moment of excitement, on the
whole Merrylands Police Station back in the eighties was so quiet
it was considered a bit of a retirement home for those who worked
there. Good if you had been doing this job for twenty years, not so
good for young police fresh out of the Academy.

Merrylands sits in between Parramatta to the north, Granville
to the east, Fairfield to the south and Wentworthville to the west.
These areas today are nothing like they were in the late eighties.
Wentworthville only opened from 7 am to 11 pm; after the station closed, Merrylands assumed responsibility for their area. Even
with the addition of Wentworthville, we could go an entire night
shift without the phone ringing, let alone being called to a job!

Working at Merrylands was good for my commitment to police
rugby league, though. The roster sergeant made sure our timetable
fitted around police footy. The day shift would have an early get-
away on game day, and we'd be given an afternoon shift the day
after, to ensure we had time to rest.

As a probationary constable, the nine months between leaving the Academy and then heading back for secondary training
required two things. First, that I not do anything to jeopardise my
right to return to the Academy – no problem, I was on my best
behaviour – and second, that I complete my typing exam at sufficient speed and accuracy – big problem! I had broken my arm
playing police footy and spent twelve weeks in a cast working the
station telephones. Lucky for me the sergeant who was supervising

the typing exam was also a footy fan and, recognising my useful-
ness as a scrum half and the sacrifice I had made in pursuit of the
station's honour, he gave me sufficient latitude to complete the typing exam. His instructions were along the lines of, 'Take as long
as you need and bring it to me when you're finished.' I typed with
one finger; it took me a while but I managed to complete the exam.

As good as Merrylands was for my footy, it wasn't really why
I had joined the force. There had to be more to being a policeman,
I thought. Twenty minutes away was a police station that would
offer a tad more variety and ensure my night shifts were filled with
plenty of excitement. I sought a transfer to Cabramatta. No one
really applied to go to Cabramatta – you were sent there – and the
inspector in charge of transfers actually rang me to ensure this was
a decision I had made of my own free will.

Cabramatta was a very different place then. It's a hub of fantastic Asian food and culture now, but when I was stationed there
you could get a deal of heroin quicker and cheaper than a spring
roll, and murders between the various gangs attracted less attention
than the opening of a Vietnamese bread shop. Still, in busy places
you learn quickly and are exposed to situations you wouldn't normally face. As a uniformed constable I investigated and prepared
briefs for matters I would never get near in other police stations.
The detectives at Cabramatta went from homicide to homicide,
simply not having the time to investigate lesser crimes.

Cabramatta Police Station was located on the corner of Phelps
and Bartley streets, directly in front of the Cabra Vale RSL Club.
Back then the diggers had a nightclub that was the place to be on
a Friday night. At three on a Saturday morning the club would
close and in they would pour. The illuminated Police sign that hung
above the station doorway may as well have read 'If you are drunk,
have lost a shoe or handbag, are sad because your girlfriend kissed
someone else, have spent all your money, need a taxi, need to go

to the toilet, need to vomit or want a friend to talk with or fight – come inside'. Because at 3 am they would arrive, half of them full of bad manners, half thinking that we police really wanted to talk to them about problems that are only important after thirty-seven beers.

My tip to everyone is this. If you happen to find yourself at the front of a police station at three in the morning after five solid hours of drinking, the cops inside don't really want to shoot the breeze with you. Go home and go to bed, go to anyone's home and go to bed, but leave the cops alone; they just want to pass the night as quietly as they can.

After three and a half years at Cabramatta, the dizzy limits came for me one Saturday morning, at 3.30 am, whilst I was entertaining the lunatics coming out of the diggers. The car crew came into the station with one party from a domestic they had been called to. They needed to offload her quickly as they were heading to another job that required their urgent attention.

This woman was deaf and dumb. I have no problems with that. She lived in a lesbian relationship. I have no problems with that. Her partner was also deaf and dumb. I also have no problems with that. They were involved in a domestic with one another, which was on the quiet side of things as far as domestics go. I think it was the sound of breaking plates that prompted the neighbours to call us. I even have no real problem with them trying to sort things out between themselves, if all things are equal, particularly on a Saturday morning between three and five when I am dealing with the witching hour.

The car crew brought her in the front door (why, given the state she was in, she wasn't taken in through the tradesmen's entrance straight to the dock in the charge room, I am not sure) and she was wired. She was going right off, thrashing her arms around and wailing at full volume. Sometimes you can step in and calm the person down if you're new to the fracas and they haven't had time to develop a hatred of you. So, knowing I had a window of thirty seconds before she decided she disliked me, I walked up and calmly tried to reason with her.

As soon as I was within two metres of the woman the car crew gave her a gentle push in my direction and disappeared out the door. With her right hand, she wound up and smacked me across the face. Obviously she didn't need thirty seconds to decide she hated me. Believe it or not I was too tired to get fired up, and so I met this with a 'Come on now, enough of that.' Then she led with her left hand, and this time it was her nails that did the damage, leaving me with a reminder of our delightful meeting for the next couple of days. By this stage I had been struck twice in the face, and some of those standing around wondering whether they should go and order a pizza realised now was as good a time as any and off they went.

Then she hit me again. More scratches down my cheek. By now I was no longer feeling gentlemanly towards her and a few minutes later she was in the dock, the station was empty and I was looking in the vacancies section of the newspaper for a new job.

During my time at Cabramatta I had managed to break my arm twice wrestling with crooks and also had my nose broken in a blue after a pretty wild car chase. Being in the police force is often described as a contact sport and it lived up to that reputation in those days at Cabramatta.

My exit out of the place, and out of uniformed policing, came about when I won a position with what is known now as the Forensic Services Group. I became a crime scene investigator long before the words 'CSI' and 'Miami' were ever used in the same breath.

Chapter 3

Our Time in the Bush

Nicole and I had been married for six months when we decided to move to Tamworth. We had grown up in the western suburbs of Sydney, living only two streets apart. We met at high school, and had been inseparable from then on. When, in April 1992, I was given the opportunity by the Forensic Services Group to move to Tamworth it was a pretty big move for both of us. We had no family there, no friends, no reason to go there other than my work.

The first few months were hard for Nicole. She had left a senior position with a department store chain and moved to country New South Wales pregnant. My job took me away from home frequently, meaning she spent a lot of time alone at home. Thankfully, after Lachie was born, Nicole spent more time out meeting people, and of course we were both besotted with the first of what would ultimately be three healthy children, Lachlan, Kelsey and Jack.

In Tamworth I started studying a Diploma of Applied Science in Forensic Investigation, which was a course designed specifically for crime scene investigators. I was part of the inaugural intake and for the next four years studied part-time, travelling to Sydney and Canberra for four weeks each year for residentials.

Twelve months into this course I found myself sitting in the witness box during a criminal trial into an arson attack. Whilst giving evidence I realised that the defence barrister, a very competent advocate obviously well versed in the law, had very little knowledge about forensic science and in particular fire investigation. Sitting in the box I made a decision then and there to commit myself to law studies so I would have knowledge of both the law and forensics.

Back in Tamworth I outlined this brilliant plan to Nicole. Her response was to suggest that we both do the course, partly because she could see that the study could work for her whilst she was at home with the kids and also because it would give us an experience that we could share. So we duly enrolled in law through the Law Extension Committee of Sydney University. For the next seven years we both studied law part-time. For the first three of the seven I was still studying the forensic science course; thankfully the semesters ran opposite to each other. The downside of this was that for three years I studied, had assignments to write and exams to prepare for, without the joy of a night off. Still, it made the last four years of law studies a walk in the park.

The week of study leading up to our exams in September 1995 was interesting to say the least. Nic was due to give birth the day after the exams. Both of us just prayed the baby wouldn't come early. Thankfully our beautiful daughter Kelsey kindly waited till the exams were over, and then held on for another two weeks just in case.

Looking back on those years when I was studying forensic science and law together, working fulltime in a job that required call-outs at all hours of the day and night, it was only though the support of one another that we were both able to complete our studies years later. I have no hesitation in acknowledging that if Nic hadn't been studying law with me at the same time, the demands would have prevented me successfully completing the course.

Our success in completing the course, without ever failing a subject and receiving numerous distinctions along the way, was not in a shared workload, but in a shared understanding of the workload. Once the kids were in bed, rather than settling down to watch television, we simply settled down to study and read judgements from the High Court.

Jack, our third child and second son, was born on Christmas Eve in 1997, which was less dramatic timing than that of Kelsey, and allowed a smoother transition into life with three kids, fulltime work and study.

Exam times were always the most difficult and as the kids got older it became more and more so. In the weeks leading up to and during exams we would take turns to mind the kids so the other one could study. It certainly was not uncommon to find one of us at McDonald's in the play area or at the local kids' gym with one eye on the kids and the other reading case law.

The forensic work I did at Tamworth encompassed the full range of jobs you might expect a country investigator to be faced with, and plenty that you wouldn't. I investigated my fair share of homicides, suicides, multiple fatality car accidents, sexual assaults and drug busts. And I also investigated some rather unusual cases, including a homicide with an unusual victim. You see, it was a bull!

This stud bull had been deliberately shot in the head and we were requested to extract the projectile for ballistic examination. So how do you break through the skull cavity of a bull when the corpse is located in the middle of a paddock? With an axe, of course. The tools of even the most prepared crime scene investigator wouldn't have been up to this task and it was soon clear to me that a scalpel wasn't going to be sufficient. Dressed in full protective gear, including disposable overalls, gloves, goggles and masks, two of us began taking turns to swing an axe and break through the skull of the bull. It was pretty solid, let me tell you. Half the job done, then it was a matter of finding the projectile. Easy with an X-ray, not so easy in the middle of a paddock. Once we'd broken through the bone we followed the trajectory of the bullet into the soft matter that filled the skull cavity until the projectile was recovered. The bull's days of siring offspring were certainly over.

My work was never run-of-the-mill, but more often than not my attendance at a job meant extreme misfortune for some poor person.

On one particularly hot summer's day in 1999, just prior to Christmas, I was called to the scene of a deceased person at Narrabri, a country town about two hours northwest of Tamworth. The deceased had been found in a house, the result of a 'concern for welfare'. This is always a hint that if there is a body inside the dwelling there is a fair chance it has been there for some time. Normally people will take a couple of days to notice the absence of their neighbour, then a few more as telephone calls go unanswered and mail remains uncollected. The call goes out to the cops then, and forcing open the door will normally be all you need to certify 'life extinct'.

The smell of a decomposing body is not something that is ever forgotten or mistaken. A crime scene investigator needs to be able to deal with it, or to transfer out, because it is part of the job.

I arrived out the front of the house in Narrabri in the late afternoon. The temperature was still in the high thirties and the sun had some way to go before it bid farewell for the day. Parked a little distance from the house was the general duties police truck.

I got out of the airconditioned comfort of my car and there it was.

15

The smell.

This wasn't going to be good.

I walked up to the uniformed police and, after the usual pleasantries, invited them to take me inside and show me what they had found.

'Bugger off, there's no way we're going in that joint,' they said.

They offered to remain outside and man the police radio in the car; the fact that we had portable radios and mobile phones seemed to have been temporarily forgotten.

I was never a big fan of face masks or all the other ways of dealing with smells, such as burning coffee or putting eucalyptus oil under my nose. It either seemed to get in the way, contaminate the scene or prove to be more hassle than it was worth.

This one was going to be different, though. Whatever I had in the car, I put it on.

I walked up to the unremarkable weatherboard cottage and pushed open the front door. As soon as I stepped inside the house I could hear them. The swarm of slow-moving, fat, overfed flies who had been gorging themselves for days and now that a door was open were heading out. I think the smell was too much even for them.

The next sensation was a crunching underfoot. With all the dead flies and the various insect larvae casings it sounded and felt as though I was walking over broken glass.

You don't see that on *CSI Miami*, do you?

Not exactly the sexiest job on the planet. Cleaning the toilets at Flemington after the Melbourne Cup and a bad serving of vindaloo would have been delightful in comparison.

I turned the corner into the lounge room and things just got worse. The deceased was lying on the floor in the corner. This wasn't the bad news, though. The biggest problem was that the floor was polished timber boards. Now, what happens when a body decomposes is that it produces what are called purge fluids. The skin and other tissues start to break down, and the casing holding the body together is no longer intact. Once this casing is breached, fluid will follow the path of gravity and leave the body.

The decomposition here was at its worst; fluid had been leaking from this body for several days and had been dammed by the presence of furniture and floor rugs. I had to walk, or more to the point shuffle, through this fluid to get to the body. The only thing going through my head at this moment was, Baines, whatever you do, DO NOT fall over.

I figured things couldn't get worse. Well, they did.

Present in the body was the largest gathering of maggots I have ever seen in my life. For your normal person that might not amount to many, but trust me, I had seen more than my fair share of the little white suckers and we were not friends.

The maggots had filled the entire chest cavity of the deceased, a man, judging by his shoes, because the decomposition had removed any hint of identity. These maggots were somewhere between fifteen and twenty centimetres deep.

I took the photos and notes I would need, trying to delay the moment I would have to extricate this poor soul from his resting place. I geared up with extra gloves, ensuring there was no flesh of mine exposed, and then went about trying to remove this person. As I leant down I picked up his arm and it felt as slippery as you might imagine. Immediately the maggots, disturbed from their feast, started crawling up my hands. I started to apply pressure to the arm and to pull the deceased from the corner, and I pulled the arm clean off his body. I tried to move his head and the same thing occurred.

I am all for showing dignity to the dead. But there comes a point in time when the practicalities of what you are trying to do overtake the desire to show dignity. I ended up loading the body into a body bag with a shovel, thus was the state of decomposition.

It was all part of the full circle of life and death, but I had happened to catch it at its ugliest point. A few more weeks and the fluid would have drained out and the insects left for newer pastures; it would have been an altogether more palatable investigation – although you might have to take my word on that.

Driving back to Tamworth that night there were numerous times I had to stop the car and get out to check that maggots weren't crawling up my legs.

Chapter 4

Murder at Bakers Creek Falls

My work in forensics was as diverse as any on this planet. However, each job always seemed to start the same way – with a seemingly innocuous phone call.

On this particular occasion Inspector John Bourke of Armidale Police was on the other end of the line.

'Peter, we have a shooting at Bakers Creek Falls near Hillgrove, and I think it's a murder.'

'What makes you think it's a murder, John?' I asked.

'Because the deceased has been shot in the head and we can't find a gun.'

'I'll see you in about an hour.'

I left home as dinner was cooking, something that becomes all too normal in the life of an on-call crime scene investigator. Lachie was still a baby and at that time our only child, so the fact that I was in and out of the house at all times of the day and night was lost on him at that age. He didn't know what was normal or what other dads were doing. Of course the unpredictability of my work was not lost on Nic, though.

Together we had made a decision that our move to Tamworth would enable Nic to stay home and care for the kids. The change in the cost of living allowed us that freedom. Whilst this was a joint decision, it still created hardship for Nic in the many long nights that she would spend at home alone. Looking back, I think the hardest part was that after a day at home with Lachie she would be looking forward to having me home to share a meal with and the parenting duties of nappies, feeding and bathtime. For me to walk in and then have to leave again twenty minutes later, knowing I would be gone for the night and at times days on end, was a disappointment. Whilst Nic had to deal with being left at home alone again, my head was quickly filled with the adrenalin of what was involved in the big jobs.

Nic was always incredibly supportive of me and understood that when I was on call, this was the reality of life. Being called out when I wasn't rostered to be working – that was never quite as well received.

It's the unpredictability of being on call that I think wears on people – both on those being called out and those left at home. There were times when I could be called out multiple times between finishing work at 4 pm and starting again at 7 am the following morning. We normally worked seven days on call at a time, and multiple call-outs in a week were the norm.

Walking out of the front door was similar to crossing over into another dimension. As I would hop into the police car parked at the front of my house and turn the key, I was not only engaging the engine, I was also engaging my head for the job I was heading to. I seemed to be able to compartmentalise the different aspects of my life quite well. When I was home, seldom did I worry or reflect on work, and when I was in work mode, I was focused on what I had to do.

On this occasion I headed north along the New England

Highway, a road that I travelled hundreds of times during my ten years at Tamworth. In fact it was the second time that day I had done the hour-long drive to Armidale.

Earlier in the day I had gone to the scene of a motor vehicle accident in which a triathlete, who had been on a long-distance bike ride for training, was struck from behind by a Japanese tourist and sustained serious injuries. Thankfully, in this instance, the man eventually recovered.

Driving to a job gave me time to ponder what I might be confronted by at the site, and I would begin planning what actions I would take when I got there. I knew that the minute I arrived at a job the crime scene would be under my sole command and how the scene was to be processed was entirely my decision. What would I collect, what would I leave behind? Always at the back of my mind was the knowledge that I would need to be thorough, because at some point in time, maybe even years later, I would more than likely end up in court explaining, sometimes for days on end, what I did or didn't do, and why.

I left the bitumen and started along the gravel roadway to the lookout at Bakers Creek Falls. I pulled up behind a marked police vehicle, and as soon as I got out of the car I was chilled by the bitter early evening air.

This was a typical country crime scene in that it was remote, so there wasn't a lot of panic or activity taking place. By the time I arrived the uniformed police had already been on scene for a couple of hours, and on this occasion they were already wondering how long it would be before they could retreat to somewhere warmer and eat their evening meal, the preparation of which had been so rudely interrupted by the unfortunate events that now required their attention.

Blue and white crime scene tape had been secured between a couple of trees, and I was suitably impressed that even on an outback dirt road about thirty minutes' drive east of Armidale the guys had still thought to put up the crime scene tape.

Inside the tape were two vehicles, a beige Sigma sedan and a brown Holden sedan. The Sigma was located off the road in among some small trees. The second vehicle was parked in a way that would make any onlooker do a double-take. It was as if somebody had just pulled up for a minute, then disappeared into thin air.

I walked over to Inspector Bourke and he gave me a rundown of what they had found on arrival, together with his report on the state of the inquiry at that point in time.

The first thing I always did at a job, regardless of its magnitude or nature, was to walk around the crime scene and try to adjust to the surroundings. I walked to the Sigma sedan; seated in the front driver's seat was the deceased man, later identified as Robert Glenn Miller. Miller's head was tilted backwards; the right side of his face was stained with black powder from a single gunshot fired at close range. He had sustained the fatal wound only in the last few hours. There was a spattering of blood on his face and around the car, but not the amount we sometimes found at a scene like this. This told me that death had occurred very shortly, if not instantly, after the trigger had been pulled and the bullet entered his head.

I wondered, as I always did in these circumstances, what he was thinking when he realised that his life was at an end. Did he scream, did he think of his family, his children, or was he just overcome with sheer panic and terror? During the next several hours I would learn a lot about Mr Miller, but we will never know what his last thoughts were.

From the way he was sitting in his car with a half-drunk can of beer between his legs, I guessed that whatever had happened to him had occurred very quickly. I was intrigued by the location of his vehicle, and an examination of the tyre marks on the soil roadway showed the direction in which the vehicle had been travelling.

An examination of the bonnet located latent finger and hand-prints on the vehicle. Two sets of handprints were developed at the scene in the cold and dark of the night, and would provide the fingerprint experts with all the information they would need to identify the offenders once they were in front of their computer screens back at the office. They showed that the vehicle had been pushed from the front to where it now rested.

After examining the rear of the vehicle it became clear why they had pushed the vehicle only this distance from the roadway. A small sapling with a trunk around the same diameter as a person's arm had prevented the vehicle disappearing into the gorge below. They had pushed the vehicle backwards and it had collided with this tree.

I am still convinced today that this sapling inadvertently resulted in a number of lives being spared, because if this vehicle had gone into the gorge below it would have been many days before it was found, such was the density and remoteness of the area. Without this crime coming so quickly to police attention, it's not a long stretch of the bow to think others who got in the killers' way would have suffered a similar fate to Robert Miller.

The examination of the vehicle and the immediate area continued into the freezing night. The second vehicle was examined and we managed to ascertain that this had been driven by the crooks. Disturbingly, we discovered in the boot several photo albums containing pornographic images of young children. Finding this evidence gave us all more impetus to find the lowlifes who had committed this crime.

So, if this was their vehicle, in whose vehicle had they left the scene? Had there been multiple offenders driving in separate cars? And if so, why had they decided to leave this vehicle behind?

I decided to increase the circumference of my search and started down the stone pathway towards the lookout wall, for no reason other than it seemed the most obvious place to search. There I found what appeared to be a blood spot on the ground. I continued walking towards the lookout and found another spot of blood. From the colour of the blood it was obvious that it had been left recently; however, its presence was somewhat perplexing. Whose blood was it, and how had it got there, some fifty metres from the vehicle?

I was confident, based upon the distribution and velocity of the blood spatter, that Miller had been shot inside his vehicle and had not been moved from the driver's seat, so I focused on the walkway. A further ten metres on I found more blood spots, larger this time. They were consistent in appearance and age with the other spots, but were now increasing in volume. The connection was obvious: the blood was coming from the same person.

I continued my torchlit progress towards the stone wall, finding even more blood spots. It was then I found something that made my stomach turn.

My mouth went dry.

It was that feeling you get when all of a sudden you realise something serious has taken place. My heart started to pound, my pupils were straining against the growing darkness to concentrate on what was in front of me. What I found in the sand were four intermittent gouge marks, the appearance of which was unmistakable. The marks had been left by somebody who was being dragged face down by their feet. The finger marks represented that person's attempt to hold on to something, anything, which might enable them to fight for what must have been frighteningly obvious was their life.

We had another victim.

I walked to the edge of the lookout and peered into the gorge below.

There are few occasions when you are confronted with absolute total darkness, when there is no ambient light and no moon. It's the kind of darkness that has a thick feel to it, as though you could almost touch it. It was one of those nights and all my torch could illuminate was the tops of the gum trees moving in the cold April wind.

I returned to the roadway and told the few guys that remained in the freezing temperatures what I had found. They didn't need to be told the obvious – that another body was located on the other side of the stone wall, within the gorge.

We were now investigating a double homicide.

We needed to enter the gorge and attempt to locate the body. The harshness of the terrain meant that this was going to be extremely difficult. Assistance was called for from the local State Emergency Service and from members of the rock-climbing club from the nearby University of New England. Calling in the local rock climbers was not something that was a common occurrence, but we weren't dealing with something that was common here. We had a body located at the base of the cliff and getting down to it safely in the middle of the night was a necessity. In the metropolitan area this would have been a job for the police rescue crew, but we were a day's drive from the closest police rescue group and this was the best solution.

A short time later the numbers at the top of the lookout had swelled. It was imperative that we find the poor soul who had been thrown from the lookout wall, firstly to ascertain that the victim was indeed deceased, and also because the sooner we established his identity, the sooner we would be able to identify the vehicle in which the offenders had left the scene.

I started down into the gorge in the company of one of the members of the rock-climbing club. Due to the very real danger of walking down into a gorge at night-time, the search party was limited to the two of us. We carefully made our way towards the area where we estimated the body was most likely to have landed. The terrain was incredibly steep and each step was taken cautiously and with great trepidation.

Within a couple of hours we had found the body of the second victim, a male Caucasian soon to be identified as fifty-year-old Anthony Ernest Percival. The body had sustained multiple injuries, including abrasions, lacerations and, all too apparent, broken limbs. Located at the end of his nose was a small bullet wound. Looking closely I realised that this had not been a fatal wound. I knew from the finger marks in the sand above us that this man had had considerable time to contemplate his last moments. I felt pity for him, for the way he had died and the horror he had faced in his last moments.

I was able to recover the wallet and identification from the deceased, and I communicated this back to the rest of the team via police radio so that the search for the offenders could begin immediately. It was apparent that the offenders were well armed and highly dangerous. Two different firearms had been used to execute the two victims: Miller had been shot at close range with a .410 shotgun, whilst Percival had been shot with a .22.

The recovery of the body was a lengthy and difficult process. A Stokes litter cage was lowered over the edge of the cliff and then, after the body had been secured to it, was manually pulled from the gorge to the top of the lookout. It was a painstakingly slow job and it wasn't completed until the chilly early hours of the following morning.

Suddenly, now that the body had been brought to the surface and conveyed to Armidale Hospital, the place was quiet again. There were still many more long hours of work required to process and record the crime scene, but that would happen tomorrow, in daylight. There were only three of us left at the scene now: Sergeant Cec Noakes, Senior Constable Graham Ridley, both from

Armidale Police Station, and myself. None of us could sleep, and as the darkness started to give way to the first glimpses of day, a discussion ensued between us about the events of the previous day and the circumstances in which the deceased had been thrown from the cliff top.

We returned to the lookout to survey the scene in daylight, and as I peered down to where we had found Percival's body only hours before, I could hardly believe my eyes.

There was the unmistakable shape of another body!

My first thought was that I simply couldn't believe, after having spent so many hours in that same location, we had not seen the third victim of this atrocious crime.

Graham made the call back to Armidale advising of the discovery of yet another victim. By this time the offenders and the description of the vehicle they were driving had been circulated and an extensive search was being conducted. It wasn't long before the vehicle had been spotted by police near the township of Bendemeer, about seventy kilometres south of Armidale. The speeding vehicle was pursued and lost several times that morning in chases across the New England tablelands.

Whilst all this was unfolding I found myself sitting once again on the side of the cliff with yet another lifeless body, that of fifty-one-year-old Gordon Geoffrey Currell. I sincerely hoped his would be the last.

At this stage of the investigation we had helicopter support from the Police Air Wing. The pilot was manoeuvring into position so that he could lower a winch to remove the deceased from the gorge, saving us many hours of back-breaking work. Just as we were ready to secure the winch the chopper banked sharply to the right and disappeared. They had left to assist the ground crew in their pursuit of the offenders, obviously a job with a much higher priority than ours.

The offenders were eventually pursued to a homestead at Kangi, where a lengthy and dramatic siege involving a large contingent of heavily armed police ensued. It unfolded that the vehicle had contained three men who were to later be identified as Leonard Leadbeater, Robert Steele and Raymond Bassett. Not surprisingly, the siege became the lead story for the six o'clock news, helped by the media themselves, who instead of just reporting the matter had become involved in the complexities of the negotiations. Media personality Mike Willesee had been talking live on air to occupants of the house, who were being held hostage by the offenders, and a helicopter carrying reporter Mike Munro was flying within the air space, now under the control of Polair, in an attempt to get footage of the siege premises.

The siege unfolded over the next twenty-seven hours, with first the surrender of Bassett, who was considered to be a follower of the other two offenders, the ringleader being Leadbeater. Both Leadbeater and Steele described themselves during telephone conversations with the media as 'psychopaths' and 'sociopaths' who had 'homicidal and suicidal urges'.

The following morning Steele would walk from the homestead into the custody of police without further incident.

At their trial it became clear that Bassett and Steele had fallen under the influence of Leadbeater and the three of them saw themselves as some sort of Kelly gang, not the murderous, cold-blooded trio they actually were. I can only surmise as to why the three victims were murdered at the top of Bakers Creek Falls that night. It seems it was for no other reason than they were at the wrong place at the wrong time. Gordon Currell and Anthony Percival may have been murdered and thrown over the cliff because Leadbeater had decided he wanted their car and didn't want to leave any witnesses. Perhaps Robert Miller drove upon the scene of the crime at some point when his two work colleagues were being executed.

Whilst the offenders didn't leave any living witnesses at Bakers Creek Falls that night, they left ample forensic evidence which would stand as a reliable witness come trial.

Leadbeater had made threats throughout the ordeal that he would not be taken alive, and that police would have to kill him. On air he said: 'I don't kill people under twelve . . . I'd rather be down in South Australia killing cops. I ain't going out without a fight. I'm going to make sure they kill me.'

The forty-one-year-old died, as the State Coroner would ultimately find, by a self-inflicted gunshot wound to the head. He shot himself just before dawn. It was a predictable end for a coward who had been a sexual predator of young children and a brutal murderer of unarmed, innocent people.

Steele, aged twenty-two, and Bassett, twenty-five, both pleaded guilty to the multiple homicides at Bakers Creek Lookout. Although not brought to trial, they were strongly suspected of two other homicides, including a fourteen-year-old pregnant girl whose charred remains were found on a southern Queensland farm, and a helicopter pilot at Mount Isa in western Queensland.

Both were incarcerated for lengthy periods.

Steele hanged himself in prison in 1997.

Chapter 5

Marlene

'Death, taxes and childbirth! There's never a convenient time for them.'

So declared Margaret Mitchell in her epic novel *Gone With the Wind* and I believe I know what she meant when writing those words.

As selfish as this may sound, it seems to me that big jobs always occur at a time that is the least convenient. This is an insensitive thing to say, perhaps, because for me a 'big job' ultimately sees the loss of somebody's life and, more often than not, the loss of multiple lives.

And this was the case on a Friday afternoon in September 2001 when I received a call summoning me to Tenterfield, a town that sits on the border of New South Wales and Queensland. The inconvenience for me in this instance was that it was my day off and I was at home looking after the kids. Travelling to Tenterfield, a three-hour drive, didn't excite me one little bit.

The reason I was called that afternoon was that a woman named Marlene Prior had failed to arrive at work on that morning.

That in itself wasn't of much significance, but what had started alarm bells ringing at her workplace was that, although estranged from him, she was married to a man with a history of violence, and it was most uncommon for her not to arrive for work without a call explaining her absence. Her work colleagues were aware she had begun a relationship with another man, which had escalated her husband's aggressive behaviour.

Marlene lived with her nine-year-old son and had been separated from her husband, Raymond John Prior, for around three months. Raymond Prior now lived at Lismore, approximately two hours' drive east of Tenterfield. When he visited his son he would stay in a caravan in the backyard of Marlene's house.

On the morning that Marlene failed to arrive at work, her workmates were so concerned that they immediately notified the local police, and Detective Steve Clark from Inverell Police Station was called in to assist. One of the first things the police did was to check that Marlene's son was safe and well. Thankfully he was, and had arrived at school as usual.

The local uniformed police then went out to Marlene's house and there they found a bloodstained face washer at the end of the bed in the main bedroom, but no sign of Marlene. Not exactly a smoking gun, but this was enough to get me into the car and onto the New England Highway.

The cops quickly made the decision that there was value in having a conversation with Raymond Prior and invited him to attend the Tenterfield Police Station to 'assist' with their initial investigation. Although he stated he was about to leave to return to Lismore, Prior consented to attend, and drove his own vehicle to the station, knowing that he could leave at any time.

After Prior had admitted that he and Marlene had argued the previous evening ('I want to be up front about that,' he said), Detective Clark thought it would be prudent to record Prior's version of events; however, the ERISP (Electronically Recorded Interview with Suspected Persons) technology at Tenterfield was not working. Detective Clark then made a request to the Glen Innes station regarding their portable ERISP machine, but as luck would have it, this wasn't operating properly either! He then managed to source the equipment required from Armidale, but had to wait for it to arrive.

After waiting a while, Prior, on the premise of being hungry and wanting to get a meal, walked out of the Tenterfield Police Station with Detective Steve Clark's consent. Outside, he turned left and hitchhiked in that general direction for a couple of hours until he hit the coast!

Steve was waiting for me at the front door of the police station. He had the pained look of a law officer who has just let a murderer walk free. I couldn't help but bring that to his attention. My comments only added to his feeling of anxiety because as a relatively junior detective who is leading a potential homicide investigation for the first time, he really didn't want to start his brief with, 'Well, you see, I had the suspect here, but I let him leave to get lunch and he never came back.'

Whilst it would have been wrong of us to miss this opportunity to take the mickey out of Steve, particularly as this was his first homicide investigation, in reality there wasn't a lot he could have done, given the information he had to hand and the resources available to him. Perhaps he could have arranged for Prior to have lunch delivered to him, but from a point of law, the moment a person believes, on reasonable grounds, that their liberty has been removed and they are no longer free to leave, then regardless of what the police say, that person is for all intents and purposes under arrest. And at this point in time Steve didn't have anywhere near sufficient information to hold Prior against his will. All that was known was that Marlene still had not fronted at her workplace and there was a bloodstained face washer on the end of her bed.

After a little more ribbing to assist Steve to see the error of his ways, I drove the short distance to Marlene Prior's house and was greeted by the uniformed police who were performing the most mind-numbing of all police duties – guarding a crime scene. The only time it gets worse for these officers is when the forensic specialists have left the premises for sleep and they must remain, usually sitting in the police vehicle out the front of the house, alone, cold, bored, hungry and tired.

Inside the weatherboard house there were no obvious signs of violence, but it did have that feel about it. Gut feelings count for a lot in police work. Standing alone in the still, quiet surroundings of a major crime scene, the air around you feels almost palpable. You literally feel the hair on the back of your neck standing up.

I spent the first thirty minutes or so wandering through the house just looking at what items lay about. I found toys in the second bedroom and dishes on the kitchen sink. I found a handbag on the main bed and a second bloodstained face washer on the slow combustion stove in the lounge room. Now there were some mounting reasons for that feeling of disquiet.

You might be able to explain one bloodstained face washer in a bedroom that has an en suite attached, but I had trouble with a second bloodstained washer at the other end of the house. Also, to my knowledge, not too many women leave the house without their handbag or purse.

I looked closely at the second washer; it was covered in blood that had been diluted, probably with water, so it wasn't likely the washer had been used to wipe up a fresh bloodstain. Tenterfield in September can be cold and it was an absolutely freezing evening, so the presence of the face washer on top of the combustion stove led me to believe that the fire had not been alight since the washer had been placed there. Given the cold, if somebody had been in the house last night, they would probably have had the fire roaring.

My instincts at this point in time were telling me Marlene had become a victim of crime and that Raymond Prior had skipped town because he had a fair degree of knowledge of what that crime had entailed. We now needed actual evidence, as courts are not too keen on police officers getting into the witness box and saying, 'You'll just have to believe me – I had a feeling in my gut!'

I returned to the main bedroom, as I had noticed a number of unusual things in there. There was the handbag lying on the bed, and the fact that the bed was covered with blankets but no sheets. There was the bloodstained washer, and on the head of the bed were what at first appeared to be small drops of blood. As I got closer I could actually see a significant amount of blood. It wasn't a massive quantity but it was a blood distribution pattern that indicated a significant assault could have occurred in which the victim sustained repeated blows.

The more I looked, the more blood I found, and what also became very obvious was that somebody had attempted to clean up the blood. This explained the bloodstained washers. I gave Steve Clark a call and confirmed his suspicions. The fact that this evidence had come to light changed the mindset of all those involved in the investigation.

I went about recording the scene in the usual manner and started to process the evidence. It was clear to me that this was going to be a prolonged investigation and not something that would be wrapped up in the one night. The first time I looked at my watch after having contacted Steve Clark I noticed the light of a new day filter into the room. It was just after 5 am and I had been working nonstop since arriving many hours previously. By this stage I was tired, hungry and cold. I always found when I was working through the night that the coldest part of the day was first thing in the morning. It was as though the coldness of the morning served to keep you awake as fatigue started to make itself felt.

Knowing there was still much to do, I decided to leave the house and check into a hotel where I could grab a couple of hours' sleep, shower and come back refreshed to start again. I woke up later that morning and rolled over to look at my phone, hoping that I had slept through the call advising me Marlene had been found safe and well. This call never came.

At the morning briefing the number of investigative staff had increased and Steve was looking slightly older than he had yesterday. We were now confident Raymond Prior was heavily involved in, if not solely responsible for, Marlene's disappearance.

At the crime scene I began an examination of the exterior of the premises, particularly the many sheds that were dotted about on this large block of land. While searching the rear sheds I wasn't looking for evidence so much as searching for Marlene's body. Each shed door I opened, each corner I peered into, I wondered if I would find her body. With each door I opened I had the eerie sensation that her body would fall onto me. I searched the vehicles that were at the rear of the land, and again, opening each boot, I wondered if I would discover her beaten and lifeless body. I inspected the caravan Prior used when he visited the house, but found nothing remarkable.

I left the scene to conduct an examination on the vehicle our suspect had left behind in his hasty exit from the police station. Prior's car was a white sedan and every foot well of the car and the boot was filled with an incredible amount of rubbish. At this point in time I had no idea what I was looking for. We had no victim, no offender, no weapon and no knowledge of the degree of injury the victim may have sustained.

As I painstakingly searched through the car, first photographing and then documenting every piece of rubbish within, I found some items I thought might be of greater value than others. As it would turn out, some were and some weren't. The things that would turn out to be of value included a roll of grey duct tape, some cable ties and a pair of King Gee trousers. There was nothing about the roll of duct tape that hinted at its significance, just one of those gut feelings again when you think, *I might just collect that.*

Examining the exterior of the car I found what appeared to be a small bloodstain on the rear driver's door handle. The colour of the stain certainly suggested it was blood, and the location of it was consistent with someone opening the car with blood on their hands. But the quantity of blood proved somewhat of a dilemma.

One of the techniques we had available to us at that time for identifying blood involved both presumptive and confirmatory testing. A presumptive test is something forensic investigators will use in the field to help them decide what samples to collect. They are normally very sensitive but not specific. So we can conduct a presumptive test for blood and get a positive result; however, a positive result is only for the possible presence of blood, and by the very nature of a presumptive test it will also return false positives. So while we might get a catalytic change that could be reacting to blood, it could be reacting to rust, a vegetable product or anything else for that matter. The real value of a presumptive test, though, is that it allows us to cull or collect samples with a degree of intelligence.

The small size of the sample on the door handle meant that if I collected it and submitted it for analysis at the forensic labs in Sydney I might not get a result at all. However, in conducting a presumptive test using Hemastix I would get a result but it would only be an indicator of the possible presence of blood, and in obtaining this sample I would in fact consume most of the sample to get the result. Any such result at this time would only tell me that it was possibly blood. It would not tell me whose blood it was, who put it there or even if it was indeed human blood.

In the end I decided that the fact there was blood on this vehicle was sufficient reason to justify my sampling the stain. I watched as the small pad of Hemastix, which was about a quarter of the size of a small fingernail, changed to green. Not only did it change to green but it did so rapidly. This is what you hope to see if you suspect blood is present.

The blue King Gee trousers I found inside the vehicle had dirt patches on the knees and small dark spots on the groin area. This was possibly the most significant find I had made during the examination of the car, which had now lasted several hours. Nothing ever did happen in reality quite as quickly as it does on *CSI Miami*.

My examination of the vehicle and its contents continued for the remainder of the day, then that night I travelled back to Tamworth to attend a ball at my kids' school. This contradiction in my life will remain with me forever. For over twenty-four hours I had been in a blood-spattered room, engaged in the investigation of a suspected homicide, wearing disposable overalls, gloves, booties and a mask to prevent cross-contamination, yet now I was about to change into a black suit and tie to go and drink, dance and laugh with a group of parents from my kids' school.

For a couple of hours I engaged in conversation that had nothing to do with what was really occupying my mind, which was the disappearance of Marlene Prior. All the time I was thinking, *Have I overlooked something? How did Marlene die and where is her body?* I tried to be an engaging and attentive husband. But I couldn't escape what I was in the middle of.

I think, well I certainly thought, that I was good at keeping the different parts of my life separate and not letting them transgress into one another. This job was different. I felt that the burden of the investigation sat quite heavily on the forensic interpretation of the scene and as the lead forensic investigator I felt that weight squarely on my shoulders.

I returned to Tenterfield the day after the ball with some of my work colleagues, Detective Senior Constable Greg Carnell from the Tamworth Crime Scene Section and Detective Senior Constable Greg Cook from the Inverell Crime Scene Section. We had a long day ahead of us, spent entirely within the confines of the main bedroom.

We measured and plotted every blood spot we could find. These spots were located on the walls, the furniture and the ceiling. It was our role to plot them onto a scaled plan and then measure the width and length of each spot. Using trigonometry these measurements would give us the angle at which they had hit each surface where they came to rest. Affixing a string line at the angle the blood spot had hit the surface, we then took the line to a fixed point. We repeated this many times over and were eventually, after a long and painstaking process, able to construct a picture of the point from which the blood had originated.

As we worked there was plenty of banter between us, much of it about the outcome of the football grand final from the previous day. There is an absolute need for those working in the forensics area to have a sense of humour; it is our way of coping and without it our jobs would be even more difficult to deal with.

Our laughter, however, came to an abrupt end when we stood back to survey the work we had done. Standing at the foot of the bed and looking at what we had spent hours creating, we could now observe a pattern of string lines that intersected at the point where Marlene had probably taken her last breath. The point of convergence was the head of the bed on the right-hand side, and this is where we suspected she lay during the attack. Sadly, it was clear to us now that it had been a savage and frenzied attack as there was blood on the roof and the three surrounding walls. We could only hope that Marlene's son, who had been in bed only metres away when this attack had taken place, had slept through that terrible night, because surely that would create nightmares no child should ever experience.

Some four days after first arriving at the scene, it was almost time to leave. Whilst we now knew a lot more than we had that first day, we still did not have a body, we still did not have a weapon, and we still did not have Raymond Prior in custody – this point alone was causing Steve Clark to age almost by the hour. That humour was now at Steve's expense, and we didn't miss an opportunity to remind him that he had had Raymond Prior in his custody but had let him walk away.

Before we could leave Tenterfield we needed to do a chemical enhancement of the scene to identify any evidence that might still be present after the clean-up attempts that had been undertaken. Luminol is a chemical that is sprayed around a room from which all light has been blocked, and if blood is present a reaction known as chemiluminescence will occur. A brilliant blue light will be given off at the exact location of any blood that might be present. Like Hemastix, Luminol is a presumptive test, therefore the positive reaction during an examination does not mean conclusively that blood is present.

My Luminol examination of the en suite bathroom returned a strong positive reaction. It was my opinion that Raymond Prior had gone about washing the blood off himself there after the assault.

There was now little else we could do. As I drove home the self-doubt began, as it always did after I'd left a crime scene. Had I taken enough photos? Had I collected enough samples? In most cases these doubts would linger until I had finished giving evidence at trial, because no matter how thorough we were, the defence lawyers would almost always find something in a photo or report that would lead to an attempt to show we had missed something at the scene. This was done to portray our evidence as unreliable.

My desk back at Tamworth CSS the following morning was a mountain of brown paper evidence bags. I had my day planned. I was required to provide the investigators with a situation report of what I had done and what my initial opinions were regarding the interpretation of the evidence from the scene.

By mid-morning, however, I received a call from Detective Senior Constable Greg Carnell. 'Bainsey, can you come out and give me a hand, we have a couple of bodies here.'

I couldn't believe what I was hearing. This was Tamworth. Once a year thousands of visitors arrived for the music festival wearing cowboy boots, belts and hats. We knew who the visitors were because none of the locals ever wore gear like that! These visitors would eat, drink, play music and then leave, and that was about the extent of the excitement around Tamworth. Records will show that in the year 2000 I led forensic investigations into twelve homicides.

What we had now was a suspected murder-suicide that had occurred on the back of a soured relationship. The fact is, I can't remember investigating a murder-suicide that wasn't the result of a relationship breakdown.

I had only been at this crime scene for an hour when a uniformed policeman arrived to tell me I was required to ring police radio immediately. I suggested that as this was Greg's case he should be the one to call them. The reply was, 'It's not Greg they want. You have been asked specifically to contact police radio BY PHONE!'

The importance of those last two words meant that the news wasn't suitable to be broadcast over police radio. Immediately my heart leapt into my throat – maybe there was something wrong at home.

To my relief the message was related to the homicide at Tenter-field. Raymond John Prior was now in custody, and he had admitted to knowing the whereabouts of Marlene Prior's body.

I left Greg in the house with the two deceased and, on the way to the office to gather the extra supplies needed to conduct the excavation of a gravesite, I received a call from Steve Clark, who sounded far happier than when we last spoke. 'We've got him, Bainsey,' he said. 'We've got him. He's in the dock at Lismore Police Station. He turned up with his mouthpiece' – his solicitor – 'and handed us a one-page statement. It details the location of Marlene's body but he won't say anything else.'

I couldn't help but smile as I had visions of Steve walking around the police station high-fiving anyone who came close to him.

I called Nicole to tell her of the latest developments and that it was highly unlikely I would be home for my son's basketball game the following evening. Outwardly she expressed to me that her only concern was that I travel safely. I am sure, though, that she, along with Lachie, whose basketball game I would miss, were disappointed once again that I would not be there, unlike the other dads.

Three hours later I was at the gravesite. It was located near a river crossing about fifteen kilometres south of Tenterfield. A branch from a large gum tree above lay over the burial site, and on close inspection it was apparent there had been a disturbance to the ground area below. It appeared that after the body had been buried, clumps of dirt had been replanted in the ground and leaf litter was then strewn over the surface. The replanted grass had not lost its colour; the disturbed soil had lost its moisture so that it no longer appeared fresh, and of course insufficient time had lapsed for any soil suppression or sinking of the site to occur. I learnt later that the State Emergency Services had in fact searched this immediate area on the Saturday after the homicide took place, but had, understandably, failed to locate the site. Prior had gone to great lengths to conceal the grave.

The technique used in the excavation of a gravesite is called the pedestal effect. The method of operation is to dig around the exterior of the gravesite in order to find the perimeter, thus ensuring the capture of any evidence. The extremities of the site are measured and plotted with string lines to allow accurate measurement and to ensure the entire site is triangulated from fixed coordinates, allowing a return to the position if required. It also allows for preparation of extremely accurate scaled plans required for any ensuing trial.

This work is meticulous, but necessary. It must always appear to uniformed police that we in forensics merely fluff around until the actual excavation commences.

Once the first blow of the shovel strikes the dirt, the digging continues until the extremity of the site is reached. Then big shovels are replaced with smaller ones, and the soil being removed is placed onto a plastic sheet so that it can be sieved for evidence.

The excavation moved at a monotonously slow pace well into the night until the first glimpse of a blue tarpaulin was revealed. The removal of soil continued until the fully shrouded body was exposed. The tarpaulin had been secured so tightly that the features of a female were quite distinct. It was almost a second skin, tied around the ankles, knees, wrists and neck with grey duct tape.

The body was then removed from the grave, and under it we found a number of bloodstained sheets, pillowcases and blankets.

To find out who was inside the tarpaulin and to begin an initial examination, we needed to remove the tarpaulin, but it was so tightly wrapped I had to use a scalpel to access the body. I had no intention of completely unwrapping the body as this would risk losing vital evidence.

It was no surprise to discover the body was Marlene Prior's, but

I was surprised by the lack of external injuries. There was blood smeared across her face and body, but after the extensive blood distribution evidence back at Marlene's house, I had expected there to be visual evidence of severe injury.

I lifted her head with my hands, feeling for palpable skull fractures. Although this is not a scientific method, it gives you a good idea whether there are any fractures, and I could feel none.

The body was then transported from its riverside grave to the Glebe morgue for a post-mortem examination, and that night Raymond John Prior was officially charged with the murder of his wife.

A lot of the evidence I had collected from Prior's vehicle at Tenterfield could now be examined in a new light. We knew now that the duct tape, together with some cable ties that matched those found beside a tree at the burial site, was of great significance. The King Gee trousers with patches of dirt on both knees were consistent with Prior kneeling at the site in the freshly dug soil. Further forensic testing proved that the blood on the front of these trousers was Marlene's. Not only was blood found outside the trousers, but it was also found inside both pockets, suggesting that Prior had stuck his bloodstained hands in his pockets. Closed circuit television coverage from a service station showed him wearing these trousers with discolouration on the knees at six in the morning when returning to Tenterfield after having spent the night burying the body.

The most compelling piece of evidence we had obtained proved to be the duct tape. I was confident that I could match this tape to the tape that had been used to firstly bind Marlene's feet and hands, and then to secure her body in the tarpaulin. After many sticky and painstaking hours unrolling this adhesive, we were able to match the end of the tape found in the car to one of the pieces taken from the tarpaulin. Now all we needed to do was to link the roll to Raymond Prior – finding it in a vehicle he was driving was not enough. To our delight, fingerprint expert Detective Senior Constable Ian Bridge was able to positively identify a thumbprint belonging to the accused under the surface of one of the tape ends.

Police had also seized a recording of a message that Prior had left on the answering machine of Marlene's new partner on the morning after her murder, saying, 'Your time is coming too.'

The brief we had to present to the court was of incredibly strong forensic and circumstantial evidence. However, Prior pleaded not guilty, meaning the case had to be heard in the Supreme Court. This meant that further preparation was required so that the evidence we presented would be clearly understood by a jury. It was our role to metaphorically take the jury to the crime scene so they could see the evidence for themselves and make their own determinations.

Prior's trial began in the Grafton Supreme Court on 12 February 2002.

I was due to fly to Grafton the following day to present the forensic evidence on behalf of the prosecution, but received a call from the instructing solicitor assisting the Crown that I was no longer required.

In a major turnaround, after the Crown had delivered its opening address to the jury, Raymond Prior had taken the advice of his defence team and changed his plea to guilty of murder. In return for his early guilty plea, the judge handed down a slightly reduced sentence.

Raymond John Prior was sentenced to sixteen years' imprisonment. The first date upon which he will be eligible for consideration for parole will be 28 August 2012.

The death of Marlene Prior was not the highest profile murder investigation that I took part in; it didn't shake the foundations of the community as many others I investigated did, nor will it be remembered outside of that family by many people. However, when I look back on this investigation it was one of the most personally rewarding that I was involved in.

The brief that was presented to the Supreme Court was not filled with transcripts of a man breaking down with guilt and remorse confessing to his murderous act, nor was the prosecution witness list filled with people who would take to the stand to detail how they saw Raymond Prior violently beat and murder his wife. There were no witnesses to the crime. The only witness was the silent witness of forensic evidence. It was there to be identified, collected, interpreted and presented to the court in a manner that would allow the jury to decide a man's guilt or innocence.

Finding the crucial piece of evidence, or in this case the bringing together of many small pieces to make the picture complete, was only one half of the puzzle. With a compelling enough argument and a certain degree of credibility you could convince the investigators that the case was solid. But the real test came in presenting the evidence before the court and having twelve impartial members of the jury make the decision as to the value or otherwise of your opinions.

I worked for months on the preparation of the forensic brief of evidence in the case against Raymond Prior and with a confidence perhaps bordering on arrogance I was looking forward to giving evidence in the trial and having my work tested. Until my opinions had been robustly tested, it didn't feel quite complete. So I had mixed feelings when I heard that Raymond Prior had changed his plea and was now pleading guilty to murder. This was a significant outcome and for a man to plead guilty to murder, when many will roll the dice without a fear of much to lose, was a reflection of the strength of the case presented by the prosecution team.

I was pleased for the family of Marlene and of course it was the best result possible, but I did feel a little empty that I didn't get to give the evidence in court and ultimately see if it was as good a forensic brief as I thought it was.

Chapter 6

Laurie

Whilst there are hundreds of jobs I have attended and forgotten about, which I sometimes think has to be a good thing, there are several that will stay with me forever.

The one job that, more than almost any other, changed irreversibly how I spoke with the families of victims began with a phone call on 23 January 1997. It was late in the afternoon and I received a call from police radio advising me of a fatal farming accident. Nothing so very unusual about that, unfortunately.

It was the peak of summer and the middle of the Tamworth Country Music Festival, which meant the weather was hot and the town was pumping with a party atmosphere. On the fifteen-minute drive to the property I decided I would knock this job over relatively quickly so that I could get back to town to share in the spirit of the festival.

I was escorted from the farm's front gate to the scene of the accident by a uniformed police officer. The property had a number of chicken sheds that, when in full operation, housed tens of thousands of chicks. However, due to a flu virus that had devastated the local industry, the property was quiet. I had a brief conversation with the police officers to get an overview of the job from their perspective.

Whilst talking with them I stood looking at the body of the deceased, lying on the ground about five metres away, covered by a white sheet put in place by the ambulance officers who had attended the scene. Not far from the body was a tractor.

I walked over and pulled the sheet from the body. I needed to see in raw terms what I was dealing with. I reeled backwards in shock. Lying on the ground, dead, was family friend Laurie Vella. The connection between the property, Laurie and his family had not been obvious to me until now. We had never visited the property; we had previously only spent time at Laurie's house, which was in town.

Nicole had met Laurie's wife, Louise, through our kids' playgroup, and both our eldest boys had become good friends. It was a natural progression through the friendship of our wives that Laurie and I would also become friends.

I pulled myself together. My immediate concern needed to be for Louise and her three children, Matthew, Jacqueline and Natalie, all under the age of five, who now didn't have a dad.

I had an absolute burning desire to get to Louise and support her in whatever way I could. It took me a few minutes to clear my head and to work out what action to take. I decided that first and foremost I had to process the accident scene. I would try to determine what circumstances had led to Laurie's death so I could provide Louise and the kids with some answers. I knew I could have asked one of my colleagues to complete the examination for me, but I just didn't want to leave Laurie lying on the ground for one minute longer than was necessary.

The forensic investigation of the scene was, as fatal accidents go, fairly straightforward. Sadly this was another farming fatality which could have been prevented but for the absence of safe work practices. Upon reflection there are very few farming fatalities that are not predictable given the level of risk those on the land expose themselves to. In their desire to get the job done quickly so that they can move on to the next one, their personal safety is often overlooked.

Laurie had died as a result of parking the tractor he was driving on an incline, not engaging the brakes to their full extent and then being caught behind the tractor as it rolled backwards and over him. It was a simple yet tragic accident, the impact of which never leaves those who loved him, his family. The rawness of the loss does heal itself in time. But as anyone who has lost someone well before their time was up will tell you, there remains a scar on their heart and that doesn't go away.

After I completed the examination of the scene I waited until Laurie's body was collected from the property and taken to the mortuary at Tamworth Base Hospital, then I left the scene and drove to Louise's, stopping at home on the way to let Nicole know what had happened. I felt sick to the pit of my stomach driving to Louise's house, and knowing that the death of Laurie had taken my work to another level: it had become personal. My thoughts went into a time frame that was new. All I could think of was how would Louise and the three young kids move forward, what was the next step for her to take? I had been involved in the investigation of death for years now; why was this so new and why did I feel like I wanted to vomit? Turning the corner into her street I knew that I was about to come face to face with something I had always tried to avoid: the inconsolable grief of a family left behind after the death of a loved one. But now, because I knew this family, it was different.

Louise had been waiting for Laurie to come home early from work on his family's property. This particular day he had planned to finish early for a reason: 23 January, the day of Laurie's death, was Louise's birthday.

She was waiting, full of excitement, for her husband to arrive home and take her to the cinema. The night was planned: the two of them would go out for dinner and a movie – which tonight was to be the blockbuster *Titanic* – and afterwards enjoy the festive atmosphere on the crowded streets of Tamworth.

But Laurie would never arrive home and Louise would never see that movie. The gift for this beautiful woman on her birthday, and for every birthday from that day onward, was a reminder of the day she lost the love of her life.

Over the next couple of days I spent a lot of time with Louise and the children. I did something that is not uncommon after the shock of a sudden death: I threw myself into work. I wanted to be constructive, to feel useful, so I took over the investigation of Laurie's death, taking all the statements from the family members about what had happened on that fateful day.

Although this was a difficult and painful time, I learnt something I had known but not quite understood before, despite having investigated hundreds of deaths. Behind every death, be it homicide, suicide or accident, there is a confused and vulnerable family that needs support and understanding.

Louise said to me some weeks after Laurie's death that the fact I had led the investigation, taken the statements from the family and cared so much had helped her and her family deal with the worst situation they could ever have imagined. It was at that point I realised I had stopped caring about the families left behind.

Thinking about it now, perhaps it wasn't that I had stopped caring, but I had become so used to death and being surrounded by grieving families that I had begun to assume the families would deal with it as I did. I assumed they knew the process that would follow and why a post-mortem examination had to be conducted.

Why wouldn't they know? It was something that occurred every day, wasn't it? Well, not in Louise's world, and not in the world of most people.

Just in my world.

And my world is different.

Laurie's death taught me something I have never forgotten – there is always a Louise waiting for her husband to come home, to take her out to celebrate her birthday.

Laurie's death also gave me a gift. It gave me a very clear understanding of what I do for a living, and why. I do it so I can find answers for those left behind.

By investigating Laurie's death, I was able to tell Louise that her husband had died as a result of a freakish accident – no fault of anybody else – and that his death was very quick. This was important not only for Louise to know, but also for Jason, Laurie's fourteen-year-old brother, who absolutely idolised him and had been working in the same area at the time of this terrible accident. It was important for all to know that Laurie's death was a tragic accident, and nothing could have been done to help him, such was the nature of his injuries.

After Laurie's death I made sure to take the time to speak with the family of the deceased, to explain to them firstly why I was there, what I was doing and why, and what would happen next. I had learnt the hard way that in so many cases the families have absolutely no idea what steps need to be taken, beyond putting the kettle on. By taking just a few short minutes, I found I could help them in such a powerful way.

Learning these lessons was of course no use to Laurie, but I am sure that what I learnt assisted the families I came into contact with from that point on.

Chapter 7

The Bali Bombings

My gruesome introduction to international Disaster Victim Identification was on the morning of Sunday, 12 October 2002. I woke up and the world had changed. Islamic terrorists had deliberately targeted western tourists by bombing nightspots popular with foreigners on the island of Bali. News broadcasts throughout the day detailed the increasing number of injured and dead. Ultimately two hundred and two people died in the attacks, including eighty-eight Australians.

Ten months earlier, in January of 2002, I had taken a promotion within the Forensic Services Group to the position of Inspector, and was now managing a number of Crime Scene Sections and other specialist groups out of the Sydney Police Centre. We left Tamworth after ten years, having gone there in 1992 for what was an undefined period of time, and relocated back to Sydney. We would both miss Tamworth, our friends and the pace of life living in the country, which is so much more relaxed than Sydney, but it wasn't a daunting move and we were both ready for the next chapter in our lives.

Bali had always been of personal significance to me. As it is for many Australians, this tropical paradise was the destination of my first international holiday. That was in 1986 and I can vividly recall walking through customs, feeling proud that I had saved hard and was now an international traveller. I felt worldly and grown up, and I quickly fell in love with Bali and the Indonesian people. Two years after that first trip I returned to Bali with Nicole; we both loved the lifestyle and the people. It felt so peaceful and relaxed being able to wander the countryside of a foreign country, talking to people who obviously loved us being there. Back then I was oblivious to the fact that not all the Indonesians welcomed us, or our Australian values.

On that fateful night in 2002 three devices were detonated. The first was outside the American Embassy, and then the two most powerful and deadly at the popular tourist spots, the Sari Club and Paddy's Bar. A suicide bomber set off one bomb inside the crowded Paddy's, sending survivors scurrying into the street. A car bomb was waiting for them outside the Sari Club across the road. The whole tactic was planned meticulously to inflict the maximum number of casualties.

The Indonesian police were overwhelmed and did not have the training or equipment to conduct a large-scale disaster victim identification (DVI) operation. The Australian response was immediate, and I felt a deep sense of pride to be asked to be part of it. When this is what you've trained for, you feel a great responsibility to use your skills, wherever they are needed.

The bombings in October 2002 came at a time in my career when things were changing. My new role was a leadership position in which I was responsible for the delivery of forensic services to a geographic region that covered basically half of Sydney. I had been involved in a number of DVI exercises, and one of the last things I'd done in Tamworth had been to lead a multi-agency response to a simulated aircraft crash at the airport in 2001. During this exercise we had volunteers from the local community role-play a number of dead passengers and grieving relatives, but that was really the extent of any recent significant DVI work I'd done. However, the Australian DVI Commander had come to Tamworth to observe the running of the operation, and we must have done something right, because not twelve months later he asked me to head to Bali after the bombings.

The Bali response presented a number of firsts for me: the first time I would deploy overseas in a work capacity, the first time I would be involved in a large-scale DVI operation where the number of fatalities had exceeded two hundred, and the first time that I would step into a leadership position comprising teams from across Australia.

I was not the only one for whom these experiences were a first. Prior to Bali the number of NSW Police deploying overseas, particularly from the forensic area, was extremely small, and in the ten years that I had spent in the FSG to that point I can only recall one other person heading off overseas for work.

The number of deceased bodies we would be seeing wasn't something that anyone else had worked on at that time either. The identification of two hundred and two people was a first for everyone who was there.

On the day I was due to fly to Bali, I packed my bags and said goodbye to Nicole and the kids. I wasn't sure if I would return home that day or if I would see everybody in a couple of weeks. I had my ticket, but I didn't yet have ministerial approval to travel, which is required for the deployment of NSW Police overseas.

Leaving home that morning I was filled with excitement and anticipation at the thought of heading overseas and working in what was a straight-out terrorist attack against Australians and what we stood for. I felt as though I had a chance to contribute in my own way to assist those who had stood and stared into the face of this ugliness and hatred that was terrorism. 9/11 had come to Australia and I could do something. I knew that I was leaving the kids for a longer period than usual this time, but I felt there was a higher purpose. I felt proud to be going and I know that Nicole felt the same. I didn't feel guilt at leaving Nicole and the kids; this felt like the absolute right thing to be doing. Lachie was turning ten and he had a greater understanding of what was happening in the world than either Kels or Jack. The little kids knew that 'Daddy was going away to help some people and would be gone for a couple of weeks'.

I left home and travelled to the Sydney office, then went about normal business, anxiously awaiting the consent needed in time to make the 2 pm flight to Denpasar. I put a call in at eleven in the morning in the hope that approval may have come through. I recall saying to the person on the other end of the phone, 'There is no point in ringing me at one-thirty this afternoon saying I am right to go, because it will be too late by then.' I was told in no uncertain terms, 'You are not to leave the office until we have sighted the written approval from the police minister.' I reluctantly agreed with the stern voice down the phone and hung up. I then gathered my bags and said to one of the boys in the office, 'Give me a lift to the airport will you, I'm right to go.' As we were unloading my bags at the international departure gate I received a phone call saying that approval had come through, I was cleared to go. Not bad. I had just over an hour until boarding for the flight.

Arriving at the site of the Sari Club and Paddy's Bar the first morning was nothing short of surreal, partly because it was so quiet. Missing were the street vendors and the crowds of tourists in their board shorts and singlets and summer dresses. I also noticed with a pang of sadness that there were also no smiling Balinese faces enjoying the banter and honing their bargaining skills on the tourists. What had replaced these familiar sights and sounds were looks of deep despair among the local community, who were hurting profoundly in a place that now reeked of death.

The scene of the bombings was not dissimilar to many large arson scenes I had visited during my career. The structural frame of the buildings stood as a reminder of what had occupied this site prior to the explosion, but surrounding that was the charred twisted metal of the building that had collapsed as the metal fatigued under the heat of the fire. There was the unmistakable putrid smell of death that is present following the burning of a body. I had smelt this on too many prior occasions and it is one of those repugnant smells that stays with you forever once it has entered your nostrils.

On the ground and in the gutter on the road there were the traces of blood from where people had lain in desperate pain or dying.

As I lifted the crime scene tape and entered the scene I was confronted by the enormity of what had occurred.

One of the tasks undertaken by crime scene investigators is to examine the scene of a fire to determine how and where on the premises the fire had started. This meant that over the years I had seen this type of destruction many times, and on a much larger scale than either Paddy's or the Sari Club. The difference now was that two hundred and two people had died as a result of the murderous actions of a few radical but well-organised terrorists. This was new and numbing to me. These deaths were the result of a coordinated attack, with the single aim of causing the greatest possible loss of life.

As I stood inside the ruins of the Sari Club, I turned and looked back at the people who were gathered on the other side of the police tape. I felt desperately sad and a little unsettled as well. Had any of those onlookers caused this mayhem? Many were dressed in jeans or shorts and T-shirts; many were wearing motorbike helmets and backpacks. Were they here to mourn a loss, to make sense of this wanton act of destruction, or were they here for more sinister reasons, perhaps to survey their own handiwork or even inflict further damage?

I felt terrible sadness for the victims and their families, and for the people of Bali who had no connection to this but would soon feel the results of it. But I also had a feeling I had seldom experienced in my policing career. I felt afraid for my own safety. I stood in police uniform at the site of the bombing looking at the faces of the locals, and for the first time ever in this wonderful paradise I had the distinct feeling of not being welcome.

Hours later I stood in the mortuary of Denpasar's Sang Lah Hospital and looked at what was left of the suicide bomber from Paddy's Bar. His remains took up little of the stainless-steel mortuary table; there was a head and a flap of skin that was attached to the rear of the head and reached down to where his lower back used to be. I stood and looked at what remained of this once healthy young man and wondered at what point in his life he had decided, or at least been brainwashed into believing, that his mission on earth was to bring grief and misery to so many people and their families.

The Australian contingent that deployed to Bali consisted of police from all jurisdictions. We were deployed under the auspices of the Australian Federal Police, and we worked side by side with the Indonesian National Police. There were three phases to the investigation: criminal investigation, forensic analysis and disaster victim identification (DVI). I was involved in the third phase. DVI is a process used to identify multiple victims following an incident, be it criminal or otherwise. DVI, which is now an international standard, had its origins in New South Wales and had been formulated in response to a crash at Sydney's Mascot Airport that had resulted in multiple fatalities. The simplicity of DVI is that it basically involves the matching of ante-mortem (prior to death) information with post-mortem (after death) information.

This process is used when more than four people have died at the one incident scene. It is used to overcome the difficulties of relying on facial identification by the relatives of the deceased. There are numerous recorded instances where grieving relatives, anxious to bring some closure to this tragic part of their life, have incorrectly identified a body. This may be because the body has been subject to such elements as fire or water, or has sustained severe injuries in an accident, or has been affected by the decomposition process. DVI does not rely on visual identification but involves a relative providing DNA from, say, the victim's hair left behind on a hairbrush, or a toothbrush, or even a fingerprint on a personal possession.

How the process worked in Bali was that relatives, friends, or for that matter anybody with sufficient interest, would report to police their concerns about the suspected loss of a relative, friend or acquaintance. An assessment would then be made based upon the information supplied as to the likelihood of the person reported missing being involved in the disaster. Once a person had been reported as missing, an ante-mortem (AM) file would be established, recording any history likely to assist in the identification.

The three primary methods of identification in DVI are fingerprints, dental information and DNA. These primary methods may be supported with secondary methods such as physical descriptions, including tattoos, scars or any other distinguishing physical features. The post-mortem (PM) process of the DVI involves police and other forensic experts, such as pathologists and odontologists (forensic dentists), collecting information that can be used as a comparison to the information supplied in the AM process. Police will collect fingerprints, the odontologists will take dental X-rays, and the pathologists will conduct a physical examination of the body for identification signs and may collect bone and other samples for DNA analysis. Once samples have been obtained in the AM and PM process, it is then a matter of comparing the information to find a match between the two.

It is a simple process, until you have several hundred samples to analyse or, as I was to discover at a later disaster, tens of thousands.

The DVI process in Bali took place at the Sang Lah Hospital. Driving out to the area each day, we were exposed to the impact the bombings had had on the locals. Streets that had previously been a hive of activity were now deserted. The Balinese who relied upon the tourists to support their families sat outside their market stalls waiting for passing trade. But the sad fact was there was no passing trade. We would travel a different way to the hospital each day as part of a counter-surveillance measure and this confirmed to us that the entire tourist area of Bali had virtually shut down.

All of the bodies had been transported to the hospital, but the disaster had completely overwhelmed the facility, so the bodies were mostly laid on the walkways between the different wings. Hospital staff covered the bodies in ice to try to slow decomposition. Even before decomposition, however, these were victims with severe trauma to the body, either from the impact of the bomb itself, or from subsequent burning, which meant that in most cases they were totally unrecognisable.

Over the years I have been asked many times how I deal with the emotional impact of seeing so many mangled bodies and still function to do my job. The truth is, everyone handles it differently. There's an important balance to strike. On the one hand you need to appreciate the enormity of what has happened, because if you don't, you lose empathy and you miss the opportunity to recognise why you are there and what you are contributing to with your work. On the other hand, you are there with a job to do, and you simply can't do your work if you get too caught up in the tragedy of it.

At some point, if you are to do this work effectively, you realise that the best thing you can do to serve the people and their families is to do your job calmly and efficiently. For ninety-five per cent of us working in Bali, death was no stranger to us. That said, this incident was on a scale so much greater than any of us had ever experienced. Some of us handled it better than others. One day a woman in her early twenties who had just started working for the Australian Federal Police arrived, having just flown in. She was checking into the hotel and she was crying at reception. She hadn't yet been exposed to death in the line of her duty, and I believe it was a mistake to send her over, asking her to dive into an ocean of death when she didn't know how to swim. I gently suggested she return to Australia, but she courageously said no, she could manage. The next day, however, she was sobbing uncontrollably again, and this time I insisted. Part of my role as one of the senior leaders with the DVI response was to manage the deployment of the teams, liaising with their home jurisdiction, and then to monitor their welfare and needs once they were on the ground. There was no way she should have been anywhere near a scene of two hundred and two partially intact, charred corpses. It takes a certain level of experience to witness that and still do a job in a professional manner.

One of the big lessons learnt from Bali was about the communication process and how to manage the expectations of not only the victims' families but also the general public, who were demanding results and quickly. The process of identifying hundreds of people takes time, and you simply cannot cut corners. That we were dealing mostly with body parts made the process that much more time intensive. While I am proud of the work we did in Bali, I believe that one mistake we made was in our process of communicating to the victims' families and the media. Many of the people who had died in the attacks had travelled to Bali as part of a group, and not everyone in each group was out at Paddy's or the Sari Club that night. Often the victims' family members or friends stayed on in Bali to identify and collect the remains of their loved ones. As day after day went by and these people did not get an identification or even a peek at remains of their loved ones, frustration and anger began to build, which of course was understandable.

One prominent person involved was Craig Salvatore, the rugby league player, whose wife was killed. Thanks to well-intentioned hospital staff he had been allowed to do a visual identification of his wife. But he wasn't able to take his wife home because her body had not been through the normal DVI process. His understandable distress was picked up by the media, and it fanned the upset of other families. Looking back, I believe we could have done a much better job of explaining why we needed to go through the formal DVI process. There were occasions when people succumbed to the pressure and went outside protocol, with horrendous results. It wasn't just a pointless bureaucratic formality – it served a very specific and valuable purpose.

With mass fatalities, family members sometimes make mistakes in visual identification because of the incredible emotional pressure they are under, and because their desire to take their loved one home quickly is so strong. This is well documented throughout the world. Several years before the Bali bombings, there was a motor vehicle collision in Adelaide. Four boys who all knew each other were killed. Visual identifications were allowed, but later forensic test results showed that two of the boys had been mixed up and buried under the wrong names. Their bodies had to be disinterred and reburied, causing enormous additional distress to the families.

In Bali, we had husbands pleading, 'Please let me go and find my wife.' We had family members asking to at least take a picture of the body of their loved ones, to have closure. The trouble is, unless you've seen it before, you can't imagine the level of injury or decomposition to some of the bodies. It was horrendous horror-movie stuff. With so many bodies in a near unrecognisable state, the risk is that a family member will find someone who is vaguely similar to their loved one and take them home, only to find that they've taken home the wrong remains.

A reality of DVI, which adds to the length of the process, is that it didn't only involve doing the PM examinations in Bali. We also had to collect enormous amounts of AM information from the families back in Australia. For example, if a mother rang the estab-lished hotline and said, 'I have grave fears for my son. He was in Bali, travelling, and I haven't heard from him since the bombing,' a whole process gets set in motion. The son could be off hiking somewhere and could be at no risk at all. Or he could be lying on one of those walkways, dead. We had to follow each lead to its conclusion. This involved going back to the family, collecting infor-mation from their medical history, and going to their local dentist and collecting their radiographs and X-rays. When this process is replicated over and over again, the enormity of the operation becomes overwhelming. All kinds of documentation – records, X-rays, fingerprints – was going back and forth between Australia and Bali via fax, internet and snail mail.

From a forensic point of view, the actual DVI process itself is not difficult. What made it hard was the huge numbers. If you do it for a group of, say, six people, you will have six yellow forms (the AM forms) that have been completed with six lots of information. And you will do six post-mortems and you will have six pink forms. Then it is just a matter of matching those. Perhaps you have three females and three males, and you can separate them into two groups. Then you have one who was an Asian, one who was African-American, and one who was Anglo-Saxon, and so the process is relatively quick. But if you have hundreds or even thousands of yellow and pink forms, the process becomes much more difficult.

At that point you set up what is called a reconciliation centre, and you go about matching, categorising and looking for identifiers. You build a case for each person, and then that information is presented before a board made up of the most senior police officer, the coroner, a forensic dentist and a doctor. It runs just like a court. The board either agrees with the findings, in which case an official identification is made, or the board asks for more information and then the team must go back and obtain that information and present it back to the board. After the board makes the identification, we notify the Australian Embassy, who then notifies the local police jurisdiction. The local police will then go and personally deliver the death notice.

The positive identification of one of the bodies marked the end of one journey and the beginning of another. For the deceased, they once again had an identity and were no longer known by a series of numbers on a body tag. Once again they were someone who had a family, friends and a history of a life lived, but ultimately cut short. The news for the relatives and loved ones of the final identification, which comes with a knock on the door by the local police and the delivery of the news that they were dreading, marks the beginning of a new journey. Until that visit comes, the family are of course hoping that their loved one will show up alive in a hospital somewhere. This visit by the police takes that hope, albeit only a glimmer of hope, away. Now they begin again with the return of their loved one and a ceremony to mark the end of their time on this planet.

The identification of a deceased also signifies the end of a journey for the police involved. At different times investigators will be tasked to track down someone who has been reported missing, and to undertake that investigation there is a real need to understand the life of that missing person, to get to know them, so to speak. No one wants to leave a case unsolved when they have invested part of their soul into the investigation; it becomes personal.

Seeing a body placed into a coffin with the Australian flag laid with dignity over the top was the most fitting send-off we could give to someone under the circumstances we dealt with in Bali, and it certainly felt like on that occasion we had done our job. For me it felt like I had contributed to providing an answer to a family, and that ultimately is what my police career was about.

Leaving Bali I was filled with mixed emotions. I was, of course, eager to return home to my family, but I didn't feel as though the job was done. I felt I had more to contribute and wanted to return. I also felt a real sense of honour and privilege to have been asked to tour Bali in the first place. The hours worked had been long and there was no question there was a heightened level of stress. There were the constant threats to our personal safety in the form of bomb threats and threats of kidnapping of Australian police. All of this resulted in a feeling of exhaustion and it caught up with me on the flight home. Once the adrenalin stopped, I hit the wall.

I shared the flight back to Sydney at the end of our deployment with Virginia Friedman, a senior New South Wales forensic biologist. Virginia told me through her exhaustion that she had slept for no more than two hours at a time in Bali, for fear another attack was imminent. And she wasn't alone in that, I'm sure. The Bali bombings changed the way Australians viewed the threat of terrorism. It was now all too real, something that had once occurred to other people but never to us.

Not long after coming home to Australia I was invited to return to Bali for a further rotation, however New South Wales was in the grip of a bushfire season that resulted in multiple deaths and quite literally hundreds of fires. I was seconded to a position in Task Force Tronto, set up to lead the investigation of the bushfires with the role of leading the forensic response across the state. This ended the prospect of any return trips to Bali.

Three brothers were later convicted of carrying out the Bali bombings. All three were executed by firing squad on 9 November 2009. The memory of their victims lives on through their loved ones and in the memorials, both in Australia and Bali, that bear their names.

Chapter 8

The Boxing Day Tsunami

First reports of the Boxing Day tsunami failed to convey the destruction and the geographical spread of the disaster. It would take days and even weeks before the full scope of the event was known. Somewhere between 250,000 and 300,000 people lost their lives in three predominant areas: Banda Aceh in Indonesia, the southern area of Sri Lanka, and the holiday areas of Phuket, Krabi and Khao Lak in Thailand.

I watched the devastation unfold on the nightly news whilst I was holidaying with family and friends on the south coast of New South Wales. Everyone who gathered around the television that first night was deeply shocked and saddened by the images we were seeing. I shared their grief, but I also felt a strong urge to be involved, to help in any way I could. It felt like a responsibility – I had the skills, and by using those skills I could make a difference.

The television reports increased in their frequency and the graphic images that gave a glimpse of the magnitude of the disaster started to come through. The print media was filled with first-hand accounts and detailed descriptions of the growing death toll. All of us on holidays read the papers and watched the television reports with interest. Mine was deeper. I would pore over every article and study the photos with an almost morbid interest. In Nicole's words, I had checked out again. I was present at the beach with everyone – I was even a useful fielder in the afternoon cricket game – but my head was in a place and country I had never even been to before. I wanted to go to Thailand. I knew I could make a difference and knew I had skills that would be needed and this was the world stage that I wanted to work on.

The first deployment of Australian police was made up of those who were either working at the time or were close enough to an airport for immediate travel. Once the call came, there was little time for planning, packing or even goodbyes.

Within days of the tsunami, as the scale of the disaster became clearer and as the number of foreign nationals who had lost their lives grew, I received a phone call asking me to return from holidays and prepare to head overseas to join the teams already in Thailand. The phone call and the subsequent meeting when I returned to the office saw my deployment confirmed within hours of arriving back at work. I called Nicole to let her know when I was going, and there was support along with a level of resignation in her voice. She had known from the moment it first hit our television screens that I would be involved.

In a sad reflection of where my head was at the time, I don't know how the kids felt about me going. Lachie was now twelve, Kels ten and Jack seven, but I don't know if they were sad I was leaving, proud of what I was doing, or just accepted that Dad was going away again and this time it would be for longer than the usual few nights or so.

My feelings as I boarded the plane were mixed. I was almost impatient to get to Thailand and get to work, but there were plenty of questions swirling around in my head that started to lead towards self-doubt. Would I have the skills required, would I be able to hold my own in this truly international event?

This was a daytime flight, first into Singapore and then on to the island of Phuket. I struggle to sleep on planes at the best of times, and with the emotions running through me I was never going to be able to sleep. I find long-haul flights a fantastic time and place to engage in deep thinking. The seven hours to Singapore allowed me plenty of time to think of the work ahead, my kids safe at home, and those kids in Thailand, many of whom would have lost their lives. The plane was almost empty, save for a team of South Australia Police who were also heading over.

We landed at Phuket Airport in the dark of the night. The place was virtually abandoned. Only days before, this airport had been filled with excited travellers starting or finishing their holidays. Now an eerie silence reverberated around the empty terminal. The walls and noticeboards were covered with photos and descriptions of missing people placed there by despairing travellers making a last-minute plea for help before their heartbreaking journey home.

I expected to see destruction immediately upon leaving the airport, but apart from the posters and the lack of people, it was hard to get a real grip on what had occurred. The JW Marriott Hotel, which would become home for the next four weeks, was a short drive away, but it was dark and there was little to see. There was almost no traffic, though, and no people out on the streets; the place felt like a ghost town.

The foyer of the hotel was deserted except for the staff, who just seemed so grateful that we had come to their country to assist. This was a little different from my experience in Bali, where not everyone welcomed our presence. In Thailand ours was a humanitarian response to an act of nature and I never felt anything but extremely welcomed in all my time there.

There was no need for an alarm clock on my first morning.

This was partly a benefit of travelling west across time zones – I always seem to find that direction so much easier – but more to do with the desire to start work. After having watched the events unfold on television from so far away, I was now in a position to contribute, and I was ready.

The hour and a half drive to the Information Management Centre (IMC) in Phuket City gave me my first chance to see Thailand in daylight. Driving out of the hotel I expected to be confronted with destruction and devastation, but what I saw was the four-lane highway that lacked the peak-hour traffic I would be stuck in back at home. The highway traverses the island of Phuket, and it made sense when I later looked at a map why I wasn't seeing the effects of the tsunami. We were travelling down the centre of the island.

Walking into the executive committee meeting I spotted Julian Slater from the Australian Federal Police (AFP) and pulled up a chair behind him. We greeted each other as though it had only been a couple of weeks since we'd last seen one another. In fact the last time I'd seen Julian in person had been at the Command Centre in the Kartika Plaza Hotel in Bali after the bombings. The executive committee also included the commanders of each of the DVI sites that had been established immediately after the tsunami, as well as representation from some of the thirty-six countries that had arrived in Thailand to assist.

My role was that of Staff Officer, which made me a sort of fancy personal assistant to the joint chief of staff. Typically a Staff Officer has sufficient technical knowledge and authority to easily step into the role they are supporting and this is exactly what I did in future tours when I returned as the Australian DVI Commander.

Julian and I would spend the next several weeks sharing every moment bar those when we retreated to our hotel rooms late at night. We would start each day with a breakfast briefing at daybreak to catch up on any of the late information that had come in from Australia overnight. We would then head to the Command Centre at the Marriott Hotel for staff briefings, and then travel the hour and a half for the 9 am executive committee meeting at the IMC. Following that there would be site visits in between further meetings with international teams, with the Australian team, the media and family members, as well as sub-committee meetings back at the IMC. Unlike most of the others, we didn't have one site that was our place of work. The rest of the police and forensic staff working in Thailand had one site where they predominantly worked, be that Wat Yan Yao, Tha Chat Chai or the IMC.

After a day of meetings that saw us travelling all over the southern area of Thailand, we would return to the Command Centre at the Marriott Hotel and divide up the reports and briefings to be written between us. The day would often conclude late at night after dinner with the two of us reflecting on what was left outstanding from the day and planning the following day. Each day was so long and so full it felt like we were cramming thirty hours into every twenty-four.

Prior to my first tour of Thailand I hadn't toured internationally in a work capacity beyond Bali, and I must admit that I felt somewhat intimidated by the larger countries that were represented in Thailand. Teams came from all over the world, including from Britain, Germany, France, Italy and a number of the Nordic countries. I had just assumed that because these countries were from the northern hemisphere, and were much larger in deployment size than us Australians, they would do things so much better and on a much grander scale than us.

I did gain some confidence in the Australian position on this world stage when I found out that one of the Nordic contingents had arrived with their pre-packed rapid-deployment kits containing their arctic-rated snow gear! Though to be fair, I don't think anyone who came to Thailand would have professed to having anticipated or trained for something on the scale we were now facing. The challenge for everyone was to take what we did well on a small scale and multiply it.

The initial international response had been led by another AFP agent, Karl Kent, who shared the joint chief of staff position with Colonel Jon Ponprasert of the Royal Thai Police. The Commander of the largest of the four DVI sites was Australian Federal Agent Michael Travis, and heading the Thai Tsunami Victim Identification Centre was Inspector Jeff Emery of the NSW Police.

The placement of so many Australians in key positions was a reflection of the respect that Australia now had in managing large-scale events, a reputation largely due to our team's DVI work after the Bali bombings. I think it also had a lot to do with how quickly the Australians worked and the clarity that each brought to their role. The leaders all exhibited a clear understanding of what steps needed to be taken and undertook their roles without panic or a defeatist attitude, which could have been excused given the scale of the job at hand. This was a task that was never going to be done in a week, a month or, for that matter, a year. What was needed were small steps, one after the other after the other. It was a little like that idea of eating an elephant one small bite at a time.

One question I am frequently asked is why Thailand received the majority of the Australian police assistance that was made available in the wake of the Boxing Day tsunami. In fact the only request for international police assistance in DVI came from the Thais. This was largely based on the fact that the sheer numbers killed in Thailand were at a level that could only be successfully identified through the DVI process.

Due to the scale of the carnage, and the fact that the disaster was spread over hundreds of kilometres in Thailand alone, four sites had been established that would each hold many hundreds or even thousands of bodies. The four sites were at Wat Yan Yao (site 1), Bang Muang (site 1b), Tha Chat Chai (2) and Krabi (3).

The evolution of the sites was more by accident than design in the initial days. When they recovered bodies, the Thais took them, as is their custom, to their local temple, which in Thailand is called a wat. As the bodies were pulled from the ocean, recovered from the street or taken out of hotel rooms where they had been trapped, they were transported to the temples.

There they were placed on the ground under cover, but very quickly the temple buildings were overrun. Soon the bodies were placed on any free area of ground, in what resembled a level of order. In those very early days family members would walk among the rows of dead looking for their loved ones. They would plead for help from anyone wearing a uniform or appearing to have a level of authority at the site. It was now several days since the tsunami had occurred and thousands of bodies lay on the ground at Wat Yan Yao. The bodies were in a moderate state of decomposition, which was rapidly progressing to an advanced stage due to the extreme weather. There weren't just ten, twenty or even a couple of hundred bodies lying on the ground; there were over three thousand bodies at this site.

There is little anyone can do to prepare themselves for something like the scene that presented itself at Wat Yan Yao. The most experienced forensic police or pathologists had never seen anything on that scale. I recall sitting in the departure lounge of Denpasar Airport waiting to leave Bali after the bombings when a colleague commented to me, 'Well, Bainesy, that is the biggest thing we are ever likely to see in our careers.' At the time it was a fair statement. But what we were confronted with some two years on dwarfed Bali.

At Wat Yan Yao alone there were 3500 bodies. The stench of death was unmistakable. It got into your clothes, your hair and your skin, and it stayed. The scene at Wat Yan Yao was almost overwhelming, and but for the fact everyone present had a degree of experience in dealing with death, the task of identification may well have seemed insurmountable. There is little you can do to protect yourself from the exposure to death on this scale. You can physically dress up with disposable overalls, gloves and masks, but you can't escape its presence. It was often the less experienced who sought out all the physical barriers they could to put between themselves and the decomposing bodies. You would see them taping the wrists and ankles of their disposable overalls to their gloves and boots, and adding multiple layers of protection. This allowed them to strip away the layers when they had finished their job and in turn distance themselves from what they had just seen, touched and smelt. The problem in Thailand was that with every layer of protection you added, your core body temperature rose incrementally and, working in forty-plus degree temperatures, this became a significant problem.

How do you cope in this environment with the unprecedented level of death? Well, I guess you either do or you don't. Within that statement sit a number of layers. You could cope at the time, but things might unravel to various degrees later on; or you might think you are fine but start on a path of destructive behaviour; or you may genuinely be able to cope with the challenges presented in this uniquely confronting time and space. There is no magic formula for what a person needs for longevity in this job or, for that matter, just to make it through one tour at a time. But suffice it to say that the more supported people are in their personal and professional lives, the easier it is for them to do their job without complications and without being pulled in various different directions.

There is no question that a lot of support comes from those within the environment in which you are working. This is not unique to the disaster area; this is the foundation of teamwork.

Shared experiences and common goals often lead to understanding, and the further those experiences are from your normal life the likelier those people sharing your journey are to understand the impact of what you are going through.

When I first arrived at Wat Yan Yao, dry ice was being placed on the bodies in an attempt to slow the decomposition, but it gave off a smoke-like haze that added to the eerie feel of the place.

The bodies had been brought to the temple on the backs of trucks and other vehicles by both local and international police, rescue personnel – anyone who had a vehicle with the capacity to carry a body in the back. Some were wrapped in sheets, some were in body bags, and some came straight off the street.

There is no worse combination than oppressive heat and the water in which the victims were found to contribute to the decomposition of bodies. The Thais were displaying pictures of decomposing bodies on photo boards for families to review and identify. This resulted in a number of grotesquely disfigured bodies being wrongly claimed by grieving families.

Also problematic was the fact that a number of countries were operating outside the prescribed process and working only to identify victims of their own nationality. Often it would turn out they were simply marching to the beat of a diplomat back home who had instructed them to find someone of 'immense importance'. The trouble for these diplomats, some of whom ironically lacked a degree of diplomacy, was that those of us in charge considered every one of the people who had died of 'immense importance' and none more so than any other.

We needed to quickly establish an orderly process that met international standards for the storage and systematic examination of those bodies. All the bodies were tagged with a unique identifying number that remained with the body throughout the identification process. They were each then placed into a body bag and covered with ice awaiting the arrival of refrigerated shipping containers, in which they remained until a post-mortem examination could be conducted. The process that we all worked to implement wasn't unique or even terribly difficult from a forensic science perspective. It was a process that was agreed upon and practised by all countries now working in Thailand. The challenge here was in the scale of death and ensuring that everyone worked within the process.

The temple was soon transformed into the busiest locality in all of Khao Lak. There were hundreds of people at the site every day: forensic specialists from around the world, a huge number of Thai volunteers, family members looking for their loved ones and people who were drawn to the site just because they wanted to help in any way they could.

The DVI work that is undertaken in such a large-scale event will pass through a number of stages. The first is the recovery of the bodies and the tagging, which establishes an ordered system. Once the bodies have been placed into the refrigerated shipping containers, another stage of the operation has passed. It was at this point in the process that we hit a snag. The one hundred and ten shipping containers couldn't remain in the temple grounds – there simply wasn't enough space for all the people and resources; besides, the temple was never intended to function as a morgue.

The containers needed to be moved to Tha Chat Chai, but the locals didn't want this to happen, and their protests closed the roads. Their concern was that if we moved the bodies two hours south of their village to Tha Chat Chai, when it came time to bring their loved ones back home to their villages the families would be responsible for the costs of transport, which would have been beyond many of them. We could understand their point of view, of course, but those bodies had to be moved.

After days of diplomatic negotiations, with an undertaking to return the bodies at no expense to the family, the streets were freed of protesters and the shipping containers made their journey south.

Julian and I spent a lot of these early weeks crisscrossing Thailand, visiting the various disaster sites. At that stage there were a lot of resources being thrown our way and thankfully a helicopter was available as we travelled from Khao Lak to Phuket, from Phi Phi Island back to Khao Lak and then back to Phuket for endless meetings.

The helicopter was not what you would call modern by any stretch of the imagination and it certainly didn't resemble any I had flown on from the NSW Police Air Wing fleet. It looked like a relic from the Vietnam War. On the doors were a number of open windows that channelled air into the interior; I assume this was what used to be called airconditioning.

On one of the helicopter trips from Phuket City to Khao Lak all on board were quiet. When the occasion presented we all took time to rest and gather our thoughts, because we knew that as soon as we landed, we needed to be switched back on.

I was sitting back, almost dreaming, when all of a sudden pandemonium broke loose. Shooting through one of the open windows in the door at warp speed was a bird. As it hit the vent the bird was ripped in half. It was propelled in through the vent and its trajectory had it on a collision course with a dozing Julian. Before we could warn him, the half-bird smacked fair into the middle of Julian's chest, sending blood and feathers to all corners of the helicopter.

It was almost as though everything happened in slow motion. Julian was woken from his slumber and, just like someone being punched in the solar plexus, his head and shoulders lunged forward, his feet lifted up off the floor, his eyes bugged out and, with all the blood, I am sure he thought he was being shot at. Suddenly it was not only the helicopter that was from the Vietnam War – we had crossed borders and eras and he was under enemy fire.

Meanwhile everyone on the helicopter was now awake, alert and slowly becoming aware of the situation.

Then, after a moment of stunned silence, everyone began roaring with laughter. I was laughing that hard I thought I was going to expire from lack of breath, and the pilot was also laughing uncontrollably, so much so that the helicopter started to shake as he struggled to hang on to the joystick.

When the helicopter landed at Wat Yan Yao Julian had found the humour in the situation, but walking back into the scene of devastation our laughter quickly evaporated.

Chapter 9

Tha Chat Chai

I am sure the infrastructure that was put in place at Tha Chat Chai would surprise a lot of people. In the weeks following the tsunami I was present as the site took shape. Concrete slabs were poured, buildings erected, footpaths built and power and phone lines connected. There was even a fountain of remembrance for the families who would come to receive the bodies of their loved ones. It really was an example of what can be achieved in a remarkably short period of time, when it just needs to happen.

The site was designed with a core administration area, tunnels where the post-mortems could be conducted and housing for the shipping containers filled with bodies. Unlike Wat Yan Yao, this was a clean site and outside the tunnels you weren't confronted by the stench of decomposing bodies.

Once Tha Chat Chai had been set up, the real DVI work could begin.

And it was hard work. The days were long and physically demanding. We would frequently be on the road by 6 am, and more often than not people were still working in the command centre at the Marriott Hotel at midnight. These hours might be sustainable in a different environment, but working in the oppressive heat under such difficult conditions, without a day off at the weekend, took its toll on everyone.

It wasn't only the long hours, the heat or the physical nature of the work that wore people down. The inescapable fact was that everyone had their days filled with death from the time they woke in the morning till when they rested their head on the pillow at night. For the unlucky ones, their sleep was also filled with images of the devastation they had seen during the day.

Those of us who work in areas where you're constantly challenged on an emotional level will often use humour as a safety valve. There was so much sadness everywhere we looked that I think we would have gone mad if we hadn't been able to laugh.

Oddly enough, humour was often found when lifting the bodies from one of the top shelves of the freezing shipping containers. We worked in pairs, and wore gumboots whilst walking across the ice-covered floor, which was worse than a skating rink. The gumboots were great ninety per cent of the time. It was the other ten per cent that brought grief to all. Getting inside the container without falling arse over tit was a challenge in itself, but at least we had one hand to grab the shelves and steady ourselves. When we slipped, and we always slipped at some point, it was just a matter of whether we fell to the ground and onto the mank that covered the floor, or whether our fall was broken by our knee crashing into the ice-covered metal at the base of the container. And that was the easy part. Then we had to reach above our heads and drag the body down off the shelf and negotiate our way back out of the container – this time walking backwards, shuffling with the rhythm of two drunken sailors, seemingly always pulling against one another. The only thing that would make this worse was when the bag had become brittle from its time in the container and, as we pulled it down, it would tear, exposing the body. At times the bag would completely separate. What can you do but laugh when all of this happens – and you know it is going to happen each time you walk into the container – if not to you then to one of your mates? Strangely enough, it was always funnier when it happened to your mate.

When we lifted a body down and could tell by the weight of the bag it was a child's body, there was no more laughter. We would fall silent and be reminded again of the horror of our task. Often we would deliver the body to the morgue and then take a break, remind ourselves that we were in the world of the living. We would pick up our phones and then quietly walk to a secluded area for a few moments' peace and distraction from the work at hand. It was then that we would telephone home, just to hear the sounds of our own kids' voices, and when they'd ask how we were going we would just tell them it was bloody hot and we were counting down the days until we would be home with them.

These times we shared created powerful bonds between workmates. You become incredibly close to these people in a very short period of time, partly because of a shared understanding of each other's struggles.

The DVI process in Thailand proceeded pretty much as it had in Bali after the bombings, just on a larger scale. That is how DVI is supposed to work: it can be implemented for the deaths of four people on the same principles as for the 5395 bodies in our charge in Thailand. What was different was the complexity of the management of the process, but the matching of the AM and PM information leading to the identifications was the same.

Following the post-mortem examinations the bodies were returned to a refrigerated container until the identification process had been completed. However it could be weeks or even months until the matching of the data obtained in the AM and PM processes took place. When an identification was made and confirmed by those sitting on the reconciliation board, the bodies could be given into the hands of relatives in the case of Thai nationals, or make their final journey home in the case of foreign visitors.

Meeting the relatives as they came to receive the body of their loved one gave meaning and perspective to what we were doing. I was blessed to meet many families who had suffered the worst losses imaginable. Each of them left an indelible impression on me.

The Australian victims were repatriated by the Department of Foreign Affairs and Trade (DFAT), which in this operation was headed by an old acquaintance of mine, Marc Innes Brown. Marc was an ideal person to lead the DFAT team. He could entertain visiting senior Australian politicians, yet he could also speak with grieving family members. Each felt they were the only person that mattered when Marc spoke with them. I have worked with many leaders across many agencies and most are able to communicate effectively at one end of the spectrum. They either find themselves holding counsel with the top echelon or mixing it with the workers. Marc had that all too rare ability to do both effectively.

Each time an Australian was to be repatriated a call would go out to the Australian team to attend the airport. There the coffin draped in an Australian flag would be loaded onto the aircraft with a guard of honour formed by the Australian team. This was befitting of the sombre circumstances and an indication that for us each and every body we identified really did matter.

When the international forensic community pulled out of Thailand in February 2006, just over four hundred bodies remained unidentified. This wasn't due to the decomposition of the bodies, it was because of the lack of AM information that was required for the comparative analysis.

One of the practices of obtaining the AM information from a missing person is for police to visit the home of that person and take possession of personal items as sources of DNA evidence.

Another option is for a fingerprint expert to attend the home of the missing person and examine for latent prints. This is a practice that may be employed where the missing person is not previously known on any central fingerprint database.

Of the 5395 people who died in Thailand as a result of the tsunami, close to half were international holidaymakers. The process of obtaining the AM information from their homes was undertaken by their local police.

In Australia police from the state or territory in which victims lived attended their homes and obtained the necessary AM information from their families.

For the Thai authorities hoping to obtain AM information for their missing nationals, however, the task was difficult and at times impossible.

Entire families and the houses in which they had lived had been washed away in those devastating waves, and with them any source of DNA or fingerprint evidence. Of the bodies that remain to this day buried under only their DVI number at a cemetery in Bang Muang, which is about fifteen minutes' drive south of Wat Yan Yao, it can be assumed they were Thais whose whole families, and their homes, were lost.

In 2007 I visited the Bang Muang cemetery for the first time, as it hadn't been built during the time I was working there. The unidentified bodies are each buried with a small, modest plaque. I felt very uneasy at the cemetery. It was as though those who are buried there aren't at rest yet. Their journey is waiting to be finished. But sadly, for the vast majority of them, their journey will remain forever unfinished.

Chapter 10

Balloons That Heal

It was in January 2005, towards the end of my first rotation in Thailand, that I was asked to attend a ceremony to be held at a sporting ground in Khao Lak to honour those souls who had been taken by the tsunami and those who had been left behind to grieve.

I travelled with AFP Agent Keith Tomlin and a well-educated and articulate Thai national named Kit, who had been working with the AFP.

Keith was employed in the AFP Bangkok office, and had been travelling through the north of Thailand on holidays with his family when the tsunami struck. The first call he received advised that there had been 'some damage caused down in the Patong area as a result of a large tidal wave or something similar and there may be some injuries'. It was thought prudent, given the number of Australians who holidayed in that area, to keep a watching brief on the situation and, if the need arose, to deploy somebody down into the area, just to fly the flag.

We know now the size of that understatement.

I had worked with Kit over a number of weeks and on this

particular day I sensed a change in his usually calm manner. He seemed excited and very chatty; there was an air of anticipation about him that was palpable. I only realised later that this was because he knew the significance of the ceremony we were on our way to. At that point I had no idea what to expect, or any appreciation of the extraordinary significance of it. The only information I had been given was that I was to wear a white shirt.

Fair enough, a simple direction that even I could accommodate.

As we got closer to the stadium, I had a very strange feeling of déjà vu. I had the sensation that we were doing something I was accustomed to, perhaps not in Thailand, but something I had done many, many times before. These feelings might have had something to do with the snail-like flow of the traffic. I looked into the cars next to me to see people patiently sitting in the barely moving lanes, all heading in the one direction, and couldn't help but notice the large number of overloaded motorbikes that were carrying at least one too many extended family members. Then it hit me!

I was heading to the cricket! It was just like at home as you drive from the outer suburbs towards the Sydney Cricket Ground for a one-dayer. Replace the green and gold shirts with white, and replace the noisy pre-game tanked-up crowd with well-mannered Thais, and it was exactly the same. The parking was still a problem, and yes, we drove around and around looking for a space. Of course there was the budding entrepreneur who was selling car spots in his front yard for more than he could dream of making in a month, and good luck to him.

We parked miles away and started the long walk towards the stadium, joining the masses heading in the same direction. The difference here was that as we entered the stadium there was nobody at the gate to check our bags for glass bottles that could be used as missiles to throw at the opposition if the game didn't go our way.

I was amused at the abundance of parking spots still available directly outside the ground. I made a mental note to ask Kit why we had walked for an eternity to get here when there was ample parking right on the doorstep.

I walked over the top of the hill to look down into the stadium and I saw the first of several sights from that night that will stay with me forever.

Placed in a grid over the entire playing surface of the oval were 20,000 candles. Seated behind each of these candles was a Thai dressed in white. They sat in a fashion so organised that it would have been any Olympic ceremony choreographer's dream. Only this had not been choreographed. People just understood the process. You walked in; you sat down quietly behind a candle and you were simply happy. No, not just happy, but honoured to be there. Just like the cricket. I think.

I was starting to catch Kit's sense of excitement. This was going to be something very special.

We walked towards the front of thousands of people already seated on the ground and looked around for a spot to sit down. The accommodating Thais quickly shuffled around, giving us all the room we needed. You know what? This was nothing like the cricket. Instead of that sweaty guy who takes up as much room as he can by stretching out and strategically positioning his food and drink supplies, we had these gentle Thai people encouraging us to sit near them and share their space, their candles, and then with a nod of the head or a smile, silently thanking us for being there to support them.

Arriving in the late afternoon did not mean we had escaped the heat. We sat on the grass as the blazing sun inched behind the surrounding mountains. For several hours we listened to a ceremony that was conducted in the Thai language, which I suppose is fairly natural, given we were in Thailand! But for me it was just downright boring.

I mean, I was sitting on the grass under the merciless sun, with an empty bottle of water in my hand, and for the second hour straight listening to local government officials making speeches in a language I couldn't understand. This experience wasn't an entire waste of time, though, because it taught me a lesson that will benefit my kids their whole childhood. And this lesson was: don't take the kids to the cricket and expect them to sit and watch every ball. That is why they always need to go to the toilet, or buy food. Not because they need to pee or are hungry, but because they are bored out of their minds. How do I know this? Because I got up and went to the toilet. Not because I needed to go, but because I needed a break from the boredom.

Walking back from my little adventure to the toilet, I wondered why all the seats in the grandstand were empty. I could just imagine myself sitting in a comfortable chair in the shade, rather than on the ground in the middle of the arena under the belting sun. I made another mental note to myself that I would take up this point with Kit when I found my way back to our spot.

It was then I saw the second sight that will never leave me.

Two thousand Buddhist monks were entering the stadium. In contrast to the white clothing of the audience, they were all dressed resplendently in robes of various shades of orange through to dark reds.

I then realised that the seats in the grandstand had been reserved for the monks. And I now understood why the locals had left so many vacant parking spaces outside the arena. I hurriedly sat myself down on our spot of grass and all of a sudden started to feel very privileged to be here.

Over the next half-hour or so the stands filled to capacity with the monks, who sat elevated above us, both in a spiritual and physical sense. The timing was impeccable, because as the heat and light of day diminished, the aura created by the presence of so many monks increased. I could only begin to imagine the significance for those Thais seated around me, most, if not all, of whom would have been of the Buddhist faith.

Although everything continued to be spoken in Thai, I was beginning to understand and appreciate the feeling and emotion behind this ceremony. It was as though the descending darkness had been conjured by the monks, taking away the daylight so that we could focus our concentration and give to them our mind and our spirit – even just for a short time.

Two thousand monks sat in the grandstands, each with a lit candle in front of them. Against the yellow and ruby robes, each small beacon of light seemed to reflect a glow from the monks' chests, like an inner light. Then, in a moment of utter magic and serenity, these two thousand monks began their mesmerising chant. If I saw sights I would never forget that night, I also heard sounds I will never forget. In a time and space filled with such loss, death and destruction without meaning, the sounds I heard, together with those unforgettable images, brought a level of calmness and tranquillity to me. I felt an inner peace.

When the chanting stopped, Kit, without saying a word, jumped up from the grass and started moving towards a group of people who had walked some five metres in front of us.

Kit wasn't the only one moving either.

Obviously everybody except Keith and me knew what this was all about.

Kit returned and then, with the assistance of the Thais around us, held up a paper balloon that was about one and a half metres tall and about a metre wide. The base of this paper balloon was a circular metal frame and centred in the middle with support wires was a candle.

Carefully holding the top of the paper balloon, the candle was lit, and we were to ensure the paper sides of the balloon were kept at a distance from the flame whilst the balloon started to fill with hot air.

Now I was like a kid.

I was totally focused on the job at hand, getting more and more excited by the second as the balloon filled with hot air.

Wanting some kind of reassurance that I was doing the right thing, that I was helping not hindering, I looked into the eyes of the elderly Thai lady standing next to me. Somehow she read my expression perfectly and began nodding; her beautiful toothless smile confirmed all was going to plan.

Then the balloon started to take on a life of its own. There was resistance against the metal frame we were holding, it was pulling skywards, tugging at our hands; it wanted to leave.

At this moment Kit and the old Thai lady simultaneously but in two different dialects gave the instruction to let the balloon go. From the tone of their voices I understood them both.

I let go, then looked upwards to see our glowing paper balloon lift off into the sky. It wasn't until our balloon had started its soul-healing journey that I looked beyond our little circle.

It was simply one of the most amazing sights I have ever seen in my life.

Our balloon had been joined by thousands more, and all were on a journey skywards, surely heading towards heaven, if there is such a place.

I stood in absolute wonder and amazement. Never had I seen something so unexpected and so simply beautiful. My spirit felt enriched.

After the last of the balloons had disappeared from view, the thousands of people who had shared the beauty of this night quietly started their journey home. The Thais left the stadium in the manner I had come to expect from them: with utmost understanding and respect for all.

The evening I spent at the football stadium was food for my soul. My head had been exercised in the technical work I had been doing, now my heart and soul were receiving the nourishment they needed.

It again made sense why I was away from my family and why I was doing what I was doing. The clarity had returned.

Even amidst all the death and destruction, I had fallen hopelessly and irreversibly in love with Thailand and its people.

Chapter 11

Tours of Duty

In all I did three rotations to Thailand, and all three were very different. In my first tour there was a franticness common to all large-scale disasters.

In those early days the response is totally reactive; there is no time to plan, prepare and practise. The challenges come all at once and this is where the leaders are tested. Everyone has an opinion and they are looking to leaders for direction. There is the expectation that leaders will make clear decisions with limited information, and some leaders struggle with this.

During the early days of the response to Bali, one of Australia's most senior police officers was so fearful of making the wrong decisions, he failed to make any decisions at all and had to be sent home. My experience from working in these environments tells me that if leaders consult with those they can, act with integrity and good intent, and yet make a decision that proves to be the wrong one, they will be forgiven. But if they fail to make any decision, they won't be forgiven.

In times of crisis, true leaders are identified by their actions and

their reactions. It's what people do and how they conduct themselves, not the position they hold, that is of the most importance.

In the very early days of the operations in Thailand this is what
I saw in so many of the Australians who held those senior positions. The rank or title each held back in their home jurisdiction
mattered little. It was the direction they showed that identified
their true leadership. It's having this direction and then effectively
articulating it to the team that results in people wanting to follow
that leader. The inspiration in a leader comes when they are able
to demonstrate to the team that they have a vision as to how the
seemingly impossible can become possible.

If under normal circumstances you asked your team to work
sixteen to eighteen hours a day for twenty-five to thirty days
straight without extra pay, there would probably be some level of
resistance. However, when the circumstances call for it, people rise
to the occasion, and this was certainly the case during the first
month or so in Thailand.

Those early teams set the standard for those that would follow.
The international response to Thailand was never going to be over
in a couple of weeks or months. It was clear we would be there for
the long haul.

Returning from my first tour it definitely didn't feel as though
I had done all I could, and whilst I was pleased to be home again
with my family, with an extra level of gratitude that they were safe
and well, I knew that if the opportunity to return presented itself I
would be keen to head back.

The disaster in Thailand had occupied my thoughts for every
hour of the day since 26 December, and stepping off the plane in
Sydney after my first tour I quickly realised that the enthusiasm for
information that had existed in the general community when I first
went to Thailand was now gone. Kids had returned to school after
the summer holidays, everyone was back at work, life had returned

to normal. The tragedy that had unfolded in front of our eyes in South-East Asia had been replaced with the routine of everyday life for many.

Returning to the office, I struggled to re-engage with the work that had seemed important prior to Christmas. The projects that I was involved in, the major crimes that I was reviewing, just didn't seem to carry the same weight any more. How could an exhibit accreditation project stimulate me on any level after having been involved in the world's largest DVI response? It couldn't, and whilst I pretended to be concerned and engaged, my head was back in Thailand. I wanted to return.

I didn't have to wait too long. Within weeks of returning to my role at Police headquarters I received a call from the AFP. I was heading back to Thailand.

This time I was leading the Australian team and managing the relationship between what had become the Thai operation at Bang Muang and the international response at Tha Chat Chai. Federal Agent Karl Kent was the joint chief of staff this time. Karl and Julian Slater were both technically equal to one another and both were clear leaders on the international stage. Julian was the more thoughtful and considered, whilst Karl was more of a larrikin.

There remained a level of discontent among the locals about the movement of the bodies from Wat Yan Yao to Tha Chat Chai, and my role was to liaise with the groups involved and bring resolution to problems as they arose. I spent a lot of time driving between the executive committee in Phuket City of a morning and Wat Yan Yao and Bang Muang of an afternoon, a distance that often took close to three hours to travel.

What I noticed during my second tour was that the frantic sense of urgency had been replaced by the realisation that this was a long-term operation and nothing was going to be solved by working the ridiculous hours the first tour had demanded. By now each of the international teams was rostered to take a day off once a week and it was a welcome relief. The hours the team was working came back to twelve or fourteen per day, depending upon the nature of the role.

It wasn't just the nature of the work that had changed on this second tour, but the daily phone calls I was having with Nicole at home changed as well. We found ourselves arguing on the phone and each phone call was turning into one made of obligation rather than a desire to connect. There didn't seem to be a reason for the disconnect that was occurring, but a sign of where things were at for me was when Nicole said that I could no longer be a family man and do the job that I was currently doing; I had a choice to make, it was one or the other. Things seemed to unravel quite quickly during this tour. Crisis is the critical testing ground for many things and sadly our marriage wouldn't survive this second tour.

Deploying staff into an environment like Thailand brings with it a conundrum for the leaders at home as to whom to choose. Part of my role when I was back in New South Wales in between tours was selecting the teams to be sent to Thailand. There is a temptation to redeploy those who have already worked there, as they have demonstrated their ability to deal with the situation, they understand the work and it is easier for continuity. However, there was also concern about how much of this kind of work people should be exposed to. When did dealing with death on this scale become just too overwhelming? At the command level of the Forensic Services Group we were only too well aware that we wouldn't see the impact of the exposure on our officers at the end of a tour or even weeks later. Sometimes it would take years, but there was little doubt it would rear its ugly head at some point in the future.

So when I was invited to tour for the third time, which was

unprecedented for anyone from NSW Police, I needed to convince the psychologists that I was fit and strong and ready to tour again. The fact that my marriage was in tatters didn't come through in the two-hour meeting that saw me get the all-clear. Returning to Thailand was what made sense to me and it was where, for some strange reason, I found solitude.

Chapter 12

Finding Alexander

'Why do you have to go? We miss you when you're gone.'
This was how Jack, who was seven at the time, responded when I told him I was heading overseas for another rotation to Thailand. This would be my third rotation and once again I would have the privilege of leading the Australian team. I would also be leading an international team at Tha Chat Chai. I knew this would give me the autonomy to really make a difference, and I knew, too, that by now I felt very much at home in Thailand and deeply connected to the community and the role I was performing there.

But to your kids it doesn't matter why you are away from them, they just miss you. Jack was seven, Kels was nine and Lachie was twelve at the time. I think the nature of the work I was doing mattered little to the kids at that point. All they knew was that as a family we were hurting and I was heading overseas again. At the time, and even now looking back, I don't think my marriage with Nicole could have been rescued from the flames if I hadn't toured on this third occasion. Strangely enough, going back to Thailand was the one thing that did make sense. Perhaps my desire to return to the destruction there was my way of escaping and not facing the mess that now existed at home. All the kids knew was that Mum was sad and spent a lot of time crying, and yet again Dad wouldn't be there on the sidelines at sport on the weekend, let alone around to assist them in this massive transition our family was undergoing. It made sense to me at the time that I return to Thailand, but of course it didn't make sense to the kids.

My children had watched the story of this deadly natural disaster unfolding on television, and they knew what I did for a living, but it was always a balance as to how much information to give a seven-year-old when my job involved going to the most horrendous scenes imaginable and processing body parts. How do you explain to your kids that you have to leave in the middle of dinner because a man sitting in a bathtub has blown his head off with a shotgun, or there has been a car accident and three little children still strapped in their car seats have been incinerated and you need to retrieve their bodies? How do you make sense of things like that?

Previously I would say there had been an accident and I had to go and help. But when I left Australia for the third time I realised they deserved a better explanation, and so I attempted to help them understand what was so important that I had to be separated from them for another month. I explained that on Boxing Day there were families just like us – mum, dad and the kids on the beach, all having a fantastic time. It was the day after Christmas, perhaps the most relaxing day of the year. Many of the families there would have saved, planned and dreamt of their holiday and the joy and laughter it would bring.

At 10 am on 26 December 2004 there was an earthquake off the coast of Indonesia. As the earth shifted, a massive amount of water was displaced and an underwater wave formed. This quake was the longest ever to be recorded by technology. Those who would later feel the effects were oblivious to what was coming their way.

Silently, the massive wave that had been created so far away was now building in size and travelling towards land at increasing speed.

Prior to its arrival, though, nature issued a warning. The water rapidly receded from the beach, like a fast-motion tide. The further the water receded, the more people were lured down to the shore to watch. Almost no one had seen this before, so of course it would arouse people's curiosity rather than send out a warning. People everywhere were drawn to the water; the Thais in the fishing village of Baan Nam Khem ran out onto the sand to get the fish that had been left behind.

But ten minutes after the water went out, it came back in. The water that had departed in such a hurry was returning, but in a deadly wall that was, incredibly, up to ten metres high in places. It wasn't a crashing tidal wave as you might imagine, rather a mountainous wall of water that just kept coming and coming. It hit the shoreline and, rather than break and recede, it continued over the beach and up into the buildings, homes, hotels and villages that lay beyond.

For the families that were on the beach that day, there were some kids who survived, there were some parents who survived, but there weren't too many families in which the kids and the parents survived. Sadly, the speed at which the tsunami was travelling meant that the moment people wandered down to inspect the phenomenon of the retreating ocean, their fate was sealed.

For those who are parents or grandparents, think about this. You're on that beach with your children or your grandchildren and you know that things aren't quite right, but like the rest of those standing on the beach, you don't know what has happened. Is it the sight of the water coming that alerts you to the danger, or is it the panic that is now starting to spread along the beach? People are pointing out to sea, some are yelling and some are starting to run.

Finally, you see that wall of water coming. You grab your kids and you hang on to them with all the strength you have and you run faster than you have ever run before. You see people running, falling, and you hear the screams of those now aware of the danger bearing down on them. Holding your kids under your arms, you run through the sand towards the road; it is agonisingly slow, you seem to be sinking deeper into the sand with each footstep, and the harder you push the slower you seem to move. The gap between you and that wall of water is now closing by the second. Your lungs are screaming in pain as you push faster and harder than you believed possible.

The water catches up to you and immediately you are knocked from your feet. You lose your grip on the children and cry out in horror, but you're being propelled, out of control, towards the cars and buildings that previously sat well beyond the shoreline. You are fighting now to draw your next breath, you need another mouthful of air before your lungs explode. You are struggling to find which way is the surface; the water is littered with missiles such as deckchairs and beach umbrellas that continually crash into you. With your head under the water there is a strange silence, until you break free and are able to take what you pray is not your last breath.

Through some strange twist of fate you survive. Thousands of others on that beach die, but you don't. For some reason you can't understand, you survive but your children or your grandchildren don't. So what do you do? You spend every minute that you remain in Thailand searching for your children's bodies. You go to the hospitals; you go to the mortuaries; you go to the victim centres; and you even search the surrounding villages.

There comes a time, though, when, despite every fibre of your being telling you to stay, you have to leave Thailand and return home. For some it will be weeks, others will hold out longer, but the logistics of remaining in a foreign country away from your home and source of income soon forces your hand. You have a job or business to return to, and the cost of staying to continue the search becomes prohibitive. Alongside this sits the realisation that you are no longer searching for your living child, you now simply want to recover their body and take it home. When you leave Thailand you go home without that most precious thing in your life – your child. And when you get home you hope and pray that the phone will ring and at the other end it will be someone saying, 'It's okay, we found them and they are alive.' But common sense tells you this call will never come.

How can you possibly start to grieve properly until you know the fate of your missing child? Till you have brought them home to you?

So I explained to my kids that this was my job, to help put in place a process that would identify the children, the mums and dads and grandparents, so that we could send them back home to their loved ones.

And I told them about Alexander.

When you work in my field you will have hard days – it is inevitable. The only way you can deal with your hard days is to understand why you do what you do. This for me was represented by Alexander, a fifteen-month-old boy who was lost in the tsunami.

His photo, with blond hair, striking blue eyes and gorgeous smile, had been placed on the outside of one of our refrigerated shipping containers, alongside hundreds of others, by his desperate parents. They were pleading that if anybody had seen him to please contact them.

So I said to my kids, 'I'm leaving you for a short time to go and find Alexander.' As a dad, the thought of Alexander spending night after night in a shipping container, alone and away from his family, drove me on through the hard times. I wanted to find his body and send him back home to his parents.

I didn't find Alexander; it would have been almost too much to hope for that I would be part of the team that identified him after he stood for so much in what had become such a turning point in my life. I do know that he was identified and repatriated home so that his parents could give him the dignity of a funeral for a life cut so short by such tragedy.

A policeman's care is for preservation of life, but it's not the same for a forensics team. We cannot save lives; we cannot bring loved ones back. I have a saying I sometimes use with colleagues as a means of conveying perspective when we're all feeling the stress of our job – 'We're not saving lives' – but the search for Alexander comes pretty close for me. It's about giving the survivors their lives back.

Chapter 13

The People Left Behind

The Disaster Victim Identification work provided some incredibly special moments throughout my rotations in Thailand, but for me the third tour was all about the people I met. There were a number of families of victims I felt privileged to meet during this tour. Memories of them will stay with me forever, together with those of the wonderful group of Australians I worked alongside. I felt incredibly honoured to lead such an effective team and I was proud of the close bonds that formed between us all despite, or perhaps because of, the extremely difficult conditions under which we operated.

It wasn't just the Australians I became close to, but also many of the Thais and dedicated officers from England. One of the members of the English team was Sergeant Gill Williams from the Thames Valley Police. Of course I didn't know it then, but meeting Gilly was to be an amazing turning point in my life. Gill was the leader of a dive team back home and her role in Thailand on this rotation was that of Body Release Officer. She would meet with the government representative or family member who arrived at

100

Tha Chat Chai to receive the body of a now identified and named deceased person.

Gilly was perfect for the job. She has the compassion and dignity necessary for the role, but she also has a wicked sense of humour, which made her an invaluable team member. She is a person with an absolute heart of gold who is also armed with a cheekiness that would sometimes make even a few of the Aussie boys blush.

You simply couldn't be serious every minute of the day or it would impact on your ability to perform the often gruesome tasks at hand. Laughter was a way of releasing pent-up emotions, a way of putting down your burden for a moment, of finding relief from within the group. I can't emphasise enough the benefit in being surrounded by people like Gill who could laugh, at themselves, at their colleagues, at the surreal situation we all found ourselves in.

I recall that when selecting the Australian team that would accompany me on this final tour, the name of a potential team member was put to me. This was a person who was without doubt one of the most technically capable and intelligent members of the FSG in New South Wales. But imposing his intense and humourless personality on other team personnel for four weeks in such trying conditions would have been very bad for morale, so he wasn't selected for the tour.

Everyone on that third tour was technically proficient, make no mistake about that. However, for me a big part of team selection was who could get along with a diverse group of people and who could have a laugh at themselves when the conditions were really daunting. It was never going to be a place for egos or precious souls.

In hindsight the team that went to Thailand on that last trip was a team that you would like to roll out every time something significant happened around the world. The team was such a unique blend that I knew nothing that was presented to us would be insurmountable.

One of the team members was Detective Sergeant David Neal from NSW Police. Dave had been on the first tour and I had spent time with him then. He was also part of the FSG back in Sydney. When I was asked to select the team he was an obvious choice because he had already been to Thailand and knew what was required of him. More importantly, though, he was someone who got along with everybody – the type of person you'd want in any team.

Dave was also a neat freak, to the point of perhaps having a touch of obsessive-compulsive disorder. It had got to the stage in the Sydney office that if Dave was on late afternoon shift and it was an unusually quiet night, he would go on a cleaning bender in the office and if it wasn't tied down, it was thrown in the bin.

Dave's obsession with order was just what we needed on that third rotation. I arrived at the site at Tha Chat Chai a day earlier than the rest of the team in order to receive the handover from the previous site commander. This was my third handover, and as such it went seamlessly. Any subtle changes were explained and the problem cases were also handed over.

The problem cases included two bodies that had been lost. When I say lost, I mean they couldn't be found on the site – we knew they were there, we just didn't know where – so not so much lost as temporarily misplaced.

At the busiest time of the identification work there were one hundred and ten refrigerated shipping containers located at Tha Chat Chai and they were spread out over the site. Each of the shipping containers had three temporary shelves installed down both internal walls, and on each shelf was a row of bodies sometimes two or three deep. All were in body bags and they were sealed with an individual tag displaying their ID number.

Some of these bodies were awaiting a post-mortem or secondary examination, but a lot had undergone all the forensic examination that was required and were now silently waiting to be sent home. Over time the number of bodies was decreasing. However, the reduction from each container was quite random, although in accordance with the formal identification process. Which shipping container the bodies came from was irrelevant to the process.

When we took over the site, we decided it was time to do a few things differently. It seemed absurd to have more than one hundred refrigerated containers running on three-phase power for twenty-four hours a day at minus eight degrees Celsius when some of them were less than half full. Clearly it was time for a reconciliation of the containers. We also knew that by conducting a full inventory of the bodies and consolidating available freezer space we would find the two missing bodies.

This process couldn't be undertaken without each and every body being removed from the containers and placed into a new one. We couldn't risk simply filling the partially empty containers and hoping to chance across the missing bodies. This was physically exhausting work. It was freezing and dark and slippery inside those containers, and we had to lift bodies, some up to one hundred kilos in weight, in frozen body bags, up and down off shelves and onto trolleys, then out into a burning sun that felt like a furnace.

People back in Australia would often ask why we worked through the hottest part of the day. My answer was that the immense size and nature of the job didn't allow us to pick and choose our working hours – we had a massive job to do and we had a lot of distraught people around the world waiting for answers.

Dave the neat freak went about numbering all of the containers in such a logical manner that it begged the question of why it hadn't been done months before. When the shipping containers had first been transported to Wat Yan Yao they were numbered according to their location. So the number code gave an indication as to its physical placement. For example, R7 was located along the side of the river and was the seventh container from the front of the temple. This made sense whilst the containers were at Wat Yan Yao, but made no sense whatsoever when the containers were two hundred kilometres away from the temple and the river!

We would remove the bodies from the containers and transport them through the site. Were these the duties I had flown from Australia to Thailand to carry out? Probably as much as had our forensic pathologist, Dr Tony Cullen, and forensic odontologist, Dr Richard Bassard, both of whom thought that if it was good enough for the cops to be out humping bodies from one container to the other, then it was good enough for them. As I have said, this was no place for egos.

The fact that Dr Cullen was a surgeon and a leading pathologist meant nothing. He was part of the team and he wanted to sweat it out as much as the next person. The only problem was that Dr Cullen was well into his sixties, and the oppressive heat had a greater impact upon him than the rest of us. It was when I saw him propped, ashen-faced, against a door of one of the shipping containers, finding relief in the cool breeze from inside, that I decided it was time to act. This was one of the rare occasions during my tour that I put on my commander's hat – I ordered him off the site and into the airconditioned meal room. Team spirit was one thing; sending a team member home in a body bag was another thing altogether.

Needless to say the reconciliation of the shipping containers revealed the location of the missing bodies and they could now be returned to their families. We were also able to remove over half the containers from the site as a result of neat-freak Dave's numbering system.

This work was not lost on the incoming teams. The Swedish team who followed us went to the executive committee and lobbied the joint chiefs of staff that the Australian team who had sorted out Tha Chat Chai should be brought back permanently to run the site. Not *an* Australian team, but the team that had been there in August 2005. Whilst that was very cool to hear, and a wonderful endorsement of the work we all had done, it was never really going to be a possibility. That team was a one-off.

The team's ability to cope day after day with the various environmental and emotional challenges was due in a large part to our ability to share our experiences with one another. Be it the heat and oppressive humidity, or the seemingly endless number of deceased, many of them young lives that had been taken before they had had a chance to grow, or dealing with the struggles of being apart from our families, there was always someone there who knew what you were going through, because more than likely they were going through it too.

Often it was the stories of the horrors that people had endured that made our work so distressing. One particular morning I ducked my head into the tunnel where the post-mortems were being conducted to talk with members of the team before I headed off to Phuket for a meeting. Speaking to our team was a party from one of the Nordic countries, there to receive a body to be repatriated. The story they recounted of this particular deceased was that he was a paraplegic. On Boxing Day morning he was with family members who had wheeled him down onto the sand so he could experience the joys of being on the beach with the rest of his party. However, when that wall of water came in, he was simply abandoned in his wheelchair, stuck in the sand to watch as the water came in.

We turned up to work prepared to deal with the bodies of the deceased; we weren't always prepared for their stories.

Naturally enough, we had to find some way of releasing the ever-present tension, but for our team it never involved the popular bars of Patong. Don't get me wrong – we loved a beer and certainly drank our share at particular times, but we found refuge away from the tourist strip, among the locals or in our own company. Many a night ended with us leaving what had become our second home – a great little drinking spot called the Timber Hut – and heading back to our hotel in convoy, astride a local taxi motorbike whose driver had waited patiently for our night to end so that he could take us home and receive a fare that warranted the wait. I never understood why we would barter so hard and get the price down from a ridiculous starting price of three hundred baht to a reasonable eighty baht, and then on arrival at our hotel hand over nothing less than five hundred baht and apologise because we didn't have more!

No matter how late we walked out of the Timber Hut (and there were a few times that got us home just in time to have a shower, change and head back to work again), the same motorbike man would be patiently waiting for us. I couldn't believe my eyes when, more than two years later, I walked out of the same club and there was our taxi man, sitting and waiting just as he had done the last time I'd been there. I am not sure which of the two of us was happier to see the other. Of course there was no discussion around price this time, except the tip had now escalated to a thousand baht.

I didn't see him the next night. I think he was sitting under the verandah of his house smoking a celebratory Cuban cigar!

Chapter 14

Beauty and Despair

She stepped out of the van that had brought her to the site at Tha Chat Chai and seemed to have a sense of purpose about her. She was an older lady, I guessed in her early sixties, and clearly a westerner by the immediate impact the heat had on her as she left the comfort of the airconditioned van. She didn't look like an NGO worker, or a foreign bureaucrat, and as she walked over to me I realised why she seemed so familiar. She could have been my mum.

She was slightly hunched, as though injured in some way. I reached out to shake her hand and introduce myself, but she stepped forward and hugged me. It was one of those hugs that convey a deep sense of life and love. It really could have been from my mum, but this hug was from a grief-stricken grandma.

She put her head on my shoulder and started to sob. It came from deep within her and as she held me tight I could almost hear her heart crying. This was the pain of someone who had lost what was most precious to her.

What I came to learn was that this lady, who turned out to be Australian, had lost her only daughter in the tsunami.

We found her daughter, but she was dead.

Her daughter had come to Thailand for the holiday of a life-time – you see, it was her honeymoon. This lady I was hugging had lost her daughter and she had also lost her son-in-law.

We found him, but he was dead as well.

This couple had been together for a number of years before they decided to get married, and a couple of months prior to the wedding they'd received some very special news. They were going to be parents.

Well, of course the unborn baby died as well.

So this lady had lost her only daughter, her new son-in-law and what would have been her first grandchild.

The hug she was giving me should have been for her daughter; it should have been for her grandchild. The pain she was feeling wasn't that immediate emotion and shock, it was deeper. It was the pain you feel when you have had the time to contemplate the extent of your loss, when you have really had time to grasp that death is forever.

This represented the real tragedy of the work I was doing.

Joy Vogel was the lady, and she had come to Thailand in search of answers. Her daughter, Moi Vogel, thirty-two, had recently married Christian Knott, thirty-four, and Joy was now dealing with the impossibly harsh reality that she had lost them both.

I spent several hours with Joy that day talking about life, the joys of bringing children into the world and watching them grow, and we also spent a lot of time talking about death. Joy hadn't come to Thailand to search for Moi and Christian; Moi's brother Peter had done that in the days following the tsunami without success. When Joy made her journey their bodies had already been repatriated to Australia. It wasn't answers she was looking for, it was to feel the energy of the last days of Moi's life and to spend some time with those of us who had been entrusted with the duty of identifying and sending her home.

I found experiences like this the hardest and yet also amongst the most rewarding. I often felt we provided so little. We could never deliver good news. Joy had lost her daughter, her son-in-law and her unborn grandchild; nothing I could say would change that. I could not pretend to understand her grief and I did not try. To do so would have been an insult. More often than not it was simply a case of providing what information I could, to try to answer those nagging questions they had. It wasn't about taking away their pain or making things right, it was about providing families with answers.

Although I fully acknowledged the need to meet families, to hear their stories, I knew I also had to find a balance. All forensic practitioners have to maintain some distance from all that pain and suffering, otherwise it would be impossible to do the job without going mad. I had at times in my career been described as cold or hard, and for me this had been a form of protection. I hope that during my time in Thailand I learnt to balance this with compassion. This was the lesson that people like Joy taught me. They reminded me that behind every body we examined was a grieving family, and our job was to provide answers to them that would allow some degree of comfort, or at least a deeper level of understanding in a journey that was so foreign and confusing for them.

Chapter 15

An Inspirational Gift

It was a typically hot day at Tha Chat Chai and I had just arrived back on site from an executive committee meeting in Phuket City.

I pulled up in front of the administration building and for a moment sat in the airconditioned comfort of the car. I was three-quarters of the way through my third tour of Thailand and my energy was low. Being in the car gave me a few moments of respite from the death and destruction that consumed each day.

Also playing on my mind was that as the time to leave Thailand came closer, so did the reality of the situation I would face when I returned home. In between my second and third tours of Thailand things had deteriorated sufficiently to the point where I had moved out of the family home and had been camped on the foldout bed at my brother's house. This was another reason why I found solitude in Thailand. As welcoming as Dave and Dee and their family were to me, it wasn't where I wanted to be. At the age of thirty-eight no one wants to be sleeping on a foldout bed with their wardrobe in the boot of the car. In the weeks before I returned to Thailand I had worked exceptionally long hours – not because of the demands of work, but so I would be less intrusive on Dave, Dee and the kids. Thailand offered an escape from what was at home but I knew the end was nigh. When I flew back to Sydney at the end of the tour, I would step off the plane and quite literally have no home to go to. It wasn't a good feeling.

I opened the car door and the oppressive heat immediately smacked me in the face. By the time I had walked the ten metres to my office, I had worked up a sweat.

I found my way to the body release area where a family had arrived to collect a relative. Gilly was there talking with the family and working her way through the various documents we needed to sight before a body could be released. A slightly built Thai woman of middle age was waiting with the unmistakable look of a grieving relative. Her shoulders were hunched forward, her movements slow and her eyes glazed. In her hand she held a white handkerchief which she used to wipe away the stream of tears rolling down her face. She represented so many of the visitors that came to the site; a body from which the heart and soul seemed temporarily to have left.

After speaking with this lady I learnt that she was from a community located six hours north of Tha Chat Chai. She had made the long journey with a friend who had driven her in his beaten-up utility. She was here to receive the body of her teenaged son.

She was poor and didn't have the means to purchase a coffin in which to place her son. For those of us working at the site, there was nothing worse than handing the body of a child back to parents in a clinical blue body bag. The way you had to pick up the bag immediately took away all dignity.

We had been caught in this predicament only once, and after that crushing experience we had arranged for the purchase of a number of simple timber coffins, one of which we made available now.

I watched this mother practise a simple yet moving traditional

Buddhist ceremony as she received the remains of her child. The love she held for her son, as well as the pain of losing him, was deeply etched into her beautiful face. The smell of the incense she burnt was a welcome change from the combination of clinical anti-septic or decomposed bodies that permeated everything on the site.

At the conclusion of her prayers and the placing of her son into the coffin, she then gifted both Gill and me with something that will never leave us.

In a gentle voice she thanked us for the work we were doing, and for the coffin we had provided. Then this lady, this mother, began – in the most genuine way possible – to ask how we were. She inquired about our wellbeing and our health, displaying a level of grace, sympathy and compassion the likes of which I had never seen before.

At what must have surely been one of the lowest points in her life, and having travelled for six gruelling hours to collect the body of her child, this dear woman somehow managed to put aside her own grief to show to us her deep appreciation and concern.

After many tears, most of which were ours, and traditional expressions of thanks, we loaded her son's coffin onto the back of the utility and she left the site to return to her community.

This beautiful Thai lady of the most modest means left an indel-ible impression upon both Gill and me. To be honest, I felt gutted. She was able to behave with so much compassion and dignity, but there was so little we could do for her.

The cruellest thing, though, was that within days this lady once again made that six-hour journey from the north of Thailand to our site, again accompanied by her friend in his utility.

She had come to collect another of her children.

Again she displayed the same level of grace; again she conveyed to us with deep honesty and compassion her gratitude for the work we had done.

112

If the world were a fair place this mother would never have had to make that journey even once. But life is not fair. And this poor woman made that twelve-hour return trip not once, not twice, not even three times. Four times she travelled to Tha Chat Chai to take possession of the bodies of her children, until she had no more to collect. Yet each time she behaved with such grace and compassion that it felt to me like a precious gift.

She was truly remarkable, courageous and inspirational, and my time with her, albeit brief, will remain with me forever.

Chapter 16

Money Doesn't Inspire

It was on this third rotation to Thailand that I realised the importance of valuing all contributions to a process, no matter how insignificant the role in that process may seem.

By August 2005 the pace at Tha Chat Chai had slowed. Many of the post-mortems had been conducted and it was the work of the team to manage the site, facilitate the repatriation of those identified and conduct further examinations as required.

The work of the team was supported by the Thai army, whose role was to assist in the movement of the bodies from the shipping containers to the mortuary. The soldiers' job was to retrieve a body from a container and carry it on a field trolley to the examination area for the forensic process to begin. I have vivid memories of watching these strong men perform what must have felt to them like a menial task. The heat outside was oppressive, but the freezing air inside the containers brought an immediate chill to the bones. It was possible to dress appropriately for one environment but not for both.

These soldiers had been performing their duties for a couple of months, and understandably were losing their enthusiasm for the job. The movement of the bodies throughout the site wasn't the responsibility of the Thais alone – many of the international teams contributed in this area – but for the Thai soldiers this was their main task. The challenge for them each day was to muster the energy and motivation to continue their work. They were working ten hours a day, six days a week, and many of the soldiers had been at the camp for some eight months. It was clear why they struggled with motivation.

During the initial handover the outgoing DVI commander from Sweden told me that he had noticed the drop in the soldiers' morale and had attempted to lift their motivation by buying them cartons of cigarettes. Not exactly promoting a healthy lifestyle but it did work – for a short time anyway.

It was becoming increasingly difficult to get the soldiers to work at the pace required, and I was acutely aware of the impact this was having on the entire team, and in fact the whole DVI process. I saw this as an excellent example of people not valuing the contribution they were making to an important process. The role of moving bodies from one part of the site to another was the least technically challenging job, but this didn't mean it was any less important. We had forensic pathologists, odontologists, biologists and police specialists from around the world, but when the soldiers lost their motivation the whole process started to grind to a halt. Identification and repatriation couldn't be achieved without bodies to work on.

The soldiers' waning enthusiasm was, however, in stark contrast to the passion they displayed when singing their national anthem each morning. With great gusto they showed us what an incredibly patriotic lot they were. Each morning they would stand tall and proud to sing as the Thai flag was raised above the site.

Unfortunately this passion dissipated once the singing had

stopped. Shoulders would slump, heads would go down and the soldiers would wander off aimlessly. It was beginning to become a chore to find them and direct them back to work. I knew that we needed to inject some energy and motivation back into the soldiers, but the question was how?

We then made one of our smartest decisions of the whole tour. We decided that every Australian team member would learn to sing the Thai national anthem – in Thai!

Dave Neal downloaded the words from the internet and over the next few days, as we travelled the one and a half hours to and from the site, we learnt to sing the Thai national anthem.

Some days later the Australian contingent lined up behind the soldiers as we did every morning, and as the Thais began singing, so did we. The soldiers swung around in amazement, eyes as big as saucers and grins like Cheshire cats'. The expression on their faces will stay with me forever. They sang louder than ever before.

Did we sing the anthem well? No.

Did that matter? Not one bit.

Did our efforts have the desired effect? Absolutely!

From that point on, the Thai soldiers were once again walking with a spring in their step, inspired to complete the task at hand, and never more so than when it was an Australian asking for their assistance.

This experience taught me the importance of motivation. If you want to inspire a team towards a goal, you must find out what drives them. You have to understand what they connect to on an emotional level, and then, as a leader, you have to take responsibility to connect with them, with honesty and integrity.

It also taught me that I can't sing!

Chapter 17

The German Couple

One of my duties as commander of the DVI site at Tha Chat Chai was to host the many visitors to the site. Government officials from all over the world came to see how their donated resources were being utilised; forensic leaders came to see first-hand the immense scale of the operation; and there was a constant throng of media representatives who had somehow convinced the executive committee that they had significant justification to be there too.

To my mind, some people had more of a right to visit than others. This wasn't a sideshow we were running, it was a humanitarian response to a natural disaster that had resulted in the loss of several thousand lives in this area alone.

The easiest way to separate those who came with a legitimate interest was their response when we showed them the tunnel where the PM work was being conducted. The tunnel was basically a row of flat-pack buildings that had been constructed on site. It looked much like a row of demountable classrooms connected end on end; we had simply replaced the desks and chairs with washbasins and X-ray equipment. The tunnel was twenty-five metres or so in length and allowed for the movement of bodies through one end and out the other.

For those without a genuine interest in visiting the site it was normally as we gowned up and approached the entrance to the tunnel that they recoiled and decided they had seen enough. Their visit would then be confined to the mess area.

On this particular day one of the Thai security guards came to my office and requested that I speak with two visitors who had presented themselves at the gate to the compound. I have exaggerated somewhat when I say he requested I speak with the visitors. It was more a case of him standing in the doorway, smiling and pointing at two people waiting at the security point. I don't know why, I should have known better, but I asked him who they were and what they wanted, to which he responded with a very broad smile and replied, 'Thank you.' Of course I should have saved him the discomfort of asking questions and just got up and gone to the gate. It wasn't this poor guy's fault that I was in his country and didn't speak his language.

Walking down to the security gate I could immediately tell that these people were not government officials; they were not forensic representatives from some faraway laboratory, and they didn't have that impatient look the media have where you are simply a stop along the way to something more important.

The man looked to be in his mid-thirties and was dressed in a pair of board shorts; the woman accompanying him was very attractive and looked to be in her late twenties.

Dressed in regulation hospital scrubs and wiping the sweat from my brow, I approached the couple, and I knew immediately from the strained expressions on their faces that they were relatives or friends of a tsunami victim. All of a sudden I wished I were dressed a little more appropriately. I stuck out my hand and introduced myself. They were German, and their grasp of the English language was only slightly better than my grasp of German, and that happens to be restricted to what I learnt from watching *Hogan's Heroes* on television as a youngster. The only other person available who might have been able to help us through the language barrier was the Thai security guard, but he didn't speak English or German.

The German gentleman had in his hands a number of documents sealed in plastic sleeves. He told me he was looking for photographic evidence of his wife who had died. It wasn't the first time I had come across this type of request but I had learnt not to judge what was right and what wasn't. I hadn't lost someone I held so dear to me, so how could I know what was best for him? He had with him a reference number, which I readily identified as a PM number allocated to all victims that had been previously identified. I excused myself to go and check on the computer to see if in fact we had the photographs they were wishing to see. We did, but just as I had anticipated, the photos depicted the body of a grossly decomposed Caucasian adult female; she would have been identified through the process of matching DNA analysis, dental records or even fingerprints. Even if visual identification was a process that was permissible, which it wasn't, it would have been impossible to identify her due to the advanced state of decomposition.

I decided not to show the man these photos. For the life of me I couldn't see how seeing his wife like this would help. I understand the thinking that seeing the body helps bring certainty, but I also know that few people really understand the horrendous changes bodies go through. The image of his wife in such an advanced state of decomposition would, I was sure, haunt him forever. It would be much better for him to remember her as she was in the photographs he had lovingly attached to the official documentation.

I returned to the security gate and invited them into our mess room where we could sit and talk without perspiration running down our faces. We took a quiet table in the corner to allow us some privacy.

I spoke firstly to the man and asked him to tell me his story. He started by telling me, in broken English, that he had come to Thailand with his wife for a summer holiday, just the two of them, a romantic escape away from Germany's bleak winter. They had stayed in the Khao Lak region and had been on the beach at the time of the tsunami. His story was similar to many others I had heard. The water receded at a speed and to a level that made no sense at all. Such was the mystery that, like many others, they felt almost compelled to walk to the water's edge to better understand what was happening. He recounted how they had stood looking at the beach now void of water and then that moment of realisation had hit them. The water was on its way back to the beach in a massive surge.

He grabbed his wife's hand; she had been a second or two slower to realise the threat. They turned to run and his wife stumbled in the sand; he almost dragged her up the beach, such was his desperation to escape, but the water quickly swept them from their feet. He held on to his wife's hand until the force of the water was too great and they were separated.

Here his voice started to grow softer and then to break. He described how he looked into the eyes of his wife as she was swept away. He told me of the fear he saw in those eyes. That was the last time he saw his wife alive.

He said that he sustained many injuries and he showed me the scars from that day. I wondered about the real scar, the one on his heart that he could not show me, and I imagined the pain he must feel every day.

He went on to confirm that the body of his wife had been identified and that she had been repatriated home and laid to rest.

I asked him what had brought him back to Thailand at this

particular point in time and why he had specifically come to this site. He continued his story by saying that he had returned to Thailand to again to visit the hotel where he had shared his last night with his wife. He would visit the restaurant where they had eaten a last meal together, and when he found the courage he would visit the beach, perhaps the location where he had last held his wife's hand before she was swept away to her death. He said that his visit to Thailand constituted a journey that he hoped would help him start to recover from this devastating episode of his life, and hence his request for the PM photographs.

As he was telling me his story, he also told me much more about his wife and their life together. He showed me many photographs of her and their young children and I reciprocated with photos of my own kids, for no reason other than it felt right to do that. We spent a lot of time talking; we spent time crying together, but thankfully we also spent time laughing too.

Whilst the two of us had been talking, the young woman had hardly said a word. I assumed that her English was not as good as the man's. I turned to her and said, 'Tell me your story.'

In her best English she began to explain that her mother had been on holidays in Thailand at the time of the tsunami and that she had died as a result of it. She said that the body of her mother had been identified and sent home to Germany and she had been buried. I asked why she was now in Thailand and she said that she, too, was on a journey of healing. I asked her who her mother had been holidaying in Thailand with, and she looked at me and then pointed at the man next to her. I looked at him then, very confused, and said, 'I thought you were here with your wife?'

To which he responded, 'Yes, I was.' I looked back to the young woman and said, 'Your mother was on holidays with this man?' 'Yes,' she said. I looked back to the man and said, 'You were here on holidays with your wife and also this lady's mother?'

'Yes,' he answered.

I sat there for a moment, thinking. This man had told me he had been in Thailand with his wife on a romantic escape; how had I got this so wrong? I sat there looking from one to the other and for a fleeting moment had a vision of this man on a romantic holiday with two women. Perhaps this was pretty cool if you were a German.

Then all of a sudden it made sense to me!

We had spent almost two hours talking and sharing stories and it was only at this point that I realised what was going on. I felt quite brilliant that I had worked this out. I looked at the man and said to him, 'This is your daughter.' I then looked to the girl and said, 'This is your father. The woman we are talking about is the same person.'

I'm quite sure I sounded as though I had just cracked a mystery to equal Dan Brown's in *The Da Vinci Code*.

I sat back, smiling.

The two of them looked at each other and the girl said something to her father in German, probably something along the lines of, 'This man is a fool. Of course you are my father, we said that at the beginning.'

To demonstrate to them that I wasn't completely useless I gave them both an ice cream and a cold bottle of water, which was probably the least I could do. I said that whilst I could understand the journey they were both on, I wouldn't give them the photographs of their dearly departed wife and mother. Having seen the state of decomposition and knowing there was little that resembled the lady in the photos, I encouraged them to remember her from the lovely photos we had spent the two hours laughing and crying over. This was how a relative should be remembered.

I also advised them that if this was something they felt incredibly strongly about, they should make an application for access to the photographs through the German coronial jurisdiction. To help them make this choice, and to facilitate any further requests they might have, I made a number of phone calls and found the German liaison officer who was working in Thailand to support the many relatives of the victims from that country. In Thailand alone Germany had suffered significant losses, with approximately five hundred nationals losing their lives. Sweden was another country that lost a similar number, with only Thailand losing more than these two nations. These numbers were of course only confined to Thailand and the work that we were doing around the identification of those who had died. It's estimated that between 250,000 and 300,000 people lost their lives, and most of this loss was in the province of Aceh, in Indonesia.

I provided them with the name and contact details for the liaison officer and advised them that she was expecting them to make contact with her. I arranged transport from the site for them and saw them on their way.

Two nights later at a social function I saw the German LO and I asked her if the father and daughter had made contact with her. She confirmed they had, and then said, 'You know the two of them absolutely love you.'

Apparently the German pair had, prior to coming to see me, gone to the German team and sought advice and assistance from them. However, not only had they not been given any answers, they had just been told to go to Tha Chat Chai and ask there. The LO went on to tell me that the two hours I had devoted to this couple had made an incredible difference to them and they appreciated the fact that an Australian had taken the time to sit and listen to their story when their own countrymen hadn't been willing to do that.

I felt very humbled and of course pleased that I had taken the time to sit with this couple.

I then got to thinking about the lessons I could take from this.

I realised that the German team member, in dismissing the couple, had forgotten why we were here and the privileged position we held. Although few people in the world would know more about the mass identification of bodies than those teams who worked in Thailand, we weren't really there to identify bodies, we were there to provide answers to families, and the German officer had forgotten this.

This man and his daughter were on a journey. It was a journey they had never made before and one hopefully they would never make again. I have no doubt that although they would have been aware that there were another 5394 victims who had died in Thailand, all they were concerned with at this point in time was their own loved one. And they deserved to be treated by us as though they were the only ones who mattered.

The risk when you operate in an area like this is forgetting the importance of what you do. You can easily slip into assuming that everyone understands the process, because you know it so well, and it's easy to forget that this is a life-changing journey for the person involved, although it may not be for you. That father and daughter deserved, as does every victim's family, for us to be the best that we could possibly be every time.

This was another enduring lesson that I would take from Thailand, and as it turned out it would be one of the last. I spent the final couple of days of this tour in discussions with the senior executive of the Royal Thai Police, who had asked me to lead a project on Phi Phi Island. I had flown to the island a number of times to scope a project which concerned the raising of a sea wall that had collapsed at the time of the tsunami, and where it was feared a number of bodies may have been buried. It would be a significant project which would take several weeks to complete and I was earmarked to lead it.

Any return to Thailand would require approval at a number of levels within Australia and I held out little hope that such a request would be given the green light. My final trip from Phi Phi Island back to the mainland was taken aboard a police launch and, sitting staring into the crystal blue waters, I had time to reflect on the events that had seen my life turned on its head since 26 December 2004. In the space of several months I had watched my marriage fall apart, I had left home, I'd led teams in the world's largest DVI response, and soon would be boarding a flight back to Australia but without a home to go to.

During the last tour I had spent several hours trying to secure rental accommodation back in Sydney for when I returned. Given the strong demand for rental properties in Sydney at the time, I was lucky to get a response from real estate agents, let alone hear anything encouraging. I was destined to return to Sydney from this tour and start the most unpleasant task of finding somewhere to live – and quickly.

I knew I had to return to Sydney and start to sort out the mess that awaited. I resigned myself to the fact that this was indeed the last tour I would make to Thailand in my capacity as a forensic investigator. Although as Phi Phi Island slipped into the distance, the escape that the island offered from the reality that I faced was appealing.

Leaving Thailand also meant leaving Gilly, with whom I had formed a strong friendship, and I felt I was leaving an older sister without being sure if I would see her again given the tyranny of distance between us both.

The flight back to Australia was not taken with team members – I travelled alone. The others had left a few days prior but I was required to stay to perform a handover to the incoming team. It was a sombre trip, one that had started under such different circumstances eight months previous. Although I had been backwards and forwards to Australia a couple of times, this journey did feel like the end. The overriding emotion I felt on the flight home was sadness.

The adrenalin that had been present with the first tours was long gone and I had plenty of time to be present in my head and with my feelings. The sadness I felt first and foremost was for my kids and for Nicole. They had been left to pick up the pieces of the destruction that landed at their feet whilst I was off overseas, my head filled with the work that I was doing. I felt sadness for the thousands of people who had lost their lives, the families who had been torn apart by the loss of loved ones. And I also felt a deep sadness for where I now found myself.

Chapter 18

Hands Across the Water

Through her work on previous tours to Thailand, Gill had met Khun Rotjana, a Thai lady who was looking after thirty-two kids orphaned as a result of the tsunami. The children were now living in a tent at Khao Lak. It was a good-looking tent, with a timber floor and power to run fans and lights, but it was still just a tent.

Of these kids, seventeen had lost both parents and the other fifteen had lost their mum. The fifteen who had lost their mum were living there because their own family could no longer provide for them.

Khun Rotjana was working for the Duang Prateep Foundation (DPF), an organisation that was formed in 1978 to support street kids in the Khlong Toei slums of Bangkok. DPF was formed by Khru Prateep Unsongtham Hata with the aim of providing education to those who were not at school and, because of their family's financial position, had no chance of receiving a formal education. Khru Prateep's first student was Khun Rotjana.

Khun Rotjana graduated from the school established by Khru Prateep and committed her life to repaying the opportunities she had been given. In time the student became the teacher and Khun Rotjana started to work at the school and within the community. She quickly found a love of teaching through music, dance and art and developed a reputation for travelling throughout Thailand teaching the poorest of the people lessons through puppetry.

After the events of Boxing Day 2004, Khru Prateep asked Khun Rotjana to go down to the Khao Lak area and see what assistance could be provided. Little did Khun Rotjana know the impact this would have upon her life. She quickly established herself in the worst affected area of Khao Lak. Here, with a handful of children who had no one to care for them, she formed a temporary home. A home that was a tent, which would grow in size as the demand for her services grew. More children came seeking somewhere to sleep, something to eat and someone to hug them. Khun Rotjana provided all three of those necessities of life.

Whilst Rotjana provided the food, care and love the children needed, living in a tent was not the answer long-term. Gill had asked Khun Rotjana on her last visit what she needed most and, no surprise, Khun Rotjana had said, 'A home for the children.'

But she did not want a home at any expense. Options existed within the Khao Lak community to provide some of what Khun Rotjana was looking for or needed for her children, but many of these options came with conditions. These conditions might have been the need to move out of the community that was home for the children, away from the schools they attended and away from any friends or relatives they might still have. The conditions imposed by some organisations required Khun Rotjana and the children to take on a new religion. She was wise enough to know that she didn't need to compromise what she stood for; she needed to be strong and to stand up for what she thought was in the best interests of the children.

Khun Rotjana's commitment to Khru Prateep was that she would spend two years living in Khao Lak to help the children get on their feet, to bring about some stability, and for Khru Prateep to build a structure that would allow her to go home to Bangkok where her husband and five-year-old awaited her return.

In the early days of the operation all the work was done by Khun Rotjana and Khru Prateep. Staff were recruited on a local level, and in the beginning no one got paid. There simply wasn't any money. Staff who came to work at the orphanage came because they, too, had lost their families and for many their sense of purpose in life. Thankfully, DPF funds were diverted from their projects in Bangkok to this region to provide food for the children.

I was standing in the kitchen of my newly rented house having a long-distance phone conversation with Gilly, who had also returned to her home in the UK. She was telling me about Khun Rotjana and the kids, and she said, 'So, do you want to raise some money and build the kids a home?'

'Let's do it,' I said without hesitation.

'What are we going to call ourselves?' Gilly asked.

I answered immediately. 'How about Hands Across the Water?'

It was as simple as that.

All I had to do now was work out how I was going to raise the amount of money that would be needed.

I thought back to a lunch meeting I had had between my second and third tours of Thailand. The lunch was with a family friend, Craig West, whom I had known for the last twenty years, and Matt Church, a speaker on the corporate circuit, whom I was meeting for the first time. Matt was, in fact, one of Australia's most sought-after speakers.

Westy had set up the lunch after I had shown him photos from Thailand and talked about the challenges we had faced and how we had overcome them. At the lunch Matt told me about the speakers' circuit and how lucrative it could be; he told me my story needed to be told and encouraged me to get out there and tell it. Quite frankly, I walked away from the lunch without really believing too much of what Matt had said.

Who, I thought, would really benefit from hearing my story? What did I know about business, because that's the world I'd be pitching to. I'd only ever worked for the police. And surely he was exaggerating the amount of money that could be made. I doubted it so much that I returned to Thailand for my third tour without giving the idea much more thought.

After I made the commitment to Gilly, though, my thoughts returned to that lunch. If even half of what Matt had said was true, then this could have possibilities.

The biggest obstacle I faced in breaking onto the speaking circuit was my scepticism about whether there was value in my story and whether or not people would want to hear it, let alone pay big dollars to do so. I really questioned my value and relevance to others outside the industry.

My first speaking events, arranged through connections and with encouragement from Matt, seemed to confirm my doubts. I began travelling from one networking group to the next, selling my wares, so to speak. I recall speaking one day at a Returned Services League club on the north shore of Sydney to a group of retirees. They could have replaced me with bingo cards and everything would have looked as though it was in order.

Halfway through my talk I could see a lot of heads resting on a lot of shoulders. The occasional snore emanated from the crowd, but I just spoke louder, pretending I couldn't hear it. Often I was saved by an ever-diligent wife who would thrust her elbow into the ribs of her drowsy but obedient husband. He would wake with a start and nod approval to whatever it was I had just said as though he had been awake and paying attention for the entire time!

Amazingly enough, there was applause at the end of the address, not only from those who had stayed awake for the story, but also from those who felt it was appropriate to applaud although they didn't quite understand why. Many began to form a queue in front of my table, with the majority wanting to shake my hand and make a donation to Hands. This was exactly the response I had hoped for.

I have never asked for support for Hands from the stage – especially given that many of the groups are paying me to speak. I have always believed that if people connect with the story and what I am doing they won't need to be asked to donate, they just will. This day, as the line diminished, the pile of notes on the table grew. They were handing me fifty-dollar notes as if they were no longer legal currency.

At the end of the day I had several thousand dollars in donations and a method of raising even more.

Over the ensuing years I have travelled throughout Australia and overseas delivering keynote presentations. The audiences have ranged from thousands to a handful, and each time I have tried to take people on a personal journey, to challenge them to reflect upon what is most important to them and how they would feel if that were taken away. I try to build to this moment, and for many it comes as a surprise as it is on the back of some humorous stories. As I stand and lead the audience on this journey I can quite literally feel and see that I have them. It's a special feeling to know that you have several hundred people hanging on your next word.

On occasions you can walk offstage and know that you have nailed the presentation. You have hit the mark and it really is a great feeling. People can be incredibly generous in their offerings after hearing a presentation that resonates deeply with them.

The first time I received a standing ovation, it caught me by surprise. I left the stage and walked to the back of the room; it happened to be an event Matt Church was MCing and he told me that I had to get back up on stage. I did this, acknowledged the audience and again walked towards the back of the room. Matt caught me halfway down the room and said, 'You need to stay on stage until they finish, otherwise it's rude, mate.' Back I went, and shortly afterwards walked to the back of the room for the final time.

It was an amazing experience and one I won't forget. Not just because so many people in the audience liked what I had to say, but because one particular person didn't, and was very clear about that.

When the conference concluded, people lined up to say how much they had enjoyed the presentation. Standing to one side was a lady and I knew by her actions she was waiting to speak with me privately. She waited until everyone had gone and then approached me.

She said, 'Can I help you with something?'

I thought she was going to offer her assistance to Hands in some way. 'Of course, we'd love your assistance.'

For the next five minutes this lady dissected my presentation, telling me what I had done wrong and what I should have done better. I was shocked, I was stunned. Hadn't she seen what had happened in the room? Didn't she realise that at this point in time I was the self-anointed rock star of the conference?

People can be very generous in their summations and people can be incredibly honest as well.

Once, and only once, have I had harsh feedback from a client about a presentation. I am not naive enough to think there haven't been other occasions when the client wasn't thrilled, but only once in several hundred presentations has the client come back with negative feedback – and when I say negative, there was not a shred of anything positive at all.

I had been flown to Singapore to speak to a group and beforehand I had had so many phone briefings that I figured I had actually delivered the keynote in totality prior to getting to Singapore.

The delegates were from the US and the UK and it was a small dinner keynote with about fifty people in the room. I delivered the address, stayed for dinner and drinks with the client, and spoke to many of the other people in the room prior to leaving them to drink on. At this point I thought things had gone quite well; there were certainly the usual complimentary comments, although that may have been through good manners more than anything else.

A few weeks later I received the written feedback from the client, who did nothing short of slam me from pillar to post, with comments such as, 'We would have got more value from the general manager juggling at the front of the room for an hour.' Ouch, that hurt.

When you stand and expose yourself (not quite literally) there will be people who like what they see and others who are less impressed. You can pretend not to be interested or influenced by the feedback, but I haven't met a speaker yet who doesn't want a good response. The negative feedback, and thankfully I haven't had to deal with too much of it, is just part of putting yourself out there. There will be people who turn up at a conference with a pissed-off attitude towards the world, before they even know who the speakers are. They will detest what every speaker stands for and will put them into a pigeonhole as a cheesy motivational speaker before they have even taken to the stage. There are people who sit waiting to be convinced that you have the right to the stage rather than coming with an open mind and, having learnt my trade as a speaker, I'm okay with that, now.

But being okay with people not liking what you have to say or what you stand for requires either a thick skin or getting really good, really fast. Having spent twenty odd years in the cops, I was used to about fifty per cent of the population despising what you stand for, so I could say I had a thick skin, but actually that was far from the truth. Therefore I decided to get good – fast.

The first time I spoke at a conference in Thailand was for Bill Hindmarsh from Goldwell, which provides high-end haircare products. I was thrilled to be asked to speak in Thailand, let alone to be getting paid for it. During a briefing call with Bill he inquired as to my international fee and I told him. He said that was out of his budget and I said, 'Well, Bill, whatever your budget allows I will be happy with,' and I was.

My presentation came at the close of the three-day conference and the room was full of women who owned hair salons, with only a few men dotted around in the room. Sitting in the front row were two guys, one who owned a salon and the other who was his partner.

I finished speaking and was honoured to receive a standing ovation from the audience, which is incredibly humbling, no matter how many times it occurs. After the conference was over the two guys approached and the first one said to me that they had been in a personal relationship with each other for seven years and this was the first time he'd seen his partner shed a tear. But what I thought was really cool was to follow.

The most pernickety of the two had been keeping a log of everything that was wrong with the hotel. He had a dossier of what had gone wrong, and at what time and on which date, and he was going to present it to the general manager upon check-out. However, after hearing my address he went back to his room and tore up his meticulously kept log of all his complaints. He said it had something to do with having just received a shot of perspective!

It is a privilege to be given the trust of the client to speak with a group, no matter how large or in what location. I had given my

audience insight into a world that was far removed from their own.
I had found a way to raise money for Hands, but more importantly,
I was reminding people of the tsunami and the children left behind
in its wake.

Chapter 19

The Home of the Stream of Love

In the early days after the tsunami, the kids either found their own way to Khun Rotjana and her tent or were brought there by family members. At that stage there was little filtering of the children: if they needed a place to stay, they could stay in the tent. It wasn't as though viable medium- or even short-term alternatives existed for the kids who were arriving. The truth was, the entire community needed help.

Friends, relatives or carers who had provided some type of temporary shelter for the kids brought them to Khun Rotjana because they could no longer provide for them. Grandparents who had relied upon their own children to provide for them now found themselves struggling to look after themselves, let alone their grandchildren. Single fathers just couldn't see how they could work and support young children. Without their extended families, which they had lost, the problems seemed insurmountable.

The land for the orphanage had been secured from the local community, with a commitment that if the money was raised to build a home for the children, they would donate the land. Plans were drawn for a two-storey building with accommodation for the boys at one end of the second floor and a couple of bedrooms for the girls at the opposite end. There was a small office and a kitchen that seemed to defy the number of meals that would need to be produced each day. Construction would start once a significant portion of the money had been raised. Thankfully, interest in supporting the Thai community was still strong at this point in time and a number of people were prepared to put up their dollars.

As the speaking work I was doing increased, so too did the funds that I was starting to raise. Along with Gill and myself, a commitment had also been made by a community within the Thai stock exchange to raise funds. Each of us worked independently of the others and each was committed to raising as much as we could, with the ultimate goal being the AUD$250,000 the building was estimated to cost.

By early 2006 signs were good that the money was going to be raised and, as the head of the Duang Prateep Foundation, Khru Prateep entered into a binding contract for the construction of the building. My role was little more than raising whatever money I could. In the early days I certainly considered myself as nothing more than a contributor of funds to a project that was led by DPF.

The building works were undertaken by local building contractors in accordance with a tender process managed by the Duang Prateep Foundation. It was decided that rather than enlist volunteers from abroad to assist in the work, locals would be employed so that the community would benefit more broadly from the project too. And besides, this wasn't a building that could be knocked up in a week with a group of good-hearted volunteers – this was a significant structure that would take several months to complete.

Construction of the new building commenced in early 2006, with the opening scheduled for August of that same year.

Although Gill and I shared a common bond in what initially

led us to Thailand and the work that we did there, the ways we went about raising money for the children were very different. Gill formed a team with her husband Ian and a number of colleagues and set about raising a significant amount of money quite quickly. She employed what you might call a traditional fundraising approach of holding dinners, gala balls and doing basically whatever she could to raise awareness of the kids in Thailand and money to support them. In doing this Gill was very successful and but for her efforts and commitment to the children, they would have spent a lot longer living in that tent.

I returned to Australia after my work in Thailand without a home to live in myself, so I certainly didn't have the same capacity as Gilly to pull fundraising events together. As when any married couple splits, you immediately lose half of your friends and connections as they choose who they will side with. I wasn't in any position to leverage contacts, even for a great cause, so I did what seemed to make sense. I took up the opportunity to speak at conferences on leadership and the lessons I had learnt working in Thailand. The funny thing was these weren't fundraising events – I was booked as a leadership speaker – but upon hearing the messages people decided to give. The amount of money I raised initially was small and slow. It took time to build momentum, but with the momentum came a sustainable model, and by year three after forming Hands I turned over in excess of AUD$1 million in a calendar year and this has been repeated year on year ever since.

Just as the fundraising paths that Gill and I took were different, so too was the formation of our charities. Our commonality was limited to our desire to help the children of Thailand and in the name we shared, Hands Across the Water. Gill's charity work was in the UK, and therefore complied with UK law and regulations, and mine was in Australia. This set-up wasn't the result of any falling out or disagreement between us; it was just that logistically it was so much easier to run our own operations from our own country. However the differences between the two organisations grew as time passed.

In the course of the fundraising work that Gill had undertaken in the UK she had come into contact with the parents of Sarah, a young girl who died in the tsunami but whose body was never recovered. Sarah was one of the very few non-Thai people whose body was not identified in the DVI process. There is no question in my mind that her body is not one of those that rest at Bang Muang cemetery, rather that her body was taken out to sea and never recovered.

Sarah's parents made a financial contribution to the building of Baan Tharn Namchai, as the orphanage had been called, and asked that some acknowledgement be made in memory of Sarah. One of the bedrooms at Baan Tharn Namchai is now known as 'Sarah's Room'.

In my mind, Baan Tharn Namchai is best described as a home. Nothing more and nothing less. It's not a 'facility for the housing of children'; I don't even like referring to it as an 'orphanage', because that brings with it connotations that are simply wrong. It is a home that is filled with love and warmth; the children, whilst they don't share common parents, all share a common bond, and that is the loss of so many in their families.

That this was a real home for the children was quite clear to me the first time I stepped inside the building, twenty months after the Boxing Day tsunami, and twelve months after my last DVI rotation. The building that the kids now called home was so different from what you might think an orphanage would look like. It is a two-storey building with open stairs at both ends, and is open to the light that filters through the many windows, filling the building with warmth and sunshine. The building was divided into boys' and girls' areas, which were separated by a corridor that displayed the pictures the kids had completed at school. It didn't have the regimented feel of a boarding school, nor did it have the smell of a place where kids are left too long in wet and soiled nappies. During my police career I learnt what a house smelt like where kids weren't cared for. This place didn't have that smell.

The beds were all brightly painted in various shades of pink, yellow, blue and red, and soft toys sat on each. Musical instruments were scattered around the building and it had fresh flowers: beautiful orchids of rich deep purples, soft pinks and calming yellows were everywhere.

Baan Tharn Namchai felt like a home filled with love.

Of course, the children's journeys were not over just because they had a new home and their own bed to sleep in. Their resilience is testament to their courage and strong belief, yet it doesn't truly reflect the scale of their loss. Each of the children had their own story.

Two children who were sister and brother came to live at Baan Tharn Namchai in the middle of 2007. They were aged four and two at the time of the tsunami and they lost both of their parents. They were taken to live in the jungle outside of Khao Lak by an old man who was like a grandfather to them. They lived with this old man in a corrugated-iron shed for two and a half years. Neither of them went to school and neither of them mixed with other members of the community; they lived in a very remote area with just this old man to care for them. The old man became gravely ill and was taken to hospital. What exactly happened next, we don't know, but it seems the children were left on their own in the shed. Three weeks later, clinging to life, the children, then aged seven and four, were found alone, on the side of the road, by police. They were both sick, malnourished and incredibly frightened. How long they had spent in the shed alone, how many nights they had wandered through the jungle in search of food, we don't know.

The children were taken to hospital and Khun Rotjana was summoned by the police. They explained the situation to her and asked her to take the two children into Baan Tharn Namchai, because shortly the children would be discharged from hospital and they knew of no other options. Of course Khun Rotjana agreed; how could anyone turn children away under these circumstances? The trauma they had been through wasn't erased by a warm bed and full tummy, of course. For the first six weeks the girl, who was seven, wouldn't speak – at all. Her brother constantly ran away. But with the passing of weeks they settled into their new home and made many new friends. Both now attend school and their smiles are as big as the other children's.

Since opening Baan Tharn Namchai we have continued to add to the building and to the quality of life for the children living there. There is a large playground, there is now a computer laboratory where the older children can work and complete their studies, and each of the children has their own bed. But this wasn't always the case.

After opening Baan Tharn Namchai in August of 2006 (and to this very day), new children arrived on an all too frequent basis seeking a home. Some came in the back of a police car, rescued from a situation in which they had been psychologically, physically and sexually abused by those purporting to care for them – those who see it as their right to take from the children what they want in lieu of providing them with a bed and meal. When children arrive under these circumstances, how can they be turned away?

When a single mum struggling to provide for her children, and often for the children of dead siblings too, takes a new man into her life who brings with him an income but also alcohol abuse and violence, she sees few options for herself. Hearing this in Australia we probably think the best option is for mum and the kids to stay together, to receive government support and for the abuser to be removed and even locked up. But when such options don't exist, where do families like this turn? Giving the kids up and seeing them live at Baan Tharn Namchai might not be the best option in our eyes, but until there are significant changes to the levels of community support in the region it becomes the only option for those without means.

The kids who come to Baan Tharn Namchai from families who aren't able to care for them right now aren't locked away from relatives or parents forever. There is a strong culture at Baan Tharn Namchai of ensuring the kids spend time with their relatives during the school holidays. We provide financial support for this, so those important family connections can be maintained and indeed fostered where at all possible. We also provide short-term care and meals for the kids, parents and carers who struggle on and do manage to provide for the kids in their own home, but sometimes trip and fall.

Just as there have been many children who have come to live at Baan Tharn Namchai as a result of family breakdown, there have also been many children over the last five years whose families have recovered to the point where they are able to leave Khun Rotjana and return to their family unit. It's always sad to see the kids leave, but it is a wonderful thing to see a family recover and reunite.

Not all children who arrive at Baan Tharn Namchai will be taken in. It is a reflection of what we have created there that many children enjoy a higher standard of living within Baan Tharn Namchai than in many of the homes in the region. In January 2010 I was in discussions with the head monk of the local temple and he said to me that the children we cared for were no longer considered underprivileged. This fact is not lost on members of the community, and there have been many occasions when a mother has arrived at Baan Tharn Namchai requesting Khun Rotjana take in her children. In discussions with the mum, it is quickly gleaned that the children are not at risk of harm, they are not being abused, they are attending school and are healthy; mum just sees Baan Tharn Namchai as a better option.

In building what we have at Baan Tharn Namchai, I am committed to ensuring the kids have what they need to have a real chance at life. But without pretending to be an authority on child welfare, it appears to me that the best place for a child, if all things are equal, is with their family. Sometimes the family constitution is different from what is normal, but our first priority is always to keep children within their community and families. If the children are being well looked after but are in a poor home, that doesn't mean they should be with us. Our children live at Baan Tharn Namchai because they have nowhere else to go and no alternative sustainable means of living. Whilst the kids have plenty to eat, a computer to do their homework on and a pillow at night where they can rest their head, that of course doesn't make up for the loss of their parents, their brothers and their sisters. Nothing ever will.

I have become acutely aware that the first of anything is usually the hardest. This includes the first time I stood on a stage to present my keynote on leadership, the first dollar that I raised or the first building that we were able to build. People want to see evidence that you have done it before, that there is substance behind what you are claiming you are going to do.

As the second, third then twentieth keynote addresses were delivered I was able to start to position myself within the space as an authority on leadership in times of crisis. As the dollars started to multiply, there was an increasing degree of rigour behind the fundraising efforts. And this was the pattern of the progress following my conversation with Gilly in the days after my return from the disaster work up until we opened Baan Tharn Namchai. I continued to repeat what was working. I refined the process, I eliminated what wasn't striking a chord, and took every opportunity I could to speak and become better at what I was doing. The more I spoke, the more bookings I got, and the more bookings I got the more money I was able to raise for the construction of the home for the kids. The driver for me was an easy one. I was enjoying what I was doing, I had a clear purpose and the outcome of doing it well was improving the lives of kids. It just made sense to keep going.

Chapter 20

The Charity Space

The decision to step into the charity space wasn't something I contemplated for a long time, weighing up the pros and cons as you might a business decision. It just seemed like the right thing to do at the time. This in turn reflects a lot of career decisions I have made – it just seemed like the right thing to do.

Apart from working at a food van in Sydney, handing out food to the homeless from around 2003 to 2005, I hadn't spent time in the charity space. I wasn't raised to support charities or donate money; God knows, Dad still has the first dollar he ever earnt. Dad's idea of giving is giving advice. He's always on hand to tell people what they are doing wrong and how they can do things better! Although he has certainly mellowed in his later years.

Mum and Dad were both from working-class families and my brother and sister and I lived a modest life growing up in the western suburbs of Sydney. Mum and Dad separated when I was about thirteen and money only became tighter. Mum in particular worked incredibly hard in the years she was alone with us to provide what she could. There wasn't much left at the end of each week after she had fed us and paid the bills. So there certainly wasn't a history of charity work within my family, but there was a history of hardworking people having a real go to make the most of what they had.

The support and interest from both Mum and Dad for Hands and the work that I do has grown to the point where it now plays a major role in their lives. Mum avoids a good part of the Canberra winter by taking up residency at the orphanage for a period of time that grows each year. In 2011 Mum will spend all of June and July with the kids at Baan Tharn Namchai, and Dad's involvement is based around our fundraising bike rides in January.

The opportunity to step into the charity space and formally establish Hands Across the Water came along at the right time in my life. Having spent three months working in Thailand, and seeing the changes that had come about in my personal life as a result, I felt like a piece of me had been left behind and a piece of Thailand was now deep inside my soul.

I am often asked these days how to set up a charity, how people can get their own personal cause or fight off the ground. I am frequently surprised at how logically many have approached the process. They ask sensible questions like, how do you structure a charity, how do you get tax deductibility? Their thinking is so much more mature than mine was. I just started with the desire and then addressed the issues as they arose.

One of the very first times I was asked to speak was at a networking breakfast in the eastern suburbs of Sydney. David Baurgmentan was the CEO of a business development group and he asked if I would speak to a group of small business owners. Doing a happy dance on my side of the phone that someone wanted me to speak to their group, but of course being too cool to let on, I put my best negotiation skills forward and demanded I be paid for the event. 'How much?' was David's response, and whilst trying to conceal the hesitations I had over my value, I responded with, 'Five hundred dollars.' Eyes closed and teeth clenched, I was thinking, *Have I gone too high? Yes, I know I have gone too high*, so I hardly heard when David asked who he should make the cheque out to.

I arrived for the breakfast and sat in the car for half an hour, waiting for the doors to be opened. As nervous as you can imagine, in I go. Feeling sick to the stomach I pass on the eggs and wait to be called to speak. Up on stage I give it my best shot and it appears to work. Afterwards, a lady walks out of the audience and stands to the side so she can speak to me on my own. Patiently she waits; occasionally we make eye contact whilst I am speaking with other people who want to pass on their thanks. She has a devilish grin and there is a twinkle in her eye. Finally, as the last person leaves, she steps forward and takes my hand in hers. I can feel the warmth of her touch as she looks me in the eye and says to me, 'I want to take you home with me.' She is seventy if she is a day, and she stands about five foot tall. She follows that up with, 'I want to adopt you as my son, you're just lovely.' Yes, I am a rock star!

After my heart returns to a resting pace, David appears full of thanks and praise and hands me a cheque made out to Hands Across the Water. I am chuffed and the charity now has five hundred dollars; this is the first donation. A problem immediately presents itself. How do I bank a cheque that is made out to Hands Across the Water, when formally no such entity exists? Suffice it to say, not only did I not have a bank account, I didn't have the legal authority to be raising money either. Given my profession you would think that was something I would have taken care of.

Off to the bank I went, looking to open a bank account for Hands Across the Water. 'No problem, just bring in your company registration, ABN and a copy of your constitution.' Okay, big problem, I didn't have anything like that. I had this cheque, but I had no means of cashing it.

After a number of rejections from banks, who were too caught up in compliance and laws governing bank accounts for my liking, I headed to the Police Credit Union. After some creative work I walked out with a bank account in the name of Hands Across the Water, which had a balance of five hundred dollars. I was able to open a social club account with two signatures, mine and that of my boss, Superintendent Mark Sweeney.

My commitment to Hands started to take up more and more of my time and headspace. It was what I thought, talked and wrote about. I was still working fulltime with the Forensic Services Group, but the work that I was doing wasn't new to me and certainly wasn't challenging me on many levels. Professionally I lacked enthusiasm for the work and felt frustrated at many people within the group who couldn't get out of their own way and spent their time looking for excuses.

The work in Thailand had certainly challenged me on a professional level and had taken me to places and situations that I couldn't have expected. My perspective on life had changed, which was no surprise considering I had been exposed to death on such a large scale and had witnessed the resolve of the wonderful Thai people. I was losing sympathy and patience for work colleagues who didn't seem to appreciate the gifts that fill our lives in Australia. We hadn't lost half of our community to a natural disaster, we weren't grieving the loss of our husbands, wives and children, we remained in reasonably well-paid employment, we all had a home that was beyond what we needed to survive and our food and medical services were not in short supply. The Thai community I had come to know didn't have what we had, but they seemed so much happier with their lives than we were on a daily basis. But I knew that I was the one who had changed at work, not everyone else. I was the one who had had my eyes opened to new and very different experiences, and it was not fair to expect others to see things the way I did.

Realistically I was always going to struggle to find motivation back in my old job. To match this lack of enthusiasm I found I had a lot of time on my hands after work, as I was now living alone. Without the kids and their busy lives to fill the void in between finishing work each day and crawling into bed, there was a significant gap. I filled it by pouring my energy into Hands. Here I felt I could make a difference. I didn't need the permission of several layers of a slow-moving and massive organisation to bring about change; when an opportunity presented itself and I thought it would benefit the kids in Thailand, I could take it and pour my energy into doing it well, without someone making a unilateral decision to stop it. It was an exciting place to be and was giving me that feeling of adrenalin that I had got from working in crisis situations.

Whilst Hands was starting to grow in my life, much was happening elsewhere as well. Gill was hard at work raising money and awareness in the UK. Her path was more traditional. She built a committed team around her and they raised a truckload of money that would be used in the construction of the first orphanage.

The fundraising that Gill and I undertook complemented each other. Gilly had a lot of momentum in the early days and moved quickly to leverage support. My methodology was slow to begin with but built a sustained momentum over time. Certainly the majority of Gill's money was raised in the early days. However, the pendulum swung the other way as time went on and, interestingly, the more time passes since the tsunami, the greater success I seem to have at fundraising. It is by no means an understatement to say that the last million I raised was so much easier than the first $50,000, by a long shot.

Chapter 21

Interpol

At the end of 2006 I was offered a position on secondment with the National Institute of Forensic Science (NIFS). NIFS was an external agency to the NSW Police and was funded by contributions made by each of the police forces within Australia. Its charter in part was to take a national approach to forensic science and assist in bringing together the various stakeholders who had an interest in forensic science within the criminal justice system. It was an appealing opportunity on a number of levels.

More and more I was losing the drive for what I considered routine police work, dominated by meetings that seemed to be for meetings' sake, and dealing with people whose level of comfort they had in their work bordered on negativity. What I would come to realise years later is that in a service industry it is often harder to measure the return on investment than it is for those who operate profit centres and cost centres. Things weren't moving at the pace that I thought they could or should. The presence of a balance sheet to reflect productivity can have a real impact upon the way organisations and teams spend their time. It felt like the more that

I could see there was to do, the slower we moved. There were too many committees formed to deal with matters where people just needed to demonstrate courage and leadership and make decisions. By deferring an issue to a committee or a working group or steering group, people were divesting themselves of the responsibility for making a decision.

By late 2006 I was consumed with my work with Hands, which I saw as making a difference on a much larger scale than I had previously experienced in the police force. My new awareness of the environment I was working in and the organisation that I was a part of didn't sit well with me, and I was becoming as negative as many around me, but for a different reason.

I recall quite distinctly the feeling I had standing in a fairly affluent area of Sydney one Sunday morning watching my daughter Kelsey play soccer. I looked around at the houses that circled the sports field and realised that, for me, the burning desire to keep improving the house I now lived in was no longer present. The drive to accumulate wealth had gone.

The secondment to NIFS offered me a chance to work on some projects that were outside my immediate area of expertise, and as such would provide personal growth too.

At the interview for the secondment I had only one request should I be selected – that I be allowed to take annual leave, a day at a time, to speak at corporate conferences as a way of continuing the fundraising for Hands. Thankfully Dr Tony Raymond was the Director of NIFS at the time and a man of great compassion and understanding. His condition was that if I took annual leave a day at time, it couldn't interfere with my commitment to NIFS or the projects I was running.

It wasn't clear to me at the time, but if I hadn't taken the NIFS secondment, the momentum I had started to build with Hands would have stalled. There certainly wasn't the support for the work

I was doing at the highest level of the Forensic Services Group, nor the latitude. Without the support and flexibility offered by Tony, things may well have been very different for me and for Hands.

The secondment was initially to last for twelve months, and my brief was to look at the threats, trends and future direction of terrorism and how those threats might impact. My main focus was on CBRN threats, which are Chemical, Biological, Radiological and Nuclear. I conducted research over the first six months and then wrote an unclassified paper, with the intention of later writing a classified paper. An extract from the classified paper was to be presented to the delegates of the International Forensic Science Symposium, which was held in Lyon, France, in October 2007.

One of the unexpected things to come out of the symposium was the intense interest in the work I had done around the management of crime scene teams within Australia, and the different review processes I had implemented in response to major crime. This caught the attention of the delegates far more than the counter-terrorism work I was in Lyon to speak about.

A large number of the delegates were true forensic scientists and a very small number were sworn police. Although having completed university studies in both forensic science and law, I always considered myself a police officer who worked in the area of forensic science. What captured the attention of a number of these scientists was my view of the introduction of forensic technology into developing countries and jurisdictions. At the risk of making a sweeping statement, my experience in the judicial system is that it is not normally the science per se that is attacked at trials, but how the evidence got to the laboratories, the procedures in handling that evidence, and the possibility of contamination at any point along the way.

For example, if a sample of evidence is found at a scene and the crime scene investigator deems it worthy of collection, there will be a clear and precise process to be followed. First the evidence will be recorded in situ and there may be some interpretative work done on the presence of the evidence. Presumptive testing might be conducted to give the crime scene investigator some strong indications as to what the evidence may consist of and if it is indeed worth collecting. Once the sample is collected it will subsequently be submitted to a forensic laboratory for confirmatory testing.

The results that are produced by the laboratory are in most cases accepted by the courts, but it is the process of how the results were obtained and what happened to the sample from the time it was detected at the scene until the time the final results were produced that the defence team will analyse in an attempt to find holes.

My view is that assisting developing countries to enhance their own forensic capabilities is neither as simple nor appropriate as just building the laboratory capacity. Introducing a new mass spectrometer to analyse samples, for example, can do more harm than good to the advancement of justice if the same advancements are not made in the processes that are undertaken prior to the sample reaching the laboratory.

Unless those advancements are made in tandem during the entire process from the crime scene to the courtroom, those deficiencies will become obvious and can be detrimental not just to that particular case before the court but for any police agency or laboratory found by a court to be unreliable or to have contamination issues.

It was through this work that the United Nations Office on Drug and Crime invited me to assist them with some development work in South-East Asia around building leadership capacity in the forensic and police laboratories. These were traditionally strong in drug crime analysis but other areas of forensic science did not match that capacity.

The secondment was due to finish in November 2007. Thankfully, NIFS still saw value in the work I was doing and I was invited to stay. An application was put through to NSW Police to extend my term and the request was granted for two further periods of six months, the second carrying the caveat that it was to be the final extension. I would end up spending two years out of NSW Police working with NIFS.

NIFS was a different organisation altogether from the NSW Police; it was relatively small and had fewer layers than a large organisation like the police. The greatest difference I noticed was in the approval process to make things happen, particularly around domestic and international travel. If Tony thought the trip was justified, it was approved. It didn't take the submission of a report to half a dozen people for approval. I enjoyed working in an organisation that had the ability to make decisions quickly, and the longer I was away from the police the more difficult it was going to be to return to such a slow-moving beast.

NIFS also offered flexibility in working conditions. The focus was more on the work output than where I was or what hours of the day I did the work. Being able to work on the research and writing till two in the morning if that fitted with my schedule made things so much easier for me. I found I was much more productive sitting at home and working in a pair of board shorts at eleven at night than actually spending time in an office and getting caught up in the politics and the constant distractions. Tony's only requirement was that I get the work done and meet the deadlines that had been set.

Around the time of this second secondment I met an Australian woman working in Singapore – how else but via a speaking gig. Nicole Perry was working with Standard Chartered Bank in Singapore, but not long before she'd left corporate Australia to take up the Singapore role she had come along to a breakfast I was speaking at in Sydney. She'd connected with the message and Hands and had convinced her company to donate $15,000.

I could tell you that Nic made this donation as a way of capturing my attention, of wooing me, but that would be a lie. Because apart from the initial phone call to advise of the donation, it was almost another twelve months before we made contact. Not long after Nic had moved to Singapore, she wrote to me to let me know that she was no longer the point of contact at Swiss Re for the donation as she was leaving Australia for a job in Singapore. As I was about to head there for a speaking gig she suggested we catch up for coffee. No plans were made to meet and neither of us followed up. I had a fairly full diary during the trip to Singapore and at that stage there was no real reason to meet in person. I was working through compliance issues to get the donation her company had pledged over the line, and a face-to-face meeting wasn't going to expedite that, particularly since she no longer worked with the company.

Now, the coincidence of having someone else come into my life with the first name of Nicole has not been lost on me or on others around me. If I'm catching up with someone and talking about life, often there will be the question 'Do you mean Nic, or do you mean Nic?' The funny thing is, that usually does clarify things! Nic, the 'new' Nic, was living and working in Singapore, and I was there for a speaking gig and to do some work with the United Nations. By then I had been living on my own for a while since separating from my wife Nicole a few years earlier.

It was over a year since our paths had first crossed without really crossing. For the twelve months after that, every second month or so there would be a question about the progress of the donation and a short reply to say I was still working on it.

Then the planets aligned and we started a conversation. I was in Perth for a speaking job on the back end of a national road show

I was doing for a client and had just flown in from Adelaide. It was around midday prior to my speaking commitment the following day and I had the afternoon to myself. I was about to head out of the hotel for a bike ride along the banks of the Swan River and thought I would just respond to a few emails first. There was one that had been sitting in my inbox from Nic in Singapore for quite some time and I responded. Then the strangest thing happened: she replied. What's strange about that? Well, in our previous contact an email between us had normally been followed by a delay of a month or so. The use of carrier pigeons between the two countries would probably have been quicker. So with this unusual and immediate response from Nic to my email, I broke with tradition and emailed her back. And she replied again. Next thing I knew we had been speaking online via email exchange for about fifteen minutes, and for the first time in twelve months we had discussed something other than the transfer of funds.

The following day I found myself sitting in the Qantas lounge at Perth airport having just missed a flight back to Sydney, and now had a four-hour wait until the next Sydney flight. I jumped back on the email and lo and behold, there was another email exchange between Nic and myself. The fact that the time zone in Perth was in line with Singapore may well have aided in the advancement of what would become a love affair.

The email conversation continued over the ensuing weeks, and I found that I was looking forward to turning on my computer in case there was an email from Nic, or she was online. There was a real wit and sense of humour to what she was saying and that immediately appealed to me. This online chat continued for a couple of weeks until I was back in Perth, back in the Qantas lounge and again with a few hours to spare. This time, filled with courage from the bar, I did the grown-up thing and called her on the phone.

This pattern continued over the coming weeks until we were

emailing one another on a daily basis. With the time difference between Sydney and Singapore I could anticipate what time Nic would be in the office and would look forward to that first email I would receive from her.

Then another speaking job took me back to Singapore, and on this occasion there was plenty of reason for us both to want to catch up with one another. It would be the first time we met in person, and by that stage I knew I felt something for her on a different level. I was either going to have all those feelings confirmed when I met her, which was my strongest suspicion, or find out that she had put up a front and was actually nothing like the person I'd concocted in my head.

Suffice it to say, I had concocted nothing in my head. Nic was everything plus so much more than I thought she was or could be.

After our first couple of days together I knew she was someone I wanted to spend a whole lot of time with. The clarity I had around wanting to share my life with her was something that I had not really experienced in many other areas of my life. As opportunities presented themselves, I usually made them work and learnt to be enthusiastic. This was something different. I wanted this girl right from the start.

There was something very different about her from the outset. She was in her early thirties when we met, she was an expat in the corporate world in Singapore, and living on her own she had the time and space to take care of all of her wants and needs. But what I quickly learnt was that running in parallel to her determination and strength was a level of compassion and compromise that almost contradicted the girl she seemed to be on paper. Here she was leading change programs for one of the biggest banks in Asia, yet outside of work there was peace, beauty and a nurturing soul that gave me the impression she was more at one with herself than anyone I had previously met.

I found plenty of reasons to travel to Singapore over the following twelve months. At the time my kids were spending five nights a fortnight with me, and if it wasn't my weekend with them I would put those frequent flyer points I was accruing to good use and fly to Singapore to spend the weekend with Nic. Our connection with one another strengthened with each visit, and each time it became harder to leave. However, the geographical distance between us was filled with weekend flights, and late nights on Skype also allowed us to explore our lives and potential future together. The eighteen months or so that Nic lived in Singapore and we maintained a relationship with one another allowed her to consider what life would be like with me and the various layers of my life. I did have three kids, I did travel domestically and internationally on a weekly basis, and I did have commitments to the charity work in Thailand that occupied a huge space in my life. I think that I speak with confidence when I suggest that all of those layers, in particular Lachie, Kels and Jack, have since added to and enriched her life on a massive level too.

Nic resigned from her job in Singapore and moved back to Australia where we started our journey together. We both worked from our home in Sydney, both running our own business. Nic assists senior leaders to manage and bring about change in their business and home lives, and I run my speaking gigs and the charity. The fact that when we met Nic was living in Singapore and I was travelling all over the place made our lives together much smoother. Neither of us expected a different way of living; neither of us wanted the other to change or settle down. I can't do what I do without travelling, and to be honest I love the excitement and new adventures that come with the travel. Often Nic and I went days or weeks passing one another quite literally in airports, but maybe that was how Nic put up with me – she got a break!

In leaving the life of an expat living in Singapore and working in the corporate world, Nic gave up a lot to return to Australia. She also had to get used to being part of a family. In the months prior to her leaving Singapore she joined Lachie, Kels, Jack and myself for our annual ski trip to New Zealand. Not only was this her first time on snow, but it was her first time in a relationship with someone who had three kids. She has often said that the easiest part of the transition from corporate life in Singapore to our life in Sydney was the relationship with the kids. It was testament to the kids, their mum and Nic that this transition was so easy.

Chapter 22

The Race of His Life

During my keynote presentations I do not espouse opinions or break new ground. I don't have the secrets to wealth that can only be learnt in the next sixty minutes, I merely recount stories and experiences. They are usually a mix of the situations I have been involved in and the lessons that I have learnt from them. What makes the stories so powerful is that they are real. I am, for want of better words, the storyteller who depicts the tragedy and ecstasy of life's struggles.

I invite audiences to come with me on the journey and then allow them the space to consider the meaning for them, be it in a work situation or in their life away from the office. People have the opportunity to travel with me as we pass through tragedy and beauty and ultimately celebrate the good that can come from action. Why it works so well is that often people can relate to the stories. For that short time they can transpose themselves into the stories, replacing those in my experiences with themselves, their children and their loved ones. It's not a massive departure for too many to see how they too could have ended up as part of the story

I tell. They don't have to have spent their lives training at an elite level and represent their country on the world stage at the Olympics for shared experiences. Merely being on holidays with their loved ones can at any time bring them into this world and that is a connection easily made.

The story I tell below is one that on occasion I will tell from the stage, should I think the mix is right and if decision-making or leading with courage is part of the brief from the client.

The word 'courage' is a bit like the words 'legend' or 'tragedy': rolled out a little too freely for my liking. Losing a football game by a couple of points isn't a tragedy, and scoring a century in a one-dayer doesn't qualify you for legend status. It's easy for these words to become meaningless with overuse.

Courage for me is when you are faced with a choice and you have to make a hard decision, knowing the outcome can change, or in some instances even cost, lives.

Little boys love to run fast, they love to run real fast. It doesn't matter if it is in a park, through the house or in a crowded shopping centre, given half the chance they'll run as fast as they can. The only thing better is when they can hold the hand of a grown-up and run fast. They love the strength of mum or dad or perhaps granddad running beside them flat out, pulling them along. They start to lose coordination, arms flapping, head back as they laugh with the joy of what is happening.

Aek, a five-year-old boy, was in the race of his life or, to be more accurate, the race *for* his life. He was holding the hand of his granddad and they were running, as fast as they could. At first the little boy thought it was just for fun. Then he turned and saw the wall of water that was rolling towards them.

As fast as they ran, granddad knew they would not be able to outrun the terrifying mass of water. They ran and Aek was losing coordination, not because he was filled with laughter but because his granddad was pulling him along with such urgency. People from their community were also running in fear, seeking higher ground. An old lady, unable to run, fell to the ground and was swept into the water.

The buildings in the distance offered the only hope, but that extra seventy-five metres might as well have been seventy-five kilometres – they were never going to reach the buildings in time. Granddad knew that their options were rapidly diminishing. He was an old man; he couldn't continue to run like this for much longer.

They came to the base of a tree and granddad decided this was his only option left. He knew that their lives depended on his ability to climb this tree and get above the water that was now upon them. With a new-found strength in his arms, he climbed limb by limb, pulling himself and Aek higher into the tree. Slipping and falling but never letting go, he climbed higher and higher. One hand wrapped around Aek, holding him like a sack of potatoes, the other searching for the next branch, granddad reached the top of the tree, his lungs burning, his arms shaking. Both he and his grandson were covered in cuts and scrapes, but they had survived.

Aek and his granddad had indeed run the race of their lives and won. Aek clung to his grandfather's chest and sobbed; he held on like a baby monkey would to its mother perched high in a tree.

They had survived but there was no celebration.

You see, when they were running, granddad held on to Aek, his five-year-old grandson, with his right hand, and with his left he held the hand of Aek's four-year-old brother, Tom. When they got to the base of that tree granddad knew the three of them were about to die unless he made a choice. He knew the three of them couldn't outrun the water, but he also knew that unless he survived, his two grandchildren would not.

He knew he couldn't climb the tree hanging on to both of his grandchildren. Which one of the two would he hang on to, and which would he let go of? The chances of surviving with one of the boys was going to be tough; with two he couldn't even start to climb.

How does someone stand staring death in the face and decide who lives and who dies?

How do you make that decision when they are your grandchildren?

They were so young, so innocent; neither deserved to live more than the other, but granddad had to make a choice between them. The water was now around his waist and the force was incredible. If he didn't act now the three of them would be washed away to their deaths.

He let go of Tom's hand and his four-year-old grandson was swept away.

Tom died in the water that day.

Can you possibly imagine the pain and torture that granddad must have faced when confronted with this impossible decision?

Granddad is now an old man, much older than his years would tell. He suffers from survivor guilt: how is it that he survived but his grandson Tom did not? He deals with the demons that live inside his head and each day he questions what he could have done differently. Could he have been faster or stronger? Could he have made a different choice? Could he have done anything to save Tom's life?

Aek suffers from anxiety. You don't lose your brother in circumstances such as he did and get over it just because a few years have passed. He and his grandfather both deal with post-traumatic stress disorder.

Aek lost his brother, Tom, his sister, Muk Yai, and his parents that day. He is one of the kids who lives in our orphanage now and his smile masks his loss. How does he smile in the face of such loss? Well, he chooses to. Like so many of the kids who live in our orphanages, Aek has made a choice to be happy and thankful for what he has, not to focus on what he has lost.

So where does courage come into this story? Well, I think that Aek's granddad displayed great courage. He was faced with a decision that no one should have to make. If he had not made that decision, all three of them would have died. But he did have the courage to make a decision, and whilst that meant Tom died, it also meant that Aek survived.

Each of us in our business and private lives make decisions every day. Some of them will be quite significant, but usually they are not about who is going to live and who is going to die. There are times when we are faced with significant decisions that we will spend nights lying awake trying to decide what's the right thing to do. We look for the answers before we make the decision. But often the answers don't come until the decision has been made. With action comes clarity and after the decision has been made then we often ponder the outcome and question our decision. However, this for me is a big part of courage. It is when you have a choice and the outcome can have a massive impact on you and others, but you still make a decision. The decision to do nothing is still in itself a decision, but if Aek's grandfather had made the decision to do nothing, another two lives would have been lost.

Chapter 23

Highs and Lows in San Fran

There have been a number of events along the way that have changed my direction in life and taken both the work of Hands and my speaking to a new level. The first was when I was invited to speak at a conference for the National Associated Retail Traders of Australia (NARTA) in San Francisco in August 2007. The conference program was filled with international speakers including experts out of the US, an Australian cardiologist and even Sugar Ray Leonard, a world champion boxer and Olympic gold medallist, to close the conference. I was a policeman from Sydney who had been invited to the States to share his story of work in Thailand.

Deb Claxton, who runs a speakers' bureau in Sydney, once said to me, 'Pete, there are speakers who have a large profile and will wow the audience before they speak, and then there are those without the big public profile who wow them during the presentation.' I certainly didn't have the profile to wow the audience beforehand, but of course the object was to leave them feeling moved, provoked and inspired – to wow them would be a nice extra.

Walking onto the stage I was more nervous than usual. The

travel from Australia to San Fran had in some way created the feeling of an extra level of importance for the job, and meeting all the other speakers for breakfast to plan the leadership panel which would follow the close of the conference only added to the sense of inadequacy that was permeating every pore of my body. What wasn't helping was the strength of ego that existed at the table. The conference room was full of the movers and shakers of the retail industry in Australia, and all had seen plenty of speakers in their time and had a good platform from which to judge them. They weren't going to be impressed easily. I took some level of comfort in knowing that the Managing Director of NARTA, Kay Spencer, who had engaged me to do the presentation, didn't risk putting a speaker on stage without having done her homework. She had clearly seen enough to know I could hold my own.

I delivered a mix of stories and experiences, all with a lesson on leadership. But what was new for this group was that I was a forensic police officer invited to San Fran to talk to their industry. Remembering what Deb had said about wowing audiences with a profile was about to work in my favour – and has on many occasions since. None of the two hundred–odd delegates expected me to challenge their very existence or have them question with such deep emotion their fundamental reason for existence. I warmed to my position on the stage and, with a love of storytelling that I was developing, I took them on a journey. I took them to the precipice of hope, when all seems lost, and then just as quickly led them away with roaring laughter. I was in my element. There is a special feeling that comes when I stand on stage and I can feel an engagement with the people I'm speaking to. There are a couple of times in each keynote when I have the audience; I mean, I really have them. They lean forward in their chairs, their full attention focused on what I'm saying; even those who were previously on their PDAs are hanging on the next word and the end of the story. I'd like to think that if the fire alarm went off, they would want me to finish the story before they left the building. It is very special for me and I love it – every time. San Fran on this August day was no different. I had them, and the lack of the wow factor before I spoke had again worked in my favour. This wasn't what they were expecting, on any level.

I walked off stage, hoping but not really sure whether the delegates had embraced my message. I knew without question that at a number of points in time you could have heard a pin drop and they were engaged, but was this any different from the other speakers? After all, these were international speakers, and I was a policeman just telling my story. Once again self-doubt crept in. I had done my best and hoped that it had worked, but I hadn't sat through other presentations and seen the audience's reaction to the other speakers, so I had no idea how mine rated. But self-doubt is not always a bad thing; on some level I am sure it keeps things in check, and stops me getting too carried away with the journey and the success that follows.

Following on from my keynote was Sugar Ray Leonard, who closed the conference. Afterwards all the speakers were invited back on stage to sit on a leaders' panel.

This conference had been going for a number of days. However, as I was balancing a fulltime job with speaking on the circuit, I had arrived on the last possible flight and would leave on the first flight out. I joined the other speakers on stage and Shane Leaney from Video Pro asked a question that would change things from that moment forward.

'What are the recurrent costs of running the orphanage?' he asked.

'Fifty thousand Australian dollars a year,' I replied.

Shane then said, 'I will put five hundred dollars on the table now and I challenge all others in the room to match that donation.'

Nothing further was said.

The conference then recessed for lunch. I sat down with a number of the delegates until the NARTA Managing Director, Kay Spencer, came up to me and informed me that the donation started by Shane had been matched, and in fact something quite special had occurred. She told me that the amount the delegates had kicked in was now in excess of $100,000!

I was stunned.

Never before had anything like this occurred. This was not a fundraiser; I hadn't asked for money, all I had done was relate a few stories about Baan Tharn Namchai. I had stepped off the stage with a huge amount of trepidation about whether or not they had embraced the story. Clearly they had!

I left lunch and went to my room and tried to sleep, knowing that the gala dinner was on that night and I had had only one hour's sleep since leaving Australia. As I lay down, though, I couldn't help but think of what had just happened. I had spoken to a group for sixty minutes and, without being asked, they had given me a huge donation for Hands. I thought about the kids we would be able to help, the difference this would make to the lives of so many of them. My mind raced as I thought how we could move forward with our projects at a rate that would far exceed anything we had previously thought possible.

And my thoughts then returned to my family.

I thought about my kids and I thought about my wife; although I no longer lived with her, she was still so important to me. I thought about the sacrifices she had made during our time together. I called her to share the news of what had happened at the conference and, whilst thrilled for me, I'm sure she would have given anything just to have things return to pre-tsunami days when our family was still intact.

I was experiencing a joy that was also touched by a sense of loss and sadness. Tears began to run down my face as I tried to comprehend the events of not just that day but the last couple of years.

Later, after regaining my composure, but with my head still spinning, I felt pretty excited as I dressed for the gala dinner. Here I was in a fancy-pants hotel in San Francisco, heading out for what would be an exceptional night after having just received a mammoth donation for the kids. Make no mistake, I was king of the world! I was ready to have a drink and I was ready to celebrate.

I was also about to be stopped dead in my tracks again.

This was my first chance to have a chat with the delegates and answer their questions, and of course to thank them for their amazing support. We took our seats, and as NARTA Chairman John Whipfli began to speak, a hush fell over the group.

'Ladies and gentlemen, we heard today from a young man who has done some amazing things. We have heard about his work and as an industry you have rallied like no other in support of that work. I am pleased to announce that the hundred thousand you pledged this afternoon has now risen to two hundred and fifty thousand dollars!'

If I had been stunned before, you could have knocked me over with a feather now. I sat at the table unable to speak as I tried to collect my thoughts. All I could think was, *Who goes to a conference, shares some stories, and walks away with a quarter of a million dollars?* No asking, no submissions required, just straight up and down a reflection of the generosity of a magnificent group of humanitarians.

I slowly regathered my composure sufficiently to celebrate in a style befitting the occasion. From that moment on, the night became an endless procession of celebrations. As soon as I would finish celebrating with one group, there was another to tell stories and raise glasses with. I remember getting up and putting some food on my plate and not being able to make it back to my seat because of the number of wellwishers stopping to talk to me. Not that this was a bad thing. It was wonderful. At some point an observant good Samaritan actually brought me a knife and fork so I could eat while standing up. This celebration continued through to the next morning.

I was on a high, and then I received an email that really sat me back on my heels. I was in the Qantas lounge at San Fran airport, about to board my flight home, when I opened my emails for the first time since the heady events of the dinner. This was the message, without any editing or correcting, that I received from Khun Rotjana.

> I 'm looking forwerd to seeing you But now It is bad new I went to check up my body that i do in every year but this time I fround cancer in my breasts I need to have an opertion as soon as. I would like to see you but I cound. After opertion I don;t know it will be OK or not. for myself I didn't care if I die but I worry about my daugter she is 7 year old and my 42 children. Please keep helping them. I holp I can stay longer to do more work for the children. Any way you don't worry about me. my staff will takeing care of you duing you are in Ban Than Nam Chai.

My first response to this email was to ask the question: how was this fair? How did a lady who had given so much and was prepared to give so much more deserve such an affliction? Of course no one ever deserves cancer, but Khun Rotjana? That just wasn't fair. After the initial response passed I felt a stronger sense of resolve to help her and it became important to me that she know of my resolve and commitment to the kids she cared for. The best demonstration of that resolve was in action. Too many following the tsunami had committed to action and then failed to follow through. I wanted to show her I was there for the long haul.

At least now, after the events of the last few days, I could write back to her and assure her that the financial future of the kids would be taken care of. I assured her that whilst I could travel and speak I would do everything possible to ensure we gave her kids the opportunities they deserved.

I made a commitment that with the money donated in San Francisco, Hands would fund the construction of a second orphanage. The number of kids we were supporting, and who were all living in the original building, had risen to sixty-four, twice the number for which the home had been built. We had girls sleeping up to three to a bed, and the boys would bunk down each night in the hallway on the floor. It was clear we needed something bigger, and I had just received the first instalment towards making that a reality.

The San Francisco conference set us up to make a real ongoing commitment to the kids. One of the things that different people had said to me, and which mirrored my own concerns, was how long would this last? How long could I go on telling the story of the challenges we faced in Thailand? How long could I expect people to remain sympathetic to our cause and willing to donate money?

Chapter 24

Full Circle

You don't normally get an eerie feeling walking into the grand ballroom of a five-star hotel. When I first enter any room in which I am about to speak, I feel a bit nervous, or I have an excited sense of anticipation, but the only way I could describe what I felt that day was 'eerie'. The last time I had walked into this lavishly appointed ballroom was when it was the operational command post for the largest Disaster Victim Identification response the world has ever seen.

The grand ballroom at the JW Marriott Hotel in Phuket was the place I called home for the first two months of my time in Thailand in 2005.

I tried to start preparing for the keynote address, but all that came up were doubts and fears. Maybe the audiovisuals would fail me. Maybe the audience wouldn't like what I was going to share with them. I was so unsettled I thought I might even crash and burn.

The room was packed with four hundred delegates from Optus, one of Australia's largest telecommunications companies. It was just before lunch and I was the last session of the conference. I stepped onto the stage and commenced doing what I love – telling the stories of the challenges Hands Across the Water had faced and what we had achieved. I got into the flow and it started to feel good, really good.

At the conclusion of the talk I told the audience about my desire to continue to support the children of Baan Tharn Namchai into the future. Immediately afterwards many, many people came up to me and expressed their deep appreciation for what I had shared with them.

There was one final task that had been planned for the delegates, then they could break for lunch and spend the afternoon lounging by the pool before readying themselves for the gala dinner that night.

Malcolm McLeod, a training expert and good friend of mine, had been asked by the company to close down the conference by leading the group through a team-building exercise, and he and I had conspired.

The tables and chairs had been removed from the room and now the delegates were standing on the empty ballroom floor in groups of six surrounded by lots and lots of bicycle parts. Their challenge was, in twenty minutes, to put the parts together into something that resembled a bike, for a proposed race between the groups – or so the delegates thought.

At the end of the allocated time some of the bikes that had been pieced together were pretty good, while others needed some assistance to be roadworthy.

I was standing at the back of the room observing the activity when Mal asked from the stage if I could think of anyone we could give these newly constructed bikes to. I began walking towards the stage and, using the microphone I was carrying, I said to Malcolm that perhaps, if the delegates didn't mind, we could give the bikes to the kids from the orphanage I had just spoken about. The suggestion was met with enthusiastic applause.

Then when I asked the delegates to imagine the looks on the faces of the kids as they received these bikes – shiny new bikes with shiny new helmets – the applause turned to a roar of approval.

I then told the delegates that many people with the best intentions in the world had wanted to give the children a whole lot of second-hand things: second-hand clothing, second-hand furniture, second-hand computers. But why, I asked, did the kids only deserve second-hand donations?

'Isn't it time they had something new?' I asked.

'Yeeesssss!' came the roar from the audience.

'Now, can you imagine their faces when they see these new bikes?'

'YEESSS!'

Then I asked my final question. 'Would you like to come with me and see their faces when we give them the bikes?'

The audience leapt to their feet and the roar made the hairs on the back of my neck stand up.

I shouted, 'Then throw open the doors, Mal, and let the children in!'

The doors swung back and the sixty-four kids from the orphanage, each with a number held high over their heads, excitedly burst into the room. The number they held corresponded to the team that had built their bike. There were excited kids running all through the ballroom searching for their team, and there were teams just as excitedly seeking their little tyke to give them the bike they had just built with their own two hands.

Standing on stage, the company's general manager and I noticed a number of the tiny kids whose bikes needed training wheels, and so to remove these little ones from the mayhem, we hoisted them up to ride around the stage. We had joyous kids everywhere, and the collective noise they were making was unbearably, heartbreakingly wonderful.

When something like this happens there are going to be tears, right?

There were plenty, but not from the kids. Maintaining any level of composure was totally impossible as men and women openly and unashamedly wept with happiness.

The death, destruction and horror the ballroom had previously represented for me had been replaced by something innocent, joyous and beautiful. The tears of despair that had been shed in this room were now tears of love and hope.

The story could end there and anyone would be justified in saying, 'Great outcome.'

But it gets better.

You see, those bikes the delegates built in June of 2008 made their way back into our story in January 2009, when we did the inaugural Hands Across the Water Bike Ride from Bangkok to Khao Lak. The journey covered eight hundred kilometres, and the last eight were the best.

It was at that point we were joined by some of the kids from the orphanage. Yes, you guessed it, riding the bikes they had been given some six months earlier in the ballroom of the JW Marriott Hotel. The last two hundred metres even included the kids who were too small to ride on their own and required adult assistance.

What was created in that June 2008 conference continued on and out into the lives of the children of Baan Tharn Namchai.

For me, this wonderful experience represents so much of what I do with organisations now and why I feel I am the luckiest person alive. When you give without expectation of anything in return, you get so much back. The delegates gave the kids a bike, and in return the kids gave them an experience they will never, ever forget. Malcolm and I shared our experiences with the delegates and were given a gift that far exceeded what we gave them – the memory of the pure joy and excitement that beamed from the faces of both kids and delegates during those magical moments they shared in the ballroom.

We can't take away from the kids the experiences they have been through, nor can we change the fact they have all suffered terrible losses. That is what makes them who they are now; it is part of their story. It is not about trying to erase the horrors of their past, but about giving them opportunities to go on and live rich and fulfilling lives.

Following the gift of the bikes, it was the kids' turn to give back to the delegates. Over lunch they performed a traditional dance for the delegates and then spent the afternoon in the pool, playing ball games, eating ice cream and hanging out with them. When it was time for them to leave, I am not sure who had the saddest faces, the kids or the delegates. But the giving continued. That night at dinner the delegates pledged $50,000, which was matched by Optus. We now had $350,000 from two events and that was enough to build the second home for the kids.

It really felt that in returning to the JW Marriott Hotel things had come full circle.

Chapter 25

Bike Ride 2009

When a long-time supporter of Hands, Brigid Gibson, emailed me and said she was contemplating riding a pushbike from Bangkok to Khao Lak, a distance of eight hundred kilometres, to raise funds for Hands, an enthralling adventure began.

The idea was simple – we would recruit ten riders to ride for ten days and they would each be required to raise $10,000 for the privilege of doing so.

Brig was in, and so was I, and now we needed to attract others.

The time seemed right, then, when answering questions from a lunchtime audience in Singapore, to use surprise tactics to enlist someone I dearly wanted by my side for the adventure. My partner Nic, who was still living in Singapore at the time, was in the audience and known to many of the delegates at the lunch.

The first question from the audience was, 'How do you raise money for Hands?' This is the type of question I love because it allows me to go in a direction I otherwise wouldn't go, since I don't seek to raise money from the audience and I don't use language such as 'we need your help to get this built . . .'. I am clear that when I am speaking I am there to speak about leadership. I certainly talk about Hands and the work that we do, but each of those stories has a point to them. It might be about creating sustainable leadership or removing limitations, but there is a point. So with the question that was asked, it gave me permission to talk about Hands from a fundraising point of view.

'A great question,' I replied with a grin. 'And thank you for it. Well, let me share with you our latest initiative. A group of us are going to ride pushbikes from Bangkok to Khao Lak in January of next year, a distance of eight hundred kilometres, and in so doing we hope to raise a heap of money. I am really pleased to let you all know today that Nic has agreed to do the ride as well, and I thank her for making that commitment.'

I looked across to Nic and saw her hand moving towards her mouth to catch the food that was in danger of being expelled as she gave an involuntary gasp of surprise.

Up until that point in time Nic had heard very little about the ride, and the conversation about her joining as a rider had never taken place. In fact, there really hadn't been a lot of planning or discussion about the ride at all, I just liked the sound of it and knew it would happen and be a lot of fun. I also knew I wanted Nic to join me and what better way of putting it out there? As her friends and colleagues moved to congratulate her for doing something as audacious as riding eight hundred kilometres to benefit the children, she confessed that she was not known as a rider. That was because she wasn't one; she hadn't ridden a bike since she stopped wearing pigtails and had got herself a driver's licence. However, the public nomination ensured that she would be with us for the adventure. Not without giving me an earbashing first, though, and I expect I probably deserved it.

So now we had three riders.

The numbers grew and we started the planning. Well, to be

truthful, I talked about the ride a lot and Brig did all the planning, and that was pretty much how things panned out for the entire journey. Something about our skill sets coming to the fore, I guess.

The idea was to cycle for eight days with a rest day in the middle, with the aim of arriving at Khao Lak on Australia Day to officially open the second orphanage. By now we had a group of eighteen riders from several different countries; some were friends and some I had yet to meet. I was blown away that Gill and her husband, Ian, were making the journey from the UK to join us on the inaugural ride. To have Gilly beside me at the opening of the orphanage was going to make for something special. Gill's involvement in the UK was still as the face of the organisation, and she was still leading the efforts on that side of the globe, but the money being raised had slowed to a more modest level. Gill's desire to help hadn't changed, but as a fulltime police officer and with the passing of time since the crisis that was the tsunami, the interest from the public was waning. Whilst I was also still working fulltime in the lead-up to the ride, I had structured things in a way that allowed for the speaking to complement my work with Hands, and all of this fitted around my fulltime job with NIFS. Every time I took to the stage I was able to share the story of Hands, and this meant I was reaching several hundred people a week with stories of what Hands was doing.

Also very special was having Lachie, Kels and Jack join Nic and myself on the ride. I felt so incredibly lucky to have those people I loved so much come with me on this journey. And they had come of their own free will too – well, the kids had, even if Nic had been railroaded! When I floated the idea of the ride with the kids, I had always hoped that they would want to come, but of course I wasn't too sure of the take-up. Lachie was probably the least enthusiastic to start with, but that was because as the oldest he understood the concept of riding eight hundred kilometres better than Kels and

Jack did. The younger two were keen from the minute I put it out there, as it involved a trip to Thailand and that had to be a good thing. As with any kids who live through the breakdown of their family unit, they suffered loss and hardship and it had had a massive impact upon their lives. We hadn't spent as much time together as any of us would have liked. The trip to Thailand was another chance to be together, which I craved, but also an opportunity for them to gain a deeper appreciation of Hands and why I spent so much time doing what I did. I was thrilled that they wanted to come and couldn't have been prouder to head to Thailand for the ride than I was with the kids by my side. Their mum gave us her blessing for the trip, with the stern warning that I take care of them.

The ride started on 17 January in Bangkok, with an hour and a half drive out of the city. We weren't trying to gain an advantage, but it would have been madness to consider riding the bikes from the heart of Bangkok to the city's outskirts. And if you have experienced the traffic in Bangkok, I know you are now nodding your head in agreement.

Khru Prateep, Khun Rotjana and a number of the kids from the orphanage had made the long car trip to be at our starting point and wish us well for the journey. After all the excited goodbyes, it was time to start riding, time to face the hard yards. We planned to ride eighty kilometres on the first day, which happened to be the longest I had ever previously cycled, and about ten kilometres further than I had ever done in training. That was a little frightening for me as this was not a long day; in fact, it was our second-shortest day.

Uppermost in my mind was the question of how long my kids would persevere on the ride. How long would it be before Jack and Kels jumped off their bikes and into the comfort of the support van? But as each kilometre went on, so did they. Due to the size of his bike, Jack needed to pedal twice as fast as the rest of us, yet he seemed to quickly develop a steely resolve not to retreat to the comfort of the van.

Lachie had found his spot, right in the middle of the pack and surrounded by the young women who were on the tour. Lachie was at home with the adults. My observation of his transformation during the tour was that he left Bangkok as the oldest child and arrived at Khao Lak as the youngest adult. Without doubt it was one of the highlights of the tour to see my three kids deal with the adversity of the ride. To see them so comfortable in their own skin and to see them shine individually was incredibly rewarding.

The first four days of the ride took us through salt fields, prawn farms and along the stunning eastern coastline south of Bangkok. The scenery was spectacular and the Thai people we saw along the way were their usual affable selves. The vehicles sharing the road with us would slow as they drove past, toot their horn and wave with a smile that exposed all their teeth. The townsfolk would run from their houses to yell 'Heeeelllooo' and wave as warmly and enthusiastically as they could. I now know why the Tour de France attracts so many entrants. The adulation the locals gave us was making us feel as though we were rock stars, and their enthusiasm was infectious. This type of encouragement will propel you anywhere.

Mercifully the temperature was a tad cooler than when we had left Sydney and conditions could not have been better.

After four days of riding we had a very welcome rest day to soak ourselves in the hotel swimming pool, or in the ocean or in anything else that might ease the ache in our legs and bums.

The rest was short-lived, however, and back on the bikes after the rest day saw the aches swiftly return and the arrival of the hilly country. The irritations caused by chafing from the first four days' riding or the grazes from falling off bikes were now making their mark. As a group we all needed to be warmed up again.

The second half of the ride was going to be different. There were going to be hills to face, or 'long undulations' as some liked to call them. However, as we rode into a fairly strong headwind pushing up these inclines, I can confirm they were definitely hills and not undulations! Every aching sinew and muscle in my body was relaying this topographical message with great accuracy.

Another noticeable change during the second half of the tour was that the pace of the riders had increased. We were now riding at around thirty kilometres per hour. This was up from about twenty-four when we'd first started.

We were warming to the task.

The hills and the increased pace made it difficult for both Jack and Kels to keep up. Not through their lack of courage, commitment or desire, but because it was increasingly difficult for the two kids to match the pace that was being set at the front by the adults. What was happening was that the gap between the front riders and the kids at the back was widening. And so for the second half of the ride the kids found themselves riding in the van a little more often. But when we arrived in Khao Lak, Jack and Kels had ridden approximately five hundred of the eight hundred kilometres. Lachie rode all but ten kilometres, and he only opted out of those ten because towards the end of one day we had taken a wrong turn twice and found ourselves riding back over ground we had already covered. Lachie, with the patience of most sixteen-year-olds, indignantly put his bike in the back of the trailer and vehemently informed us, 'When you get your shit together, I'll get back on the bike!'

We'd organised, on the final day of the ride, to meet a few kids from the orphanage with about eight kilometres left to ride. They would ride their bikes – those Optus bikes – alongside us back to the orphanage, in effect showing us the way home.

One of the girls who rode this section with us got a puncture.

What else could I do but sit her on the back of my bike? So after eight hundred kilometres, hills, thrills and spills and the loss of buckets of sweat, I was now riding the last few kilometres with one of the kids from the orphanage as my special passenger. The very reason we were doing the ride was to support the kids, so it felt just right that I would ride in with one of them on the back of my bike.

As we rode towards the orphanage we passed Wat Yan Yao, the place where all this had started for me. Where four years ago almost to the day the bodies of more than three and a half thousand people lay decomposing. For a brief moment the joy of what we were doing slipped away. But I then found my mate Gilly amongst the throng and caught her eye. She, too, was shedding a tear. An emotional tear for those who had lost so much, a tear for the amazing journey we had experienced together, and a tear for what we had now collectively achieved.

The tours I had made to Thailand whilst working as a forensic investigator represented a period of loss in my life on unprecedented levels, one that I hope will never be repeated. For the first nine months of 2005, I had been surrounded by death and grief. I had gone from living in a comfortable home in Sydney with my wife and three kids to spending time living out of the boot of my car whilst camped on my brother's foldout bed. Life was so different in so many ways from how it had started out at the beginning of the year. Gill had spent months working in Thailand surrounded by death, and she saw me on the last tour of Thailand dealing with foreign ambassadors one minute, grieving families the next and then trawling the internet unsuccessfully trying to find a place to live when the tour came to an end. Whilst the tours of Thailand during the disaster identification work represent a period of loss in my life, Hands and indeed the bike ride represented the start of a journey towards recovery.

Recovery for all of those families who lost one or more of their loved ones in the tsunami would be at their own pace and in their own time, starting with one small step. Whilst my losses can never be compared to the death of a loved one, my recovery was starting too, with small steps. Even more than the opening of the first orphanage, the bike ride felt like the beginning of healing for me; it felt like the time when things had really turned and I had found my strength and purpose. With Nic, my kids and Hands it felt like I was contributing in a meaningful way once again.

As we turned the corner to ride the final two hundred metres to the orphanage, we were greeted with a wonderful sight: all the rest of the kids on their bikes. There were tiny kids on bikes with training wheels, and there were some who were even smaller and required an adult to keep them upright.

It was one of the most amazing experiences of my life, without question.

At this point my speed had slowed from cruise to an absolute crawl. I was travelling so slowly that it was difficult to keep the bike upright, but I wanted to savour every second.

I wanted it to last forever.

We then entered the street where the new orphanage had been built, and it was lined with over a thousand local guests and a marching band who had come to greet us. They were waving Australian flags and the kids all had flags stuck to their bikes and poked into their helmets to acknowledge that it was also 26 January, Australia Day. Suddenly the ride was over.

We had travelled eight hundred kilometres through some stunning country in seven and a half days on the bike with a rest day thrown into the middle, and had subjected ourselves to an experience that, without exaggeration, was life changing. What had really been just a group of acquaintances nine days earlier was now a group of friends who had shared something that would last a lifetime.

The Khao Lak area of Thailand was destroyed by the 2004 Boxing Day tsunami.

Resorts in the Khao Lak area were almost unrecognisable after the disaster.

3500 bodies would be taken to Wat Yan Yao in the days following the tsunami.

Thanking the soldiers for their tireless efforts in moving thousands of bodies at Tha Chat Chai.

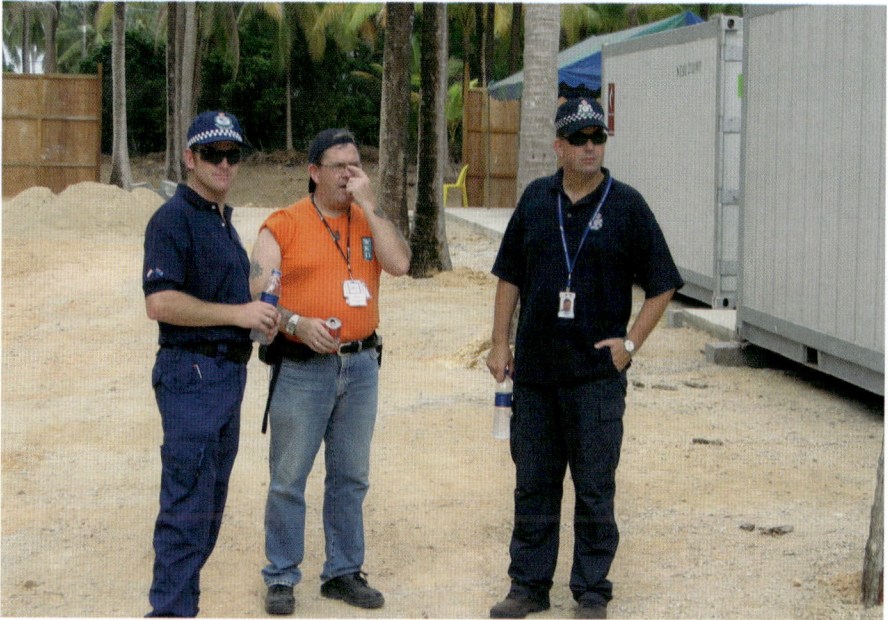

With Julian Slater (right) from the Australian Federal Police during the construction of the mortuary at Tha Chat Chai.

The release of thousands of balloons into the night sky, a sight and a night I will never forget.

With Gill Williams at the opening of Baan Tharn Namchai.

Baan Tharn Namchai was built from the ground up for the children who lost their parents during the Boxing Day tsunami.

With former NSW Police Commissioner Ken Moroney, a great man and a great leader awarding me the Humanitarian Overseas Services medal for my work after the tsunami.

The inaugural bike-riding crew in 2009.

Riding with Jack, who covered an amazing amount of territory on that tiny bike.

During the 2009 ride Kelsey spent some time with Thai locals on the journey from Bangkok to Khao Lak.

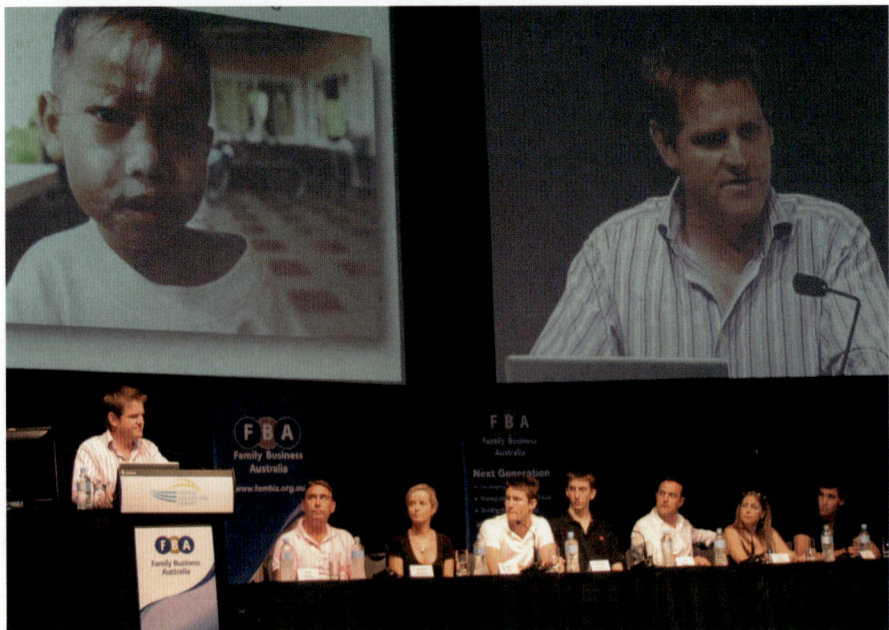

Speaking at a national conference at the Darwin Convention Centre. Seated on stage are Andrew Mostyn and Scott Evans with their families, both of whom would prove to be valuable and long-term supporters of Hands.

Nic and I celebrating the Melbourne Cup carnival in Melbourne 2009.

The cheque donated by the generous NARTA group.

Left: Lachie and I in Bangkok prior to the start of the 2010 ride.

Below: The morning of the 2010 Bangkok to Khao Lak ride. Our numbers had grown significantly from the first ride.

With Dad, Lachie, Jack, Kelsey and Nic on the 2010 ride.

At the completion of the 2010 ride the second orphanage at Khao Lak was opened. The first orphanage is located in the background on the right side of the photograph.

Opening our second orphanage meant there was a bed for every child.

Right: With Ton Hom, who had just joined us at Baan Tharn Namchai, in July 2010. At almost six years of age she weighed 9.5 kilograms and was found flea-bitten and covered in a hessian sack. Twelve months on she weighs and smiles a lot more.

Above: A bit of fun with playdough.

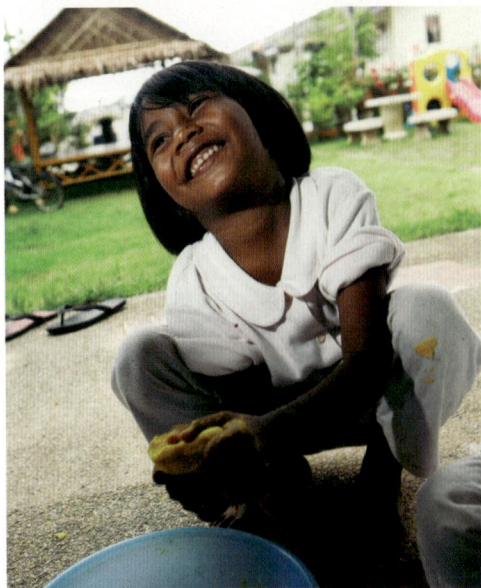

Left: Ohm is ten and lives at Baan Tharn Namchai. It is said that when she smiles the sun shines. A beautiful girl with a personality to match.

On the start of the second day of the first Bangkok to Khao Lak ride in 2011, Khun Thew joins Nic and I before we head off on the bikes.

Mealtime at the orphanage.

With kids like Ton Koa there to meet us at the end of the ride, it made the 800 kilometres – or 1600 kilometres as the case would be in 2011 – worthwhile.

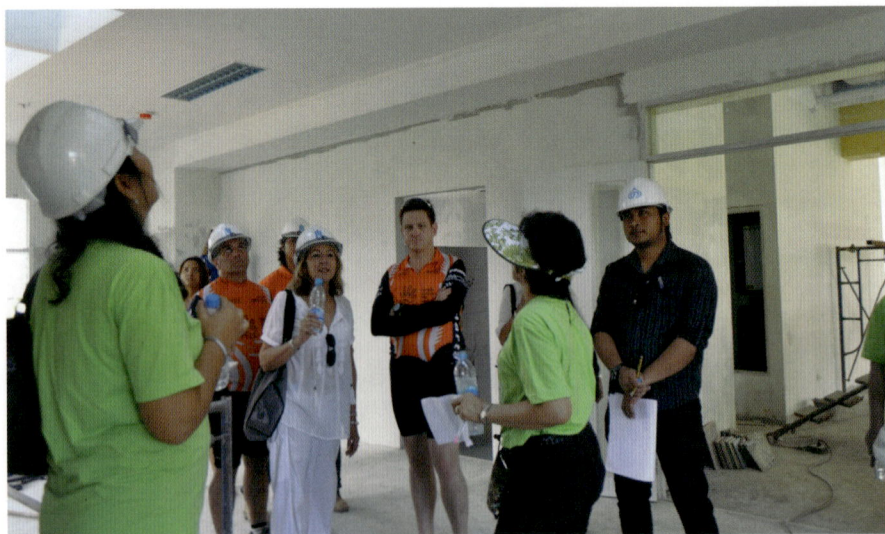

After riding 800 kilometres the last thing I felt like doing was spending an hour conducting a building inspection, which explains the look on my face. Kay Spencer is in white, and Scott Stein is looking for strength from above, having also just finished the ride. Khun Rotjana is in the foreground on the left and Khru Prateep is in the centre.

At the end of the ride we shared dinner on the beach with the kids that we ride to support.

At the conclusion of the 2011 ride we opened the new community centre at Baan Nam Khem.

The community centre also provides a nursery and child care centre for kids who otherwise would be left in dubious care.

Some of the boys from Baan Tharn Namchai.

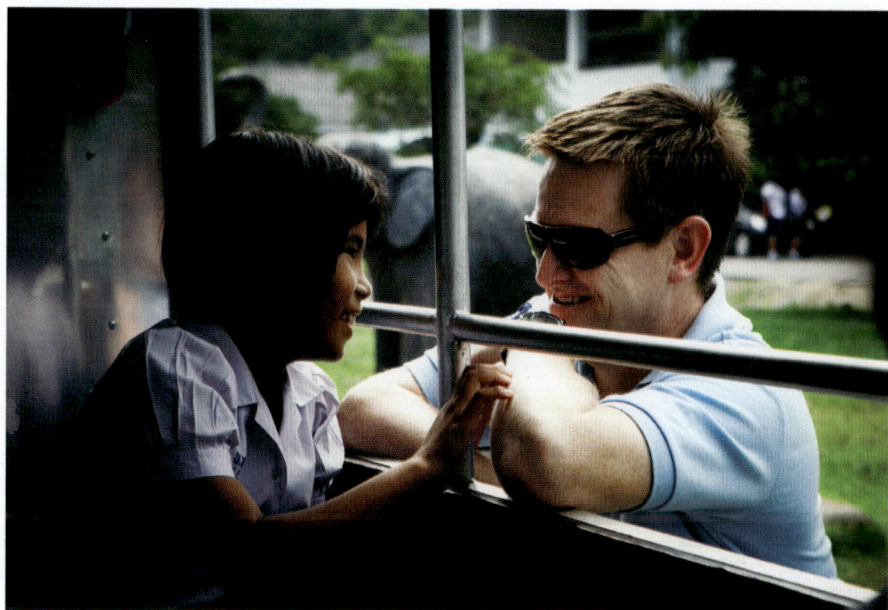

With Tip, a seven-year-old girl from Baan Tharn Namchai, on the school bus ready to head home.

With Mum in Khao Lak in June of 2011. She spends a couple of months each year at Baan Tharn Namchai, basically giving the kids hugs on demand.

My children, Jack, Lachlan and Kelsey.

Above: Looking down into the devastated area of one of the many cities in the Iwate prefecture in Japan after the 11 March tsunami.

Left: Contemplating my next move in Japan and how best to help.

Stepping off the bikes, the emotion hit us. And out came the tears of joy. We hugged, we danced, we kissed. We hugged strangers who were also caught up in the moment. This was the sweetest of all grand finals.

What a journey.

Coming to the end of the ride didn't feel like the end of the journey. It felt more like the start than ever before. I got off that bike having forged a stronger relationship with Nic, Lachie, Kelsey and Jack, and my dad, who had driven the support vehicle. I felt a stronger commitment to the children of Baan Tharn Namchai, whom we were supporting, and I felt I could take Hands to levels that I never imagined when all of this started.

There to meet us and share this magical moment were friends and supporters who had travelled to sit alongside us as the immaculate new two-storey orphanage was officially opened.

What a glorious home it was for the children who would now live there, and what wonderful sounds were emanating from the kids as they ran around their new playground, their squeals of delight almost drowning out the speechmakers. If the bike riders were excited and emotional then matching that level of excitement was Khun Rotjana. She had been there to see us off nine days prior and was here now to receive us as we arrived.

Although Khun Rotjana had not ridden eight hundred kilometres, she had certainly run her own marathon in the previous couple of years. After being diagnosed with advanced and aggressive breast cancer which threatened her life, she had survived thanks to the efforts of a surgeon and radical surgery. Her road to recovery was not without bumps as she fought infection and complications. But without us taking her out of the public hospital system and putting her into the private system her future may have been cut short. Now two years on from the surgery she was regaining strength and full health.

Not only were there health challenges for Khun Rotjana, but the two-year commitment that she had given to Khru Prateep when she'd first came to Baan Tharn Namchai had come and gone. One thing was certain: she wouldn't be leaving the children and returning to Bangkok. Her daughter Tom Palm now lived with her at the orphanage; her husband elected to stay in Bangkok and quickly that became the end of their marriage.

Taking eighteen people into Thailand to ride eight hundred kilometres involved risks, and the least of those was someone falling off their bike. The trip needed to represent Hands and what we stood for. It needed to offer a rewarding experience for all involved; those riding needed to benefit and the community we were supporting should benefit as well. Reflecting on the ride in the days that followed it was quite easy to say that all the expectations we had had were surpassed. For an idea that had started as a whim, eighteen riders had each taken part in a ride that changed their lives. You don't spend every waking minute with a group of people, ride eight hundred kilometres in eight days through the heat of Thailand, and remain unmoved. The magic of the ride was how it finished, arriving as we did to the sea of smiling faces which brought it all into perspective. Individually we had achieved something, the significance of which varied between the riders, but we all would leave Thailand changed.

As a group we had achieved what only the power of working together can achieve. The strength of the group pulled each rider along the road in a spirit that is formed in times of adversity. As the less conditioned riders struggled into a water stop, their spirits would rise once again as they first saw the group standing in their Hands jerseys and then heard the sound of the cheers and whistles, which acted as an injection of adrenalin into those tired muscles. This is the power of the team.

We had been on a bike ride; as individuals we had grown and

as a team we had shared the spirit of achieving under pressure, but was it more than a great holiday or team-building experience? There is no question in my mind that it was. This for me was evidence of how we can do good, by doing good. The riders set out to raise money and awareness of the children living in Thailand who had lost their parents. That was achieved in the fundraising work that was done, but along the way the participants found inner strength and ability a number might not have thought was possible.

One of the greatest outcomes for me was the understanding of the significance of what we had started. This ride wasn't a race from Bangkok to Khao Lak down the highway, it was a journey through villages and communities along coastal roads that allowed the exploration of willpower, fitness and strength of mind in a setting so wonderful, surrounded by people so enriching. The excitement in finishing was in the knowledge that I was going to do it all again the following year. We were onto something here.

Chapter 26

Our Steps Towards Sustainability

Hands had grown into something that required a different path. No longer was it appropriate to be managing things on the back of a beer coaster. The responsibility we had to our donors, who had demonstrated such amazing generosity, required that we consider how what we were creating could be sustainable moving forward. It was not my intention, nor that of anyone on the board of Hands, that we would just continue to raise money without raising capacity in Thailand.

After we provided each of the kids with a bed to sleep in at night and ensured they each had a full belly when they headed to school, our next commitment was to start looking to see how we could make our investment into the community sustainable. One of the things that Hands does incredibly well is act with accountability and transparency in the use of the funds that we receive. Each year we post our audited accounts onto the website for everyone to see. We want people to know how and where we spend their money. So there was no change required there, but the change we did need to make was in ensuring Hands remained a strong organisation and the money we received was used not only in a transparent way, but also in an effective way.

We resolved that to be more effective than we were, we needed to create a level of sustainability. We looked not only for opportunities that would allow for a greater efficiency in the use of funds, but also for ways in which we could engage the Thai community in that process.

One of the clear indicators that we had grown beyond the initial structure I had set up was our account balance with the Police Credit Union. Superintendent Mark Sweeney, who was my boss in the FSG and a good friend, had of course agreed to be the signatory on the social club account when I first opened it. The trust between the two of us was such that the details of the account were never mentioned again. Mark could see the money coming into the account, and over coffee I would let him know when I transferred money to Thailand and what was going on, but he didn't take an active role. That was until Mark's wife, Karen, opened the mail and read the statement for Mark's little slush fund which had – wait for it – over $263,000 sitting in the account.

This was after the Wood Royal Commission into the New South Wales Police Force and Karen immediately started to wonder how she would cope raising the two boys with Mark in jail on corruption charges. How could he possibly have $263,000 sitting in a bank account that she had no knowledge of? Was he involved in the sale of drugs? Was he taking bribes? What on earth was he up to? More importantly, if he went to jail, would she get to keep the money herself?

Mark shared this with me the next day in the office and I realised it was time to shift the money out of the social club account and into a proper, grown-up account.

It was during this time that we also made our run for deductible gift recipient status, which would mean donations could be tax-deductible. This is a major turning point for any charity in Australia and is particularly difficult to achieve for charities sending money offshore. As it should be. In effect, once you have DGR, the Australian Government, using taxpayers' money, is supporting the cause and the work you do.

Applying for DGR takes real commitment and you are best served by having an experienced legal team behind you. Thankfully we had Kevin Abrahamson and Caroline Carnegie from Middletons in Melbourne leading a small team who took up the charge for us on a pro bono basis. Any expectations I had that the standard of service would match the price we'd paid were proven completely wrong. What an amazing group of people to work with and a standard of service above and beyond my wildest expectations.

Kevin briefed me that we really had one decent shot at getting DGR. It was a process that could take up to two years and it was not uncommon for charities to be battling away more than three years after lodging their submission, still trying to get it over the line. I also spoke with other charities that said they simply ran out of puff; they were worn down by the process and gave it away.

The real worth of having DGR, in my opinion, is that it says you are a legitimate player in the field. You have been assessed by AusAID, DFAT and the ATO and have come up okay. Various organisations will use DGR as a filter: if you don't have it, don't come knocking. It really is the biggest tick a charity can get from the Australian Government.

Part of the process of getting DGR is understanding what you are applying for and how you fit the criteria. It is clear that building hospitals, schools or orphanages is not sufficient to get DGR. You need to do more. The key for us, I believe, was that, firstly, we had an exit strategy, and secondly, we had a commitment to sustainability.

Within five years of opening each of the buildings we had funded we intended to have enough sustainable projects in place that the recurrent operational costs could be met by those projects – that was our exit strategy. What those assessing the DGR application wanted to see was that we had a plan to reduce the reliance on Australian aid, that we didn't just intend on tipping money into this area indefinitely.

Our trump card was that it wasn't just rhetoric when we talked about sustainability – we had made a significant investment in this area. Early in 2008 we had found ourselves in a strong financial position after a number of large donations that built upon the money we had received from NARTA in August 2007. We now had the cost of the second orphanage covered and we had decided it was appropriate that we invest in low-risk sustainable projects rather than continuing to build projects that would all have ongoing running costs. The board considered a number of options and in the end spent $380,000 purchasing a rubber plantation in the hills northeast of Khao Lak.

Nic and I headed up in the rain and the mud with Khun Rotjana to view this rubber plantation after I had persuaded the board to agree to the purchase. There were trees and, yes, there was white stuff coming out of the trees into little coconut collecting shells. I could go home and report to the board that the money had been well spent!

The purchase of this rubber plantation serves a number of purposes. It returns a positive cash flow to assist in meeting its operational costs. Based upon the returns measured against investment, I am not suggesting you pull your savings out of your self-managed super fund and buy a rubber plantation, but it's doing okay. The plantation provides work opportunities for members of the community, who are thus able to feed their families and stay together as a family unit. The land around the plantation has its use maximised. A massive pond has been dug as a fish farm. These fish are used as food at the orphanage and are sold to members of the community, acting as another source of income. There are vegetable and fruit plantations; there are chooks, pigs and other animals, and recently bamboo has been planted, which will also be sold.

The children go up to the rubber plantation on most weekends. They all have chores to undertake and, depending upon their age, they will also have certain responsibilities which might be as simple as feeding the pigs and chickens or throwing handfuls of fish food into the dam. This teaches the children that, despite the support they receive from many generous people, they need to work to support themselves. And they do work, and work hard too.

But the greatest outcome from the purchase of the rubber plantation is one we didn't predict. You see, the soil is the richest in all of the southern area of Thailand. You ask Khun Rotjana and she will tell you. But it has nothing to do with the composition of the soil. The reason the soil is so rich and the land so valuable is because it is theirs. They own it. Everyone who works and lives at the orphanage lost everything in the tsunami; it might not have been a lot, but it was everything they owned. The land upon which the rubber plantation sits belongs to them. They can work the crops, plant trees, catch the fish – it is all theirs, and they are free to use it as they wish.

On the weekends, when the kids are at the rubber plantation, you can hear the girls screaming with delight as the boys chase them around the property. Their laughter bounces off the sides of the mountains and it is a joyous place to be.

So although the rubber plantation may have played a significant part in our being granted that highly valuable DGR status, it actually brings more to the lives of the kids and the staff of Baan Tharn Namchai than the money it earns us.

Chapter 27

Time to Go

At the end of my secondment to NIFS I knew I had a choice to make: return to the NSW Police and take up a role similar to the one I had left two years earlier, or go out on my own and resign from a wonderful job that had meant so much to me, on so many levels, for twenty-two years of my life.

I had had what you might call a dream run within the police and seemed to have consistently fallen on my feet. I often happened to be in the right place at the right time, and by the age of thirty-four I had been promoted to the rank of detective inspector. I sat on a number of national working groups and various committees, and after my experiences in Bali and Thailand I felt many opportunities still existed for me.

The more I thought about it, though, the clearer the choice became. If I went back to the police, I would no longer be able to travel and speak on the corporate circuit as I had been doing for the last couple of years. More importantly, if I stopped speaking, the work we were doing at Hands would grind to a halt. Sure, we could continue as a charity, but we'd become like so many other organisations these days who have to fight very hard in a crowded market firstly to have a voice and secondly for every dollar.

How could I have spoken to tens of thousands of people over the last couple of years about the importance of total commitment only to walk away from something I was so passionate about?

As fate would have it, Dr Tony Raymond, who had interviewed me for the secondment at NIFS, was now back at NSW Police as the Chief Scientist for the Forensic Services Group. He, along with the then commander of the FSG, wanted to know what my intentions were. Tony was keen to see me work with him once again and he certainly made me an attractive offer, one better than I could have hoped to receive. It was in part due to my respect for Tony that I made the decision to resign. He was a man I had a great deal of admiration for, and not for the first time he was going out on a limb for me. I felt I couldn't offer him my full commitment and I did not want to offer anything less than my best. Tony asked me to take some time to consider his offer before making my decision; I think he could see where I was heading.

Tony's support was humbling, and certainly in contrast to that of the commander of the group. At the end of the meeting she said she would be too busy to take my telephone call in a week's time once I had made my decision. Her response was a clear signal to me that if I returned I wouldn't have her support in what I was doing.

I headed to New Zealand with Nic for a week to recharge after what had been a busy year. We stayed in a stunning house on Waiheke Island perched above the beach with views back to the mainland. Waiheke Island is a short ferry ride out of Auckland, but that ferry ride is transformative. As you sit and stare out at the beautiful calming waters the stresses of life start to fall away. As the ferry slows and makes its approach to the wharf, the water is crystal clear and pure. Above rise the lush hills of Waiheke, home to many wonderful vineyards. I have visited Waiheke Island several times and each time arrive feeling as though layers of stress have been washed away.

Our time on Waiheke was perfect for reflection and contemplation. There is not a lot to do there and that is part of its beauty. Sitting on the deck of our temporary home, the birds, the ocean and the smell of the salt air provided everything we needed.

Nic and I talked about the decision I was faced with and what it meant. In her usual beautiful way she didn't seek to overlay her own feelings or thoughts, just to help me explore mine. She gently asked me questions that allowed me to hear the answers out loud, so that I was now saying what I had been thinking for some time.

Contemplating making the call to Tony, I was taken back almost two years to the day to when I'd started with NIFS. After my final day on the force I'd finished up and headed out to speak at a dinner for the senior management of the Reserve Bank. I arrived early and stood outside their premises situated next to Kirribilli House with views back to the Opera House. Standing there, looking out over the harbour, I thought to myself, I could quite possibly have just done my last day in the police. As fate would have it, I was right.

I guess the writing had been on the wall even then, and in some way NIFS provided me with two years to explore the option of leaving, to test the water, so to speak. Clearly I found the waters quite nice.

It was time to go.

It's a significant decision to resign from the police because you can't simply go back if you change your mind or things don't work out. Well, that is not entirely true – you can go back, but at best you return as a senior constable. You can certainly join another state police force, but again you join at the bottom. It's not like you leave one bank, try things on your own for a while and then head to another bank if things don't work out. Leaving was for good and I needed to be okay with that.

Upon returning to Sydney in the middle of December 2008, I submitted my resignation papers, to be effective from 31 January 2009. Come the middle of February, without any contact at all from the police over that six-week period, I withdrew some money from an ATM and a sizeable deposit had been made into my account. It was my long service leave. An entry on the ATM slip read Separation payment. I was no longer a member of the NSW Police. Thanks for coming, you might say!

I now needed to earn an income and that income was solely dependant upon what I did and how well I did it. Having over twenty years' service in the police I could have decided I'd had enough and gone off sick and received a pension for life. I wasn't prepared to play that card, and spend twelve months pretending I was too sick to work.

The way Hands is structured is that I sit as the chairman of the board, but as is the case with the rest of the directors, none of us receives any income or compensation for our time. I was not an employee of Hands, and I continued to personally fund all of my travel associated with Hands. I would derive an income through consulting and speaking fees as a completely separate legal entity from Hands. When I entered into a contract to speak at a conference or engage in consulting around leadership or corporate social responsibility, it was very clear to all parties, either I was being paid or it was a donation to Hands. If there was a donation to Hands, every cent went to Hands. If the engagement was between Peter Baines Consulting and the client then that was my personal income and it was removed from Hands. The only sharing of that was between the tax man and myself, and God knows he does well out of it.

Leaving was not without risk – the economy was heading into dangerous waters and what did this mean for someone trying to make a living speaking at conferences? Would the conferences continue, would I still get bookings, and would money still exist for Hands in the way it had up till now?

Those questions were to be answered quite quickly.

In early February 2009 I spoke at a conference for international construction company Laing O'Rourke. It was on a Saturday at the Gold Coast Convention Centre in Queensland. I flew up in the morning as I was the first speaker after lunch. I delivered my keynote and immediately left to return home. Adam Spencer was to follow, so I literally finished the keynote, took my laptop off the stage, walked out a side door to the sound of polite applause and jumped into the car waiting to drive me to the airport.

As usual, as I left I found myself questioning whether the message had been received by the audience in the way I had intended. (By now you are probably seeing a trend!) I hoped that those listening, which numbered more than a thousand, found benefit in what I had to say, but as Adam had followed directly after me, I hadn't had the chance to gauge the response.

The next day I received a phone call from the speakers' bureau that had booked me for the job. I don't often hear from the bureaus after having fulfilled an engagement and I had never heard from any of them on a Sunday! I thought, *Hmm, something isn't right.* David Maher, the MD from the speakers' bureau, asked me if he could pass on my phone details to the staff of the CEO of Laing O'Rourke, who wanted to meet with me prior to him returning to his base in the UK. 'Of course,' I said and diaries were matched up.

During the time between the conference and my meeting with CEO Ray O'Rourke, Hands had a board meeting at which I tabled my desire to raise $750,000 in the calendar year of 2009, allowing us the following year to begin construction of our fourth major project. This was not received by the board as well as I had hoped, with a chorus suggesting I was being just a tad ambitious, even for me. They questioned if I was aware of this little thing called the Global Financial Crisis that was sweeping the world. I spoke strongly about my belief that we were different from most other charities, and that we shouldn't limit ourselves by scaling down our own expectations.

A week later I met with Ray O'Rourke. His staff had let it slip that he was going to make a significant donation to Hands, although they wouldn't disclose the amount. Strangely, although I was excited about this, the actual amount of the donation was secondary to me. I was just thrilled that another group had heard the keynote and decided to support us unconditionally as this was a ringing endorsement for the way we were going about our business.

I arrived at the corporate office of Laing O'Rourke in Sydney and met the support staff before being introduced to the man himself. He walked into the room and it felt as though I was being reunited with a long-lost uncle. There was a bear hug from him and mock punches to the ribs.

He then thanked me for my keynote, congratulated me on doing some great work, and unceremoniously presented me with a cheque for a quarter of a million dollars!

It has to be noted that this wasn't one of those big, grandstanding 'You've won the lottery' cheques you hand over at photo opportunities, just a normal handwritten cheque bearing the beautiful numbers $250,000.

My target of raising $750,000 for the year was off to a great start.

Within days of receiving the cheque from Ray, I flew to Whistler in Canada, not because I had $250,000 but because I was on my way to the annual NARTA conference.

This was the first time their full group had come together since gathering in San Francisco in August of 2007, where they had committed $250,000 to Hands. I was attending the conference mainly as their facilitator for the last session, but also to say thank you for their support and to show pictorial evidence of the magnificent orphanage that had been built with the help of the funds they had raised.

The Whistler conference was another amazing event, not just for Hands but because a number of the children from Baan Tharn Namchai would benefit in a quite spectacular way as well. One of the sponsors of the conference and a great supporter of Hands was Steve Tipple from HSBC Bank, who had decided that rather than spend money at the conference entertaining delegates in their annual golf day, he would sponsor the travel of a couple of the kids and Khru Prateep and Khun Rotjana to join us in Whistler.

What a wonderful idea it turned out to be. From the buzz of anticipation back in the orphanage right up until the moment the kids saw snow for the first time, having these children at the conference was just incredible. Seeing the kids holding hands and giggling as they bounced on their beds in the Four Seasons Hotel, doing some wide-eyed exploring through the bag of goodies they had been given, hearing them laugh hysterically as they got hit with their first snowball – all of it was a joy.

It was an extremely generous gift to give the young children, but what they gave back to the delegates was even more precious.

During the final session of the conference, Khru Prateep spoke to the audience and told them about the history of the Duang Prateep Foundation, which she had founded thirty years before, and why the support of Hands was so vital in the struggle that continued in Thailand.

Next to speak was Champ, a sixteen-year-old boy who stood before the delegates in the ballroom and in a quiet voice explained, in English, how he had not only lost his mother to the tsunami, but it had also left his father disabled and unable to care for him. He was one of the first to move into the tents in the very early days.

Champ then thanked the audience and Hands Across the Water for giving him 'a good life'.

By now tears were flowing freely in the audience.

I returned to the lectern and introduced my dear friend Khun Rotjana, the director of the orphanage at Khao Lak. The events of Black Saturday in Victoria, when one hundred and seventy-three Australians lost their lives to the bushfires, were fresh in the minds of all in attendance. Khun Rotjana shared the story of how the children, after hearing of the devastating fires, were deeply concerned for their Australian friends. She said they crowded around the television to hear the updates on what had happened.

The children wanted to do something to thank those who had given them so much, so they baked doughnuts to sell at school, raising money to send to the Australians who had suffered in the bushfires. It was an initiative thought up and organised by the kids themselves. Six months later a cheque for $3500 was sent to the bushfire victims in Australia from the children of the Baan Tharn Namchai orphanage.

For me this is at the very core of the Thai people we are so fortunate to be working with. They are content with their lot in life, however meagre it may seem to us, and are always happy to share what little they have. The attitude of 'Once I have all that I need, once I have done all that I want to and once I have become all I can be, then I will consider others' just doesn't exist for them.

The audience was deeply moved, that much was evident just by the looks on their faces. Again they responded as an industry and pledges were made, which were then matched by so many of the generous individuals in the audience, and within an hour over dinner the pledges had grown to over $300,000!

Many in the audience who so generously donated funds were from large organisations, some were from small family operations and many individuals found the spirit of generosity within and dug deep into their own pockets as well. Those who have made contributions to Hands from the NARTA group or from any other organisation do so not because they leverage that donation to improve their profile or brand image – we are too small for that. They do it because of a shared value set, transparency in our operations and our ability to achieve what we promise.

So within a week of my declaring my audacious goal to the board, Hands had raised over $550,000. And before the end of February, we had already met the 2009 target of $750,000.

We were now ready to undertake our fourth major project. On the back of the first two orphanages, and the rubber plantation we had purchased in 2008, we were now in a position to move forward on a health care, education and community centre in the nearby village of Baan Nam Khem.

Chapter 28

Bike Ride 2010

After the success of the first bike ride in 2009, it seemed obvious that there would be a second ride. I just needed to convince myself that it was a good idea, as the pain was still fresh in my mind, legs and bum! I also needed to ensure this was the way I wanted to spend the January school holidays with Nic and the kids. I was paying the same as everyone else to be on the ride and it was a costly exercise for the five of us to participate. Whilst the experience was personally quite amazing, it did represent work for me on a number of levels, and it wasn't a family holiday where I could devote myself to Nic and the kids. I knew that as the face of Hands I had a role to play and expectations to meet. However, we had raised just over $180,000 on that first ride, and if there was sufficient interest I knew it would be difficult to walk away from.

As it happened there was plenty of interest, and this time we assembled in Thailand with thirty-four riders, including eight of us who were returning for our second trip. I began to worry that some people might be disappointed; I was concerned that we would be unable to recreate something that had been so special.

I shouldn't have worried. For reasons I haven't been able to put my finger on, the 2010 ride was even better than the 2009 ride. If I knew what the key ingredients were I would have bottled them to ensure we could bring them out every year.

The bus trip from Bangkok to Petchuburi on the first morning of the ride brought with it nervous anticipation. Having done it once I knew that, without illness or injury, I could complete the ride. But of course on the first morning, even the seasoned riders felt a certain level of nervousness. What would the roads be like? How would we cope with the heat? How would the manic drivers in Thailand affect us?

The lead-up to the ride for most is quite long. Raising $10,000 is not an easy feat. It is certainly achievable, but it takes effort. So by the time the riders got their bums on the bus seats on that first morning, they were ready to ride.

I was concerned about the numbers we had agreed to take on the journey. As well as the thirty-four riders from Hands, we also had Chris and John from the tour company, which meant that thirty-six people would be riding each day. Questions were running through my head. Would the increased size of the pack slow us down? Would there be little break-away groups, and how would that affect everyone? Would the fast riders become frustrated with the slower ones? As it turned out, there was no need to worry. For some reason that made no sense at all we rode faster as a group than we had the previous year. We were arriving at lunch so much earlier than anticipated that the local restaurants weren't ready for us. The group felt tighter as a pack and, again for no logical reason, we bonded even more strongly than we had the year before.

Perhaps that was because we had a couple of pretty special riders with us. We had invited two riders from the Baan Tharn Namchai orphanage to join us. When I put the invite out to Khun Rotjana, I was surprised at how eager she was to make the most of the opportunity to have someone from Baan Tharn Namchai ride with us. Upon reflection I was offering them a chance to cycle down through a beautiful part of Thailand with an amazing group of thirty-odd Australians and Kiwis who had each raised $10,000 and funded their own travel expenses to be there. Of course they would want to join us on the ride.

The two riders were Yong, a fifteen-year-old boy, and Nong, a thirty-two-year-old female staff member.

Khun Rotjana had first met Yong at a hospital when she was asked to assess Yong's sister, Pong, who was ready for discharge but had no home to go to. They had lost both of their parents. Rotjana tells the story of how she went into the ward where Pong was and Yong was standing in the corner of the room. He did not raise his eyes to make contact with Rotjana, instead his gaze was firmly fixed on the ground. Not that she could actually see his eyes; they were covered with a long fringe and the peak of his hat to ensure his anonymity.

Rotjana left the hospital with one of the staff from the orphanage, who suggested they take the little girl but not the boy – he was bad news. 'He looks like a gangster.'

But if Rotjana was to take Pong, then Yong, aged thirteen, would be left on his own with nowhere to go, and brother and sister would be separated. That wouldn't have been in the interests of either of them.

Rotjana did take Yong, and he turned out to be a beautiful young boy who was just incredibly shy. He didn't make eye contact because he didn't believe he was entitled to.

Several months after the meeting in the hospital, Yong got out of bed and came out to Rotjana, who was sitting alone watching television now all the children were finally asleep. Yong sat on the ground at Rotjana's feet. He then professed his love and appreciation to Rotjana for the opportunity he had been given. He felt he was unworthy of such a chance as nothing similar had ever come his way before. No one had shown him and Pong the love they were now receiving. Yong promised to do the best he could to repay the kindness.

In January 2010 Yong found himself on a bike surrounded by thirty-five other riders, thirty-four of whom were not from his native country and thirty-two of whom spoke no Thai at all. And the Thai that two of us did speak didn't lend itself to long, meaningful conversations.

Accompanying Yong on the ride was Khun Nong, who was a staff member at the orphanage.

On the morning of the tsunami Nong had left her family at Baan Nam Khem to fill her motorbike with petrol as the family was heading out for the day. Her family consisted of her eighteen-month-old daughter, her ten-year-old son and her husband. Having filled up her motorbike, Nong began riding back along the road towards her village, except that ahead of her the road no longer existed. It had been replaced with a wall of water that was now racing towards her. Not only had the road vanished, but her village, her home and her family were gone too.

Nong rescued people from her village on her motorbike and she recovered an elderly lady who was naked, her clothes having been ripped from her body by the ferocity of the moving water. Nong assisted in the rescue effort and saved lives. Unfortunately she was unable to save the lives of her family.

I would later learn that Nong was searching for the bodies of her family at Wat Yan Yao at the very same time I was working there. The body of her eighteen-month-old was recovered soon after, but it was some months before her ten-year-old and her husband were formally identified and returned to her.

For months after the tsunami life offered little meaning to Nong. She felt her life had no purpose. She questioned why this had happened; she questioned her future, and she even questioned her Buddhist faith.

She eventually found her way to the orphanage at Baan Tharn Namchai, which would ultimately provide her life with the meaning she felt had all but gone.

The bicycle ride for Nong represented a journey of transformation. In her own way she was passing from the abyss of her grief into new beginnings. She had a deep scar on her heart, but she was learning to live with that. It was a part of her and part of who she would always be.

Standing at the top of a four-kilometre hill on the morning of the last day, the tears flowed from Nong. We say that the previous seven and a half days of riding is in training for this hill. You make the top of the hill and it is quite literally and metaphorically all downhill from then on.

Nong was returning home now, she was returning to her family, which consisted of seventy-two children.

The ride is a special experience for us all, and we all take something from that, but without question, spending time with those that I love the most and people like Nong and Yong is food for the soul. Watching my three kids push through the physical challenge, being beside them as they continued to push down and pull up on those pedals when they could easily have got off and got in the van, is a wonderful journey, and as a parent I treasure the opportunity that the ride presents to be next to my kids and to see them grow.

Kels recently shared with me one of her fondest memories of all the bike rides, and that was riding along a long straight stretch into a head wind. Nic and I were both at the back riding and supporting Jack, and Kels had found herself alone along a hard stretch of road. It was hot and there were no other riders around to encourage her or even provide company, and she had run out of water. Then her big brother appeared out of nowhere. He rode with her and stopped at a roadside stand to buy her a cool drink and give her time off the bike to find her strength. Till the next water stop Lachie rode beside Kels, encouraging her all the way. When I heard this from Kels, two things came up for me. Firstly, how magical that they could share this experience and find strength in one another, and secondly, why when they clearly love each other do they fight so much at home?!

Having done the ride in 2009 the kids knew what they were in for. They knew of the hard work that was required on the long stretches of road, they hadn't forgotten about the hills we had to climb, but they also knew just what an amazing experience it was. Lachie, who was now seventeen, rode at the front of the pack whenever he felt like it; on a physical level the ride didn't really challenge him. He had the strength to ride towards the front when he chose and hang at the back with Nic and me when he was feeling a little lazy. I spent a lot of time riding next to Jack and Kels, partly because that was where I wanted to be, and also because I wanted to make sure they were safe. The only downside of this was that the opportunities to ride with Lachie were fewer than I'd hoped. Nic would encourage me to stretch my legs and ride at the front, but I just couldn't escape the thought of how bad I would feel if one of the kids came off their bike and was injured while I was off at the front of the pack. Not that I thought I could prevent them falling any more than anyone else, but at least I could be there, should that happen. The times when we did all find ourselves riding together, Nic, Lachie, Jack, Kels and I, were the most enjoyable moments of the journey.

Kelsey, now fourteen, started the tour with the resolve to ride further than the year before. What that would look like, none of us really knew. I guess I got a good understanding of her ability at the end of the second day when, with about five kilometres to go until the end of the hundred-and-ten-kilometre day, she and Jack took off in a race with one another. Spurred on by their energy, I gave chase. Jack would succumb to the speed but Kelsey and I rode at a speed nudging just over forty kilometres per hour for what seemed like way too far. It was the end of the second day and Kelsey had ridden the entire distance, as she had done the day before. The talk then turned to her ability to ride the entire eight hundred kilometres.

This pattern repeated itself day in, day out, and on the second-last day Nic, Kelsey and I were riding together. It was another long day of a hundred and thirty kilometres up and down hills. I had ridden almost two entire tours without a puncture, yet this day I picked up two within the space of an hour. This pushed me to the back of the pack each time and I had to ride hard to catch the group. It was after lunch and we had just crested a long hill and our legs were burning. We had over seven hundred kilometres behind us when Kelsey pulled to the side of the road with a puncture. Nic and I both peeled off the road to help her and the other riders rode past.

We climbed off our bikes and Kels started to get quite emotional. She buried her head in my chest and sobbed. I thought it had all finally got too much for her – the hills, the heat, more hills, more unrelenting heat . . . I asked her if she wanted to get into the van, telling her there was no need to push on. She had done so amazingly well.

Sobbing she said, 'You're going to make me get in the van now. I don't want to stop riding.' I looked over the top of Kelsey's head to Nic and she shrugged, as confused as I was. Kel was concerned that the puncture would put us at the back of the pack and therefore I would want her in the van and her bike in the trailer. The tears weren't because she *wanted* to stop riding, the tears were because she was afraid she'd *have to* stop riding.

Kelsey finished the entire eight hundred kilometres, and what she achieved on that ride serves as inspiration for me each time I start to feel the pressure of a hill climb.

Jack, having turned twelve on Christmas Eve, just before the ride, was yet to grow into himself. Let's say he's not competing for the title of tallest boy in his class. Therefore his pedal-to-distance ratio needs to be higher than anyone else's. He was fitted out with a bike that was better suited to the challenge than the bike he'd ridden the previous year and he certainly enjoyed the additional output he received from riding a larger bike.

Once again, as the youngest on tour, he found inspiration at each of the stops in between bike legs, when he would walk out of a shop with lollies and ice creams. He was never going to suffer from a sugar deficiency. For a while there I couldn't quite work out where he was getting the money to buy so much stuff at every stop. He still had a cuteness to him that ensured the other riders were buying him treats in recognition of his efforts, but surely it couldn't all have been rewards. Maybe my dad, who comes along each ride as an integral part of the support crew, was handing over cash. That might sound a likely explanation to you, but when you search frugal on Wikipedia you will get an image of Dad. It would be most unlike him to be handing over cash. When I asked Lachie where Jack was getting his funding, he reminded me that Dad was the custodian of my wallet. That explained it!

To understand one of the 'almost' highlights of the ride for me, I need to give you a bit of background to the story. I say almost, because it missed becoming THE highlight of the trip by only minutes. My dad spent his entire working life as a Commonwealth driver, which meant he drove senior politicians and dignitaries around. Being punctual was almost as essential as being able to drive. Which was good, because Dad was punctual to the point of obsession. The importance to him of being on time is not something I can overemphasise. The only thing better for him than being on time is if this is in some way going to save him money!

In Bangkok, prior to the start of the ride, we were enjoying a beer when Dad was approached by a lady from the hill tribes selling Rolex watches. Originals, of course! Dad makes the mistake of showing the slightest interest in what's inside her timber box and minutes later he is sporting a brand-new Rolex watch. He can't believe it only cost him eight hundred baht; I can't believe he paid that much.

For the first two days there is no one in between Bangkok and Sydney that doesn't know Dad has got himself a Rolex and he is there to tell you the time, whether you want to know it or not. On the third day I walked down into the foyer of the hotel for breakfast. Just about to head out the door of the hotel is Dad, hat and camera in hand. The conversation goes like this.

'Hey g'day,' I say to him. 'How's things?'

He says, 'Yeah, great, slept well. When you work as hard as me you never have trouble sleeping.' He had driven the car the previous two days whilst we rode.

I say, 'I didn't sleep that well, beds are so hard.'

He says, 'See, if you worked harder during the day you wouldn't have trouble sleeping.'

I ignore that and say, 'Have you seen the kids this morning?'

He says, 'Yeah, they were up early.' Were they? That sounds unusual.

I say, 'Have you eaten?'

He says, 'No, I am going out for a walk along the beach and will have something when I get back.'

I look at my watch and think he's cutting it fine.

I say, 'Well, don't be long on your walk – we bail out of here in thirty minutes.'

He looks at his new Rolex and says, 'No, we don't, it's still early, we've got almost two hours before we go.'

Right then it hits me – his Rolex has stopped.

I say to him, 'Dad, your Rolex is stuffed. It's not 5.30 am, it's 6.45 am – we leave in thirty minutes.'

Of course it has to be my watch that's broken, not the fifteen-dollar Rolex.

He grabs my hand and looks at my watch. 'No, your watch is buggered. Look here, its 5.30 am,' whilst sticking the Rolex in my face.

I turn him to the clock in the foyer of the hotel, which displays the correct time, which happens to match my watch. 'Dad, your Rolex is rooted. It's 6.45 am, we leave in thirty minutes.'

He says, 'Jesus Christ, my watch is broken!'

He leaves the foyer, but not without spinning his thongs so quickly he almost trips up the stairs.

Sharing the 2009 ride with Dad almost brought me to tears, such was the level of frustration I felt at times. Sharing the 2010 ride with him had me crying with laughter. Like any father–son relationship there are great times and times when distance is your best friend, but as I have shared some great experiences with my kids on the ride, so too have I with Dad. I know that we are closer than ever before and the ride has given us that time to spend together.

He is never short of a word, don't be mistaken about that for one minute. There are several times a day when I wished it were the case, but when it comes to sharing and expressing your feelings, Dad comes from that generation when that's not the done thing. But I see the way he engages with my kids and I see how proud he is when we are at the orphanage and that speaks volumes. The best evidence of what the ride means for Dad was still yet to come.

In the weeks after I returned to Australia, I received an email that was the translated transcription of what Yong had felt and experienced during his time on the ride:

Even before the ride started I was very excited. Within myself I kept asking Can I do this? But I was very determined. Rotjana has taught me that I must always keep going. She told me that she had cancer but was still and always would fight to have a life to work for the future of the children. This is what made me strong and gave me power.

The first day I was very excited and worried but every day I had fun and my confidence grew. All the time as I rode I thought, We are all the same, we are a team and we are having many adventures together. When I saw the others riding and working so hard it made me so proud that I wanted to cry.

I would like to thank all the riders who came to help the children of my home. One day I fell from my bike. I hurt a lot but I kept going.

The route was often by the sea and I enjoyed the beautiful scenery. We went through many provinces and I saw many different traditions and cultures.

Everyone on the ride took care of Nong and I, made us feel part of the group. Every night I had a nice bed and every day wonderful food such as I had never had before. Every time we had a break Tony [one of the riders] bought me milk and made special jokes for me.

One of the ladies also encouraged me and made me laugh. She would sing and joke and that always made the ride easy.

Every day I saw Peter cycling with his youngest son, taking care of him. I could see the love they had and this also made me feel very warm. I would like to have a father like this. His sons are very lucky to have a father like Peter. I don't have a father, he died already.

On the last day as we cycled towards Baan Tharn Nam-chai, sure I missed everyone at home but this was the last day of the adventure and I didn't want it to end. As I got closer and closer I finally thought, I can do it. I've reached my goal.

When we got home and I saw everyone's faces, all of them waiting for the team to come home, I was very proud. I saw Rotjana walking with a stick, she wasn't well, I saw her cry. When I saw that it made me cry too, I was overwhelmed.

I thank everyone very much for giving me this experience. Now I know how hard people work to raise money for our home. It has made me know that I must work hard and study and grow up to be a good person.

This was a wonderful memory that I will never forget until the day I die.

Chapter 29

Baan Nam Khem

Many of the children who live in the orphanages have stories that are difficult to hear and sometimes even difficult to believe because they're just so awful.

The two kids who arrived at Baan Tharn Namchai in November 2010, taking our numbers from seventy-two to seventy-four, are typical of those you simply can't turn away. The two girls were aged two and four and lived alone with their mum. She was faced with a dilemma each day. Should she stay at home and care for her children, or should she head out to work so she could feed them? If she stayed at home and cared for her two daughters, as she so desperately wanted to, she would have no money to buy food. If she headed out to work to earn money so that they could eat and survive, she would have to leave the children on their own. Faced with two evils, she chose the lesser – leaving the children at home whilst she went out to work.

Previously this wouldn't have been an issue because the mum would have had her parents, aunties or sisters to help look after her kids. But they were now gone, lost to the tsunami.

The two children could not be left to roam the house on their own, though; there was no end to the harm they could bring upon themselves. The mother decided the safest option was to lock the two girls in a cage under the house whilst she was at work. She didn't do this out of cruelty, she did it because she saw it as the best option for their protection.

Coming home from work the mother found that the safety of the cage had been breached. Not from the inside by the girls, but from the outside.

Her four-year-old daughter had been raped.

The mother decided she had no option but to give up her girls until she was in a position to provide a safe home for them.

The girls were brought to our orphanage at Baan Tharn Namchai and were of course welcomed. They weren't taken from their mother without the option of return, however. They were simply given a safe home until their mum could provide for them once again. They would continue to spend time with her, but it would be in a safe environment.

This type of situation only reinforces to me the need to continue to support a community beyond the immediate crisis.

The circumstances this young mother found herself in are not atypical amongst the broken families of the Baan Nam Khem region. Baan Nam Khem is located about ten minutes' drive from the orphanages at Baan Tharn Namchai, south towards Phuket. It is located right on the coast and is surrounded by water on three sides. It was the worst affected area in all of Thailand and it is estimated that well over half of the four thousand people who lived in this community lost their lives to the tsunami.

The village of Baan Nam Khem is a community of modest houses occupied by local fisherman. The entire area is only a couple of metres above sea level, so when the tsunami hit, the water travelled for up to two kilometres inland before it was stopped by the escarpment. The village of Baan Nam Khem was directly in its path and little of it survived intact.

Many of the children from our orphanages come from the Baan Nam Khem region. One young girl lost twenty-one members of her family in the tsunami. For a community that relies upon the extended family network to make things happen and to take care of one another, this is devastating in a way that cannot be measured just by loss of life and property.

Once we had built the second orphanage, I sought from Khru Prateep her advice on how we could best assist the local community.

Sitting in her office in the Khlong Toei slums of Bangkok, she and I talked about what was needed and what we might be able to provide.

The streets of Baan Nam Khem might have been cleaned up after the tsunami – buildings might be rising again and fishermen finding employment – but this picture of normality in fact masked the true situation. Khru Prateep told me that the community suffered from fifty per cent unemployment. With such high unemployment rates come increased substance abuse, increased criminal activity, increased teenage pregnancies and general breakdown of communities. There was a thirteen-year-old girl who was now pregnant. She had lost her parents and her grandparents – who would support her and her child? Who would provide her with the skills to care for her child and prevent further pregnancies at such a tender age? There are many examples of how a community continues to hurt long after a crisis has passed and aid been withdrawn.

Now the orphanages had been built, we had taken care of those first couple of necessities of life: food and shelter. Now it was time to focus on the next stage of the children's and the community's recovery.

We wanted the community centre at Baan Nam Khem to be a place for the provision of education and vocational training. We knew that so many members of the local community had little or no formal training and were entirely reliant upon fishing for an income. The trouble with that is if you take away the demand, through lack of tourism, or you take away the opportunity, through seasonal or climatic changes, fishing becomes a very unreliable way of making a living. The local community needed other options for employment.

Families who had lost their support network still needed to work to survive; we saw that in building the community centre we could provide a centre for the care of the children during the day when their parents needed to work. The common practice was to either leave the children on their own at home or to keep the older children home from school to care for their younger siblings.

In this community centre we also wanted to provide medical and dental care for those people who slipped through the cracks. To receive treatment in Thailand you need to have an identity card or to be able to afford higher charges imposed by private medical facilities. If you are from Burma, Laos or Cambodia and living in Thailand illegally, as a general rule you cannot afford the higher charges imposed by private hospitals or medical centres, thus putting medical or dental care out of reach. This is typical of the people living in the poorer communities, who go without the necessities of life.

In building a community centre we also needed to consider the fear that still existed for those who had survived the tsunami, the fear that another would come and, living on the water's edge, they'd be just as vulnerable as last time. The idea was hatched that we should turn any centre we built into a tsunami refuge centre.

Over lunch the plans were laid for our next major project: a community centre that would provide vocational training, health and social care, medical and dental care, childcare for working parents, and tsunami refuge.

In the end, the final design, construction and fit-out of the building cost over AUD$1.4 million, which was significantly more than we had previously invested in any other project. If you stand at the driveway to the centre the physical size of the building is quite imposing. It has several storeys and is certainly one of the largest buildings in all of Baan Nam Khem. The first time I clambered over the building site, midway through construction, I was shocked at the size of the building. It was so much bigger than it looked on the plans! But in designing what we wanted the building to provide I am convinced this was the right course of action to take.

The roof has been built at a height of seventeen metres above ground level and has the capacity to hold a thousand people at any one time. There is a stairway leading up to the roof, right in the middle of the building, and it is seven metres wide. The design is to facilitate the movement of a large group of people who may be filled with panic. When you stand back at ground level looking at this impressive staircase leading to the roof, it looks as though the stairs lead to some place beyond the clouds. We could have made the building much smaller and done away with this refuge area. Clearly you don't get such a high roof without some pretty substantial formwork underneath. But we felt that providing the refuge area was important for those members of the community who had lived through the events of 2004. Having someone tell you it was a one in one hundred year event doesn't really give you peace of mind; having a safe option, having a place of refuge should another tsunami occur, does.

There was a Thai family who lived in Baan Nam Khem, a fishing village north of Phuket, at the time of the tsunami. Dad was a fisherman, a caring father and loving husband who worked hard each day to provide for his family. He didn't set off every morning in a large boat to fish the deep crystal-blue waters of the Anda-man Sea – that was beyond his means. Instead he and his partner walked out into the water with a long fishing net affixed to two timber poles. When the water level was up to their armpits the two men walked parallel to the beach with the net stretched out between them, then walked backwards and forwards, dragging the net through the water. They circled methodically, then returned to the beach to empty their catch from the net. Such was the life of a poor Thai fisherman working to support his family.

At home his wife cared for their three children, devoting her time to meeting their needs and keeping her modest home neat and tidy. This little family, like so many in that Thai fishing village, was surrounded by relatives and a strong community.

Boxing Day is not a day of celebration for the Thais. For this family it was another ordinary day on the calendar, another day that Dad would leave the family to drag his fishing net through the water and Mum would tend to her children. She was becoming slower in her movements these days as the bundle in her stomach grew. This was to be her fourth child.

Boxing Day was never a day of celebration, but Boxing Day 2004 was a day that would never be forgotten.

The family lost their father in the tsunami and Mum lost her husband. In addition she also lost her home and many of her extended family, to whom she would normally have turned for assistance. She was relocated with her three children to another community which was being supported by foreign aid; without this aid she couldn't have kept her family intact. For twelve months she lived within this community, reliant upon the food and money she was given. She gave birth to the baby she was carrying at the time of the tsunami and now had four children to care for.

After twelve months, the aid this family was relying upon stopped. For this young widow, struggling to keep her family together, there was no exit strategy put in place, no contingency plan for leaving the aid-run community, and she received no warning that her circumstances were about to change so dramatically. Many charities and NGOs that respond to crisis situations such as the tsunami have within their charter pre-identified exit times and strategies. It is rarely their intention to stay long-term, although this is often not communicated to the people they are supporting. Or if it is, the message is often not heard by those relying upon the aid.

From an aid response point of view, I certainly understand that charities who mobilise and respond to a disaster within days or weeks can't commit to an area for the long term, as this takes away from their rapid-response capacity. However, what I have witnessed in the Khao Lak area is that too many groups focus on short- to medium-term assistance, and when they leave, a massive hole is left behind.

When the assistance was withdrawn, this young mum was forced to do whatever she could to keep her family fed. She had four children, the youngest only months old, and no ready means of supporting her family. They lived in a rough shelter which offered little respite from the elements. For the next twelve months or so she struggled to keep her family together. The children were no longer going to school as that had become a luxury they could not afford. Each day was now about survival, about securing their next meal. The family relied upon the assistance of the community and whatever offerings they could share, but this was a poor community and most other people were struggling too.

The children woke one morning to find their mum gone. Nok, the eldest of the children, assumed that her mother was out looking for food to accompany the small amount of rice they had. Her younger brother and sisters had woken with empty bellies, as usual, and were eager for something, anything, to eat.

Whilst it was not the first time Nok had woken to find her mum was not there, it was unusual for her not to have returned by now. Sadly, Nok's mother didn't return that day. She didn't return the following day either, and it is now two and half years on and she still hasn't returned.

We don't know what happened to Nok's mother. We don't know if she left of her own accord, if she was taken, or if something terrible happened to her whilst she was out looking for food for her children.

Nok and her three siblings learnt to survive. Through the assistance of the community and the local temple they continued to live in their home for another twelve months. For me, the fact that four children of such tender age could live on their own and not draw the attention of authorities to their plight is evidence of a community that is hurting and doing its best to re-establish itself. If in fact the children were known to authorities, their living arrangement may have been deemed suitable or at the very least acceptable. The children managed to eke out a living, God knows how, and Nok became the carer and provider for the little family. Nok was eight years old at the time.

Eventually the staff at our orphanage came to hear of Nok and her siblings and the desperate situation they were in. Suffice it to say, before the sun had set, Khun Rotjana was out there collecting the children and taking them to a home in which they could live safely.

I was on one of my fleeting visits to Thailand only weeks after this little family had come to our attention and I was able to meet with the kids. They each had their own bed, their own change of clean clothes and a belly full of nutritious food. One of the beautiful things was to see them smile and to learn later that Nok was fitting into her role as an eight-year-old child, now she was no longer required to be parent and provider. The children have returned to school and found new friends at Baan Tharn Nam-chai; they, too, have a tragic story to tell, just like the rest of the kids, but they also have a better chance in life than they might otherwise have had.

As for their mum, well, there remains no news of her. Khun Rotjana has told me that she believes the children's mother simply left her children, not knowing what to do and unable to cope.

For me this is what sustainability in its most basic form is all about.

As a parent, our fundamental goal is to provide for our children. It is about ensuring they have enough food to stop them going hungry, keeping them well and safe, and giving them access to education so they can eventually carve their own path in this journey of life. How desperate must this mother have been, then, to walk away from her children in the middle of the night, leaving them to fend for themselves?

Her life as a mother had become unsustainable. You see, we can care all we want, but unless what we are doing is sustainable, it won't last, it won't survive. For me, no matter what we are doing within Hands, there needs to be an eye on the future. Someone needs to be considering what happens when the aid, support or assistance stops. Love and desire alone won't sustain a family or a community, no matter how strong that love is.

At the beginning, when we were forming Hands, very little of what is clear and drives me and the other board members now was present or had such strength. We were starting from nothing, so it was to be expected that the first couple of years were as much a learning experience for us all as they were devoted to raising money and building homes for the kids. With our increased activity, the clarity has come. We know that to build long-term results we need to build long-term strategies. It doesn't matter if we are thinking about the needs of a child, a family or the broader community. I can see that evolution around our thinking and our actions when I look at what our orphanages and the community centre are doing and our differing levels of support for them. Firstly we need to take care of the children's immediate needs such as food and shelter, then we can turn our attention to education, training and sustainable projects such as the rubber plantation we have.

When we operate within the guiding principles that we have, when we focus on the long-term outcomes, it would seem we are heading in the right direction.

Chapter 30

Home Hug

Increasingly I receive emails or phone calls from people seeking the assistance of Hands. Some merely want advice as to how to start their own charity; some will want to drill down and gain a deep understanding of why our model works so well; and others will want the financial assistance of Hands for a particular cause.

I have received numerous requests to take Hands into places such as Sri Lanka, India, Nepal, the Middle East, Africa, Pakistan, Cambodia, other parts of Thailand and most recently Japan following the disaster that has befallen that country. They have all been worthy causes, and we are always willing to share what has worked for us, but it wasn't until January 2010 that we were in a position to look beyond our project in the southern area of Thailand that encapsulates Baan Tharn Namchai and Baan Nam Khem.

I was preparing to leave for the second of our bike rides when I received an email asking me to take a look at a project in the northeast of Thailand, run by the Suthasinee Noiin Foundation and affectionately known as Baan Home Hug. The email came from a Thai-Australian now living in Australia, who had read an article in Australia's largest circulating Thai newspaper. The article talked about Hands and the impending bike ride.

Exploring the web I started to learn about the Suthasinee Noiin Foundation in a place called Yasothon, 530 kilometres northeast of Bangkok. The foundation was established some twenty-three years ago and provided care to children who had been impacted by HIV-AIDS. Kids living at this orphanage either suffered from the virus themselves or were there because their parents had the virus and were now too ill to care for them or had in fact died from AIDS or an associated illness.

Janet Gilchrist, a Thai-born lady who now lives in Australia and with whom I work on a number of projects, was with me in my office as we explored the website, learning what we could about the Suthasinee Noiin Foundation, or Home Hug.

We decided it was time to give them a call. Speaking in Thai, Janet asked them the questions I wrote on paper in front of her and then translated the answers for me. We learnt a number of key things that day. One hundred and fifteen children lived at the orphanage and their ages ranged from a few weeks to eighteen years old. Approximately one third of the children were infected with HIV; a number of the younger children showed enough markers to indicate they had the virus, however these cases had not been confirmed; and in the year previous many children had died from associated illnesses. The income the orphanage received was sporadic and relied upon the founder, Khun Thew, working to raise awareness and funds, mostly in Bangkok. Sadly, Khun Thew was suffering from pancreatic cancer.

I had heard enough. I knew I had to travel to Thailand to see the place for myself.

The trip to Yasothon was made in March of 2010, after the January bike ride. It was always going to be difficult turning up at Home Hug as a *farang* who spoke little Thai while trying to convey the right intent, and more importantly, find the right way to ask the sensitive questions I needed answered. I had to understand their financial position, who was giving them money, how much and how often, and how was it spent. To be brutally honest, I needed to understand how they protected the children from sexual abuse, and to be sure that the operation they were running wasn't in any way associated with pedophiles. I also wanted to explore personal issues such as the succession plan Khun Thew had in place for when the cancer overtook her body. Some of the questions were quite probing, and normally it would have been best to try to build a friendship and demonstrate a lasting commitment to the enterprise before delving into these areas. But these questions needed to be asked, and I knew that when I returned to the board room and spoke to the Hands faithful, they would expect me to have asked the questions and to have the answers. The flipside was also true, of course – Khun Thew would quite rightly be sceptical of me and my intentions; she would want to know why I was there and what I really wanted out of all of this.

Khun Thew had huge barriers to overcome in talking openly to me. Many of the children at Home Hug had contracted HIV after being sexually abused or raped. I would come to learn that there weren't any men in Khun Thew's life whom she trusted completely. There were very few whom she trusted even remotely. For over twenty years she had seen the results of men behaving badly towards children. Her guardedness towards me was protection of her children and I found it a reassuring quality. It meant that I needed to earn her trust and I knew that would take time, but it was a road I would need to travel for us to make any progress.

In addition to her distrust of men, she, along with Khun Rotjana at Baan Tharn Namchai, have had experience after experience of people turning up filled with pity for them and the children and believing they have the answers. But once the feeling of pity dissipates so does any support they might have had. Most pledge to return to their country and raise money, and yet are never heard from again.

Having arrived in Bangkok late at night, Nic and I had five hours in between flights to get some sleep. Like me, Nic works for herself, running a successful change management consultancy, and this brings us both a degree of flexibility. The advantage of this is that we both travel nationally and throughout the Asia Pacific region quite often, so when the chance arises for one of us to share the other's journey we grab it. We can effectively work from anywhere, and if we can string a couple of days together in Singapore, Thailand or elsewhere, that is a bonus. At the time of the planned Yasothon trip, the planets aligned and we were able to travel together. An additional plus was that it was her birthday at the end of the trip, and I found a sneaky little place overlooking the Mekong River for a couple of days' holiday.

After checking into the hotel in Bangkok, we were up after what seemed like five minutes and heading to Ubon Ratchatani, or Ubon, as it is also known. Ubon Ratchatani is the province that is located in the region of Isan, and Yasothon is a much smaller adjoining province. The quickest way to get to Yasothon is to fly to Ubon out of Bangkok, a journey of 530 kilometres, and then to drive the further one hundred kilometres northwest to Yasothon. At the domestic check-in counter of the airport it was clear we were heading somewhere unusual when the locals stared at us, assuming we were in the wrong line. Why would we be heading to Ubon? This was only confirmed when the bemused check-in lady greeted us with, 'This flight is for Ubon Ratchatani.' Clearly what she meant to say was, 'You should have read the sign correctly, you are in the wrong line!'

The flight was typical of many domestic flights in Asia – as soon as the passengers heard the landing gear being lowered, they interpreted that to mean, 'Get out of your seat, grab your hand luggage and run for the front exit door; if the flight attendant gets in your way, push her to one side.'

Walking into the terminal at Ubon Ratchatani, it was a delight to see the smiling faces of Khru Prateep and Khun Rotjana, both of whom had made the trip to Ubon to accompany Nic and me on the visit to the orphanage. I thought it was important for a number of reasons: firstly, so that they could explain to Khun Thew who I was and what Hands was all about, and secondly, to engage them in the process. I didn't want them to think we were stepping away from Baan Tharn Namchai in any way at all.

The Isan region of Thailand is very different from that of the south around Phuket or Khao Lak. It is the poorest region in all of Thailand, and the standard of living is quite low. The average monthly income is approximately half of the national average. It has fewer doctors and fewer hospitals per head than any other area of Thailand. The main source of income is agriculture and, although diversification does exist in the form of cash crops, the main crop remains sticky rice. Due to the lack of rainfall in this area the production of the crops is lower than elsewhere in Thailand, and it is not uncommon for only one crop per year to be harvested. The region also has the lowest literacy rate in all of Thailand, which contributes to the ignorance, fear and gross discrimination of the kids who have HIV that the orphanage faces. The other major difference between the rest of Thailand and Isan is that there are certainly no tourists riding around in tuktuks.

Standing at the hire-car desk in Ubon airport was an unusual experience, though probably more so for the Thai staff behind the desk who kept smiling and laughing behind their hands at the *farang* who had come to this area. It just didn't happen on a regular basis. I enjoyed the experience of driving through a rural Thai city such as Ubon, which is large enough to be busy with traffic but small enough for all of the road signs to be in Thai. The trip out to the orphanage confirmed that the driving was no better in the northeast than it had been in the areas I was familiar with, and it was still acceptable to overtake a vehicle whilst you were being overtaken. There's always enough room on a two-lane road for two cars and a truck side by side. You just make it fit.

On arrival at the orphanage I was immediately struck by a number of things. The children smiled and giggled just like the kids at Baan Tharn Namchai, and it was clear that the love Khun Thew had for these children filled her heart and soul. But the kids' appearance lacked the freshness the kids at Baan Tharn Namchai had. I wanted to throw them all a cake of soap, get them a haircut and some new clothes. There was an institutional smell about the place, too, which was quite different from the orphanages at Baan Tharn Namchai. But what seemed most out of place to me given what I had heard about their dire situation was the construction of a new building at the front of the premises. I thought to myself, *How is it that they have the money to build a new structure, and yet I am hearing that they don't have enough money to feed and care for the kids?* I couldn't leave without finding out what this was about, but that would have to wait for a while.

After the initial greetings and sharing of food, we got down to the real business. Khun Thew was joined by a Catholic nun, Sister Nong Luk, who actually speaks more English than anyone else at the orphanage, not that she used it a lot in this first meeting. When she looked at me, I felt as though I was in trouble and needed to apologise. She was a tiny thing, but I was in her territory and I got the feeling she wasn't all too happy about it.

Throughout the meeting Khru Prateep translated into Thai for Khun Thew and into English for me. I wish I could speak more than a little Thai – it's something I would love to do – but making the commitment and finding the time is the only obstacle. To be truthful, it's an excuse, it's not really an obstacle that can't be overcome. At one point, though, there was no translation required. Khru Prateep and Khun Thew were speaking in Thai and I was sitting on the opposite side of the table. Khun Thew looked at me pointedly and her eyes screamed, 'Who is he and what does he want?' The look in her eyes was one of a mother protecting her children from a threat she had experienced all too often.

Khru Prateep, in her soft and comforting voice, turned to me and said, 'I haven't given Khun Thew much of your story. Now I am going to do that.' For the next twenty minutes Khru Prateep spoke only in Thai to Khun Thew and explained to her the journey of Hands Across the Water, what we had done for the children and, more importantly, that we had done it without imposing a religious or political view, with only the intent to help the children and the communities who had suffered so much.

In those twenty minutes Khun Thew's face softened and the distrust left her body. She turned and looked at me with an almost apologetic smile as her eyes welled up and a few tears ran down her face. For that moment I shared the love and understanding that I am sure each of her kids feels when they're with her.

Khru Prateep went on to explain that we didn't come with unfulfilled promises, we had indeed seen through the commitments we had made. Khru Prateep achieved more in twenty minutes than I think I could have achieved in twelve months of work and visits. After she had finished speaking we were accepted into the lives of the children at Home Hug and into the trusted circle of Khun Thew.

Walking around the orphanage with Khun Thew, we were shown the bedrooms and the kitchen – if that is what you call three free-standing gas burners – where one hundred and fifteen children were housed and fed. The youngest of the children was four weeks old and had positive HIV markers.

It was obvious to Nic and me that Khun Thew loved these children and really enjoyed their company. There was a very special moment when we were standing outside one of the buildings discussing the issue of the provision of water, and Khun Thew made her hand into the shape of a gun and began play shooting with a four-year-boy who was along for the walk.

Unfortunately, however, the orphanage needed a whole heap of love and attention; it was dirty and it smelt. Khun Thew was a sick lady and she was running short on energy. She needed to be taken care of herself.

The dormitory housing the older girls was full of broken hospital gurneys which were the kids' beds. They didn't have one of these beds to themselves either; there were at least two or three to each bed. These beds sent a clear message to the children that they were sick and all that they deserved was what other people no longer wanted.

Before we could leave I needed to find out what the new building at the front of the premises was all about. My question drew a response from Khun Thew indicating she wasn't happy. It wasn't the question that upset her but the building itself. The Thai Royal family had decided the orphanage would benefit from a library and funds were committed to build one. Khun Thew's say in the spending of the money or the appropriateness of the decision wasn't a consideration. A monument was required and one would be built.

This was another classic example of people with money coming into a charity and deciding what they needed. I'd have thought the money would have been better invested in the children's health. I am all for education and kids having access to books to read. But if they are dying because of lack of food and medication, a book isn't of much use to them.

Leaving Khun Thew that day I had no doubt of the next course of action to take. And it wasn't just a dream: I knew I could return with some friends and transform this place. It was simply a matter of picking the dates and making it happen – that's how confident I was about what we could do at Hands.

I was excited by the change we could bring to these children. I saw Khun Thew as a lady who carried a heavy burden and had done so for a long time. I saw the opportunity to take some of that load from her and let her rest a while. She could spend her time with the kids, loving them as she did and as they deserved, without the burden of having to raise funds to keep the orphanage going. We could bring some hope and comfort into her life and into the lives of her children.

However, I doubt Khun Thew shared the same level of enthusiasm and certainty about my return. Too often people would come to visit her, bring food, take photos and hug the kids, leaving with promises of returning but not living up to those promises. Gradually, though, as I returned to Yasothon several times over the ensuing months, she started to believe that I would keep my promises.

Back in Australia I presented the board with a pretty emotional and compelling case as to why I thought this orphanage was right for us, why I believed we should expand our reach beyond the tsunami orphanages we had built. There was resistance from key supporters who thought it would distract us from the work that we were doing in Khao Lak, which was what they had signed up for. But having seen the kids, having seen how they lived, and knowing what resources we could bring to Yasothon, it felt completely right to me.

Thankfully the board signed off on my recommendation at that meeting. Kay asked me to stop halfway through my presentation as it was too confronting. To steal a line from Hollywood, she said, 'You had me at hello.'

I would visit Yasothon several times within the first six months

after my initial visit. There was much to learn, a great deal to prepare for in taking a group of volunteers to the region and it was
also important for me to spend some time with Khun Thew, letting
her know the first visit wasn't a one-off and giving her reason to
believe we might be different from others.

Each of the ensuing visits was made on my own and during this
time I got to learn more about the struggles the kids faced. I would
learn from Khun Thew of the dilemma she faced when one of the
non–Thai national kids became ill. She didn't discriminate about
which children she took in, but the public health system did. If you
are not Thai, you pay cash for treatment. The treatment can be
inexpensive at the public hospital by western standards, but for the
children to receive specialist treatment when they were sick with
AIDS they needed to go to the private hospital and this is where
the problem was. Each visit that Khun Thew made to the private
hospital for one of the non-Thai children was equivalent to the
cost of feeding the children for twenty-five days. Her choice was
to take the sick child to hospital for treatment and do without the
money to buy food, or buy the food and let the sick child die. On
many occasions she would take the child to hospital. Then, without the money to buy food, the older children living at Home Hug
would head out into the scrub that surrounds the orphanage to
catch rats and lizards that they could eat. And of course when this
becomes their diet, even those children who weren't ill at the time
eventually become ill and require medical treatment themselves. It
was becoming clear why children were dying, and it also became
clear that we could make an immediate difference just by inject-
ing enough money on a regular basis to ensure Khun Thew could
afford both food and medication.

In the early days of visiting Baan Tharn Namchai I would often
leave the orphanage with a heavy heart, saddened by the stories
I had heard and touched by the smiles and happiness of the kids

despite their losses. I think a part of the heaviness that weighed on me was wondering if or when I would return. Leaving Home Hug I had heard equally tragic stories, some more so than I was hearing out of Baan Tharn Namchai, but I didn't leave with the same heaviness or sadness. I also left in a hurry, wanting to get to the airport or on to Bangkok so I could do something to change things straight away. As soon as I was on the plane from Ubon to Bangkok I would have my laptop out and be firing off a paper to the board full of ideas for what we could or should do. There was no longer the question of if I would return; I knew I would be back within a couple of months, even if nothing was planned. I always left Home Hug feeling inspired to make a difference and I wanted to do it quickly.

The idea of taking foreigners into Thailand to undertake the work was new for Hands and not something we had engaged in before. All of the work had previously been done through local contractors, ensuring that employment was generated in the local community and the financial benefit went to the families of the contractors. I was also aware that just because people had the desire to volunteer and engage in this work didn't mean they had the skill set. Desire doesn't always equal capability. But the project at Yasothon was different from in other areas.

Westerners on holidays in Thailand didn't visit Isan, Ubon or Yasothon. I struggle to meet anyone who has ever heard of Yasothon before. I certainly hadn't. What that means is people are not calling into the orphanage and learning about the kids or their needs and then making a choice to support them, or at least having an awareness of their plight. Your typical Australian tourist heading to Thailand will go to Phuket, Phi Phi Island, Koh Samui, Krabi, or Chiang Mai in the north. No one heads to the northeastern part of the country without good reason, and I can understand why. It is a dry, poor area that offers very little even for the intrepid traveller. However, I was confident that once people learnt about the kids here, a steady stream of travellers looking for something beyond what Patong has to offer would put Yasothon on their list of places to visit.

And this turned out to be the case. In the twelve months from April 2010, when I first presented the concept of assisting Home Hug to the board of Hands, over one hundred and fifty visits have been made to this area by people directly associated with Hands.

The second major reason for taking people into Yasothon was a direct result of Khun Thew's experiences and desires. There exists such a fear and high level of ignorance about HIV-AIDS in the broader Isan region that contractors simply won't go to the orphanage to undertake paid work. Their fear of catching HIV from painting a wall or digging a garden bed stops many of them even considering the work. And for those who will put their prejudice aside, some of them have seen the opportunity to take advantage of the kids at the orphanage.

So rather than taking work away from the local Thais by bringing westerners into the region, we were initially completing work that wouldn't otherwise have been done, and the presence of the team generated work for the hotels they would stay in, the restaurants they ate in and the drivers who would provide their transport for the two weeks. In fact, the group that would go in all likelihood injected more money into the local economy in tips alone than would have been paid in wages if Thais had been engaged to do the work.

I began planning a return trip to Yasothon later in the year, this time with some friends. As usually happens within the Hands community, you just need to float half an idea and it gains enough momentum that it very quickly becomes reality.

I decided that my friends and I would put a lick of paint on the walls and spruce the place up a bit. But just like the Paul Kelly,

Kev Carmody song, 'From Little Things Big Things Grow', in the end sixty-three people from five different countries descended upon Yasothon in November 2010 for a two-week period to change a few lives. Along the way lives were changed, and it wasn't only the children's lives but the volunteers' too.

What became known as Task Force Yasothon brought together people from very different backgrounds for a common purpose. It was like our own mini United Nations. We had people from Australia, New Zealand, Hong Kong, Singapore, the UK and Thailand joining us there. Each of them paid for their own flight, accommodation and meals, and each brought a different skill set. There were some pretty seasoned travellers amongst the group, but none had previously ventured into this part of Thailand and none had ever heard of Yasothon, let alone visited the place.

Our very clear intention was to renovate the buildings, paint some walls and build a new kitchen. But there was always going to be more. We could have spent the money and engaged local tradespeople to undertake the work, but that would have negated two of the greatest gifts to come out of the project. The first was the engagement of the task force members. In giving the western volunteers an experience at Home Hug that engaged their hearts as much as their hands, I knew they would become advocates for Hands and return home talking about their time there, about the lives they had changed and how their life was changed in the process. You don't get this sort of meaningful experience donating one hundred or one thousand dollars. But once the experience has been had and the hearts and minds engaged, there is more likelihood of ongoing support from people, both financially and emotionally. It was giving them reason to be involved.

The second greatest gift was the message our involvement conveyed to the children. That we cared about them. The kids who live in this orphanage are ostracised by their own community because of their HIV status, and they seldom see any *farang* who come for more than a stickybeak.

This is not to underestimate the physical changes that were brought to the premises. The three gas burners were replaced by a state-of-the-art commercial kitchen; the bedrooms were painted and the kids received new beds; the gardens were tended and a grey-water system was put in place.

At times people may question our spending and the high quality of the buildings we construct. I operate from a paradigm that our commitment is long-term, therefore we need to build for the long-term, and that what we provide for the kids conveys a message to them about how we measure their worth.

Khun Thew recounted something quite remarkable that occurred during the two weeks we were there.

Death is not new to anyone living at the orphanage. Khun Thew made it very clear to all the task force members that she can't afford to show grief when one of the children dies. Statistically, one child will die each week. In the twenty-three years she has been caring for children affected by HIV-AIDS, she estimates that over one thousand children have died. How on earth do you cope with something like that? For Khun Thew it is about sticking to the routine and keeping her grief inside. She does not let the children know the hurt and sadness she feels each time there is a death. That grief and sorrow is kept for herself when she is alone at night. Personally I can't begin to understand the journey this lady has made, nor the loss she has had to deal with on a continual basis.

Dealing with death is typified by the story of one of the seventeen-year-old boys who lives and works at the orphanage. You see, he fulfils an important task – he is the gravedigger. Each time one of the children he has shared a meal with, played soccer with and sung songs with passes away, his job is to dig their grave. In recognition of the loss of each of these kids he will stand and say something at the burial. He writes something unique that captures each child and their individual journey, however brief that may have been, and then he turns it into a song which is sung at the orphanage.

So what happened during those two weeks that was so remarkable? Well, a couple of the children were very ill and were not expected to see the night out. But they did survive the night, and in fact their health improved and in this short period of time they regained their strength. What was different then? There was a group of people who had come to help, and for no reason other than that they wanted to make the lives of the kids a little bit better. The mere presence of the volunteers and the work that was being done was enough to lift the spirits of these sick children.

For me the transformation that I witnessed in the lives of the volunteers was somewhat predictable. I had been living and travelling this journey ever since I formed Hands. I knew more than anyone the rewards that came from giving of yourself from deep within your heart when you did it for no other reason. Time and time again I witness people who give without expectation receiving so much back in return. But the key is to give without the expectation.

A classic example of the change that came about for the volunteers was in one of them whom I have known all my life, my brother Dave. Dave is a few years older than me and is a successful executive who has a lovely wife Dee and two gorgeous daughters Georgia and Kate. Even before leaving school Dave was driven by the dollar. He saw the struggle that both Mum and Dad had in living hand to mouth and committed himself to not being in the same position. Through his work he achieved a level of financial security that sees him live a very comfortable life, but one that he works very hard to maintain. In this pursuit to reach an ever-increasing level of financial wealth I have witnessed him suffer health issues that I attribute to the stress in his life.

Whilst Dave was clearly aware of Hands and what I was doing, he was not actively involved in a meaningful way. I was totally okay with that – Hands is my journey and it doesn't have to be for anyone else. I know why I do it. Dave would come to the annual fundraising dinner which we held in Sydney and stump up an auction prize. This had pretty much been the limit of his involvement, until the Yasothon project came around.

For some reason the project that we were planning for Yasothon appealed to him and clearly appealed on a deep level, because he didn't just commit himself but also convinced a group of his mates from Canberra to sign up to travel to Thailand at their own expense and engage in unpaid manual work for two weeks.

Dave and the mates of his who went to Yasothon are all very successful businessmen in their own right. They are all well travelled and live very comfortable lives. So what was it that took them to the poorest region in Thailand for a couple of weeks to dig channels, fell trees and build walls? The opportunity to be part of the Yasothon task force didn't come with any promises. It wasn't about improving anyone's CV; we didn't even give them a T-shirt. They went because they felt it was the right time and the right opportunity.

Dave and the boys from Canberra are typical of people I meet on a regular basis as I travel around speaking at conferences. To generalise, they fit into the following group: they're aged in their mid to late forties, have kids at private schools and doing well; they are successful in their business or career; they are not looking for further career advancement; they live a very fortunate life – but something is missing. When I talk with them what I usually find is that they feel as though the challenge of making money for themselves or someone else doesn't reward them on a soulful level. It meets their material needs, it provides them and their families with everything they need to live, but there remains a desire to do more.

Yasothon gave all of our team the chance to feel the personal reward that can come from doing something for someone else. When you stand to gain little other than an experience, you are not looking for the return; instead you focus on the gift of giving. Every one of the men and women who were part of our task force experienced this real emotional connection.

Up until about six weeks out from the Yasothon trip, Nic and I were both planning on heading there with the team, and I was going to lead the response. Flights were booked and we had our diaries cleared for the two weeks. An opportunity was then presented to me to work for BHP at one of their mining sites for a week. The week was, of course, the first week of the Yasothon trip. It was the type of offer that was just too good for a self-employed consultant to refuse. I was also aware that I had kept my diary free of speaking work for the month of December due to a major project I was working on, and January would be spent riding through Thailand. That meant two months of no income, with plenty of expenses heading out the door.

My decision to step aside from the Yasothon trip was something that I deliberated over for a week or so and it gave me plenty of sleepless nights. I was worried that I was letting the team down, and continually asked myself if I was doing the right thing by the children at the orphanage. Upon reflection I think the decision not to go has been a good thing for Hands. What it did was create opportunities for significant projects to occur without my personal involvement. I know that I could fill every waking day with Hands matters, but doing that is not sustainable for me. I need to earn money to support my family and spending all my time on Hands wouldn't allow that.

I remained in contact with the crew during the renovation work and every phone call gave me mixed emotions. I was so pleased to hear what was going on and to hear the excitement in the voices of those working there, but I was also missing being part of the action. I knew the personal rewards and satisfaction that the team would take away and I wanted to be part of that. But this was not my time.

When I'd first returned from Yasothon and presented my report to the board of Hands in April of 2010, suggesting this was a place we needed to be, the board agreed. They asked probing and relevant questions, but at the end of the day they trusted my lead on this decision. Nonetheless it was very satisfying for me when Willie Moulden, a Hands director, called me midway through the Yasothon project from the building site to tell me how right it was for Hands to have taken on Home Hug and the kids. Now that he had been there, seen the kids and seen the opportunity for Hands, he had that deeper level of engagement, as did all the volunteers who attended.

A measure of the success of the program at Yasothon can be gauged by the changes it brought about for the kids. Did the two-week visit meet the objectives of transforming the building? Would the volunteers return, or recommend the experience to others?

The changes for the children were both physical and emotional, and I am not sure how you judge the importance of one over the other. On a physical level their health improved, they stopped getting sicker and – to put it bluntly – they stopped dying. That in itself is a fairly significant outcome, and if it had been the only outcome it would have been sufficient. How did the work that the team undertook in that two-week period save lives? Well, quite simply, the kids have an incredibly low immune system as a result of HIV. They are susceptible to illnesses that healthy kids would fend off. One of the biggest problems we pinpointed was the mould and mildew that grew in the buildings where the kids slept each night. Due to the high humidity in the dry season and the rain in the wet season, mould and mildew were a constant cause of illness. During the team's visit, ventilation was improved and the walls of the bedrooms painted with a mould-resistant paint. Such an easy fix, but with such significant outcomes.

On an emotional level the kids saw that people cared. The mere presence and commitment of the volunteers in turning up and working hard from sun-up to sundown told the kids that they mattered and were worth helping.

The transformation of the building was substantial but it was just the start. The new commercial kitchen was now in place and each of the kids had a new bed to sleep in. No longer did they have to share a broken-down gurney.

Our final measure of the success of the project was whether the volunteers would return or recommend the experience. The team each gave one of two responses to this question. Many said yes, they would return in a heartbeat – and fifteen of them did just that in April of 2011, to continue the renovation work and install water tanks that would give the orphanage a storage capacity of over one quarter of a million litres of filtered water to get them through the dry season. The other response was no, they wouldn't return. Why not? They had formed such a strong attachment to some of the children in that two-week period that they couldn't bear the thought of going back to Yasothon to find that one of those kids had died.

The chance that a child might die before a volunteer's return visit was a very real issue for each to consider. But since Home Hug has become a part of the Hands family, not one child has died. In the first twelve months after the visit I made in March of 2010, Khun Thew has had the resources to ensure her kids eat three meals a day. They all have the medication they require on a daily basis and they make the trip to hospital for treatment as the need arises. For the first time since the orphanage was formed, children no longer die on a weekly or monthly basis.

However you choose to measure the success of the work that the volunteers did in November 2010, or the presence of Hands at

Home Hug, the greatest outcome has to be that kids are alive today who wouldn't be otherwise.

The orphanage at Yasothon is now well and truly a part of the Hands family. At a board level we have made a long-term commitment to support them financially. Because of the support and trust of our many donors and hardworking supporters, we have grown to a point where we don't need to fundraise for every individual project before we can start making a difference. When I first started Hands, and during the following couple of years, it would be a process of identifying a suitable project and then raising money to see it come to fruition. The amount of time it took to get the project off the ground was obviously dependent upon the scale of the project and how successful we were at raising the money. But we have grown, and now have the capacity to made immediate change when required. So when the board agreed to implement a financial strategy that would stop the kids from dying and bring about the renovation work at Home Hug, we didn't have to raise the money first. We had the strength as an organisation to carry that expense, knowing we would raise additional money through various means as the project progressed.

The task force's visit to Yasothon ignited the passion amongst a new group of supporters that will bring about change to these kids. Upon return from Thailand, Lisa, a volunteer from Adelaide, immediately began production of a calendar which was distributed through the group and raised several thousand dollars. She has also taken to speaking at different functions to raise awareness of Hands and the work that we are doing. A number of the original team returned to the orphanage in April 2011, and plans are well under way for the third trip, which is planned for November of 2011. Each of the team members now has a level of ownership of the project, and each is acutely aware of the difference even a single person can make.

Chapter 31

2011: A Ride with Greater Meaning

In 2011, due to increasing demand for positions on our annual bike ride, we decided to hold two rides, back to back. There was another new element to these rides, as well. Having committed Hands to supporting the kids at Yasothon, one of the things I wanted to do was ensure there was integration between the two areas we were now supporting: the tsunami-related projects in Khao Lak and the HIV kids in the northeast at Yasothon. This meant having a couple of people from each orphanage on each ride. When the offer was put to Khun Thew at Yasothon that she could have a couple of riders join us if they were interested, there was immediate interest in the idea. However, there appeared to be some confusion, as she kept suggesting she would be one of the riders. Another message lost in translation, I thought; I needed to work on my Thai language skills.

I asked Khun Gae, the Thai part owner of the bike touring company that we use each year, to speak to Khun Thew and explain what I was offering and what the ride entailed. It turned out Khun Thew wasn't confused – she knew what was on offer and she wanted to ride. This was a lady who looked quite ill when I met her for the first time in March of 2010. When I'd seen her a couple of months after that she was using a walking stick and I wondered if she would survive the year, or whether the cancer that had invaded her body would claim her. Now in August she was suggesting she would ride. In the lead-up to the ride I was managing the fifty-odd Australian and New Zealand riders who would soon make the trip to Thailand and ensuring they were supported. I must admit that I didn't follow up with Khun Thew, thinking that she would come to her senses or, if push came to shove, I'd let her join us and she could ride in the van once she appreciated what the ride was about. Anyway, I thought it might be good for her to have a couple of days relaxing in the van away from the orphanage.

What a limiting mind space I had drifted into. And on reflection, what was personally disappointing for me about this was that one of the key messages I try to convey when speaking at conferences is not to let other people impose their limitations upon us. Yet that is exactly what I did here. I was assuming that because Khun Thew was battling pancreatic cancer and in June had needed a walking stick to get around, she couldn't ride.

Khun Thew set off on the eight-hundred-kilometre journey towards Khao Lak on 5 January, along with twenty-seven other riders. And just like my kids had done in 2009, Khun Thew just kept riding. She finished the first stage of the first day – a distance of about twenty-three kilometres – as she'd started, smiling and with grim determination. Then she rode into lunch at the end of the second stage, and before we knew it we were all standing outside the hotel at the end of the first day cheering and yelling as she rode into the car park.

I shouldn't have been surprised. This was a lady who nine years before was diagnosed with pancreatic cancer and given six months to live. She watched her father battle and then die from cancer and she was now fighting a battle for her own life that was beyond the scope of any bike ride. For the previous twenty-three years she had fought on a daily basis for the lives of thousands of children, and sadly had buried over one thousand in the same period. She knew what a struggle was about and was going to teach us a lesson about determination, courage and commitment.

Khun Thew had rejected western medicine in her fight to beat cancer, having witnessed what her father went through and how he died a painful death. She had adopted her own philosophy and treatment, which included getting up at 3 am each day to undergo a three-hour detox process before the the rest of us dragged ourselves out of bed. Riding with Khun Thew was an inspiration for every one of us. People on the ride had the good sense not to complain about minor niggling injuries or soreness given the commitment that Khun Thew was putting in every day.

On day six we rode into a large town called Surat Thani, located about 170 kilometres from our final destination. We had pre-arranged for a large coach filled with kids from Yasothon to travel to Khao Lak, to be at the end of the ride to welcome in Khun Thew and the rest of the riders. It was also an opportunity for the kids from the north to see the ocean for the first time in their lives. The kids couldn't wait until we arrived two days later to see Khun Thew, and had travelled back to Surat Thani to see her that afternoon. For the riders it would be their first opportunity to see the kids that we were riding for, and it was a chance to put the pain of the last six days into perspective.

Day six is the longest day on the bike and although not the hardest, it is close to it. We ride around 138 kilometres that day, but it is not the distance which is the hard part, it is a couple of long straight stretches, some of which are accompanied by an unwelcome head wind. Arriving at the hotel on this occasion there was barely time to get out of the lycra and back to the car park before the bus filled with kids from Yasothon pulled in.

Even before the bus came to a stop and well before the doors opened, we could hear and see the excitement of the kids, and it wasn't just the little ones. The coach stood a real risk of toppling over as everyone inside rushed to one side to catch the first glimpse of Khun Thew. The little kids raced from the bus to be first to throw their tiny little arms around her. They weren't racing one another, they just wanted to hug her. The older kids and staff left the bus in a more controlled manner, many choosing to use the steps that the younger kids had seen as a mere impediment to getting to Khun Thew as quickly as they could. I am sure the older kids and staff were also filled with a sense of relief that Khun Thew had not only survived the journey so far, but was looking as healthy as she was.

After the car park rendezvous, it was soon time for the kids to board the bus again and return to Khao Lak. Before they left the hotel, Scott Stein, one of the directors of Hands who was on the first ride, presented a gift for the children. He had received several hundred pairs of Ecco shoes from the company in Australia as a donation for the kids, and each of the riders had added an extra suitcase to their luggage filled with the shoes.

Because they come from an HIV orphanage in the poorest area of Thailand, the Yasothon kids aren't use to receiving new clothes, new shoes or for that matter anything new at all. So when these leather shoes, which retail in Australia for several hundred dollars a pair, started to be pulled out of boxes and suitcases, the kids stood with wide eyes staring at them. The smell of fresh leather filled the air as the kids stood back, not daring to touch, watching as the pile of shoes on the ground started to grow. It took a lot of convincing before the kids understood the shoes were for them. They were free to take a pair and try them on.

Once the situation became clear the children's eyes widened

and their faces were filled with excitement for the second time in twenty minutes. The kids didn't rifle through the shoes looking for the right colour or style – it didn't even matter to them what size they were. The kids simply could not believe that they had a new pair of shoes. The fact that it might take them another eight years of growing to fit into them didn't concern them. They had just been given something that was theirs to keep, and something that was shiny, new, and smelt new as well.

Seeing the joy that a new pair of shoes had brought to these kids, on top of the unbridled love and affection shown between Khun Thew and all of those who got off the bus, was too much for those of us standing in the car park. We were now two days away from finishing what had been a ten-month project for many. The emotion overflowed. The scene had shown us what all this was really about: it was why we were riding, why we had done the fundraising. It was for these beautiful selfless children, who through no fault of their own faced a daily fight just to survive. This experience had given our riders a degree of engagement that you can't simulate or plan, you just have to be a part of it.

I stood towards the back of the group, watching how this played out for everyone. Our two strongest riders, Henry and Rob, who had joined the group late without a great personal knowledge of Hands, stood side by side sobbing. CT, Kel, Branka and Lisa, four girls who had worked hard in the fundraising and equally hard on the bike, had their hearts captured in that car park that afternoon by these kids. Our two Irish girls, Davina and Ailish, who worked harder than anyone to raise their money, revelled in the events as they unfolded.

We all tried not to cry in front of the kids because we didn't want them thinking we were sad or we were filled with pity, because we weren't. We cried because of how lucky we were to have been part of something so special. This was a time and a place that would never be forgotten by anyone standing in the car park in Surat Thani that afternoon.

For Nic and me, watching the kids pick out a new pair of shoes had a heightened significance. When we'd first visited the orphanage at Yasothon in March of 2010, we'd been shown plastic bags that contained one shirt, one pair of shorts and one pair of shoes. We were told that each year the kids handed over their clothes to someone younger than them. Even the clothes they wore on their backs were on loan, so we knew what a pair of shoes that would be theirs alone must have meant to each child.

As they struggled to comprehend what was going on, shoes clutched to their chests, the children reboarded the bus to return to Khao Lak and await our arrival in two days' time. The unscheduled meeting of the kids that afternoon was the highlight of the ride for many.

Standing in the car park watching the events unfold was the moment that encapsulated for me what the last twelve months of work had been for. I took so much pleasure in watching the riders share an experience they would never forget. I was filled with pride and a deep sense of accomplishment that what we had started several years earlier had come to scenes like this. Every one of the kids from Yasothon and the riders from Australia and New Zealand were winners that day; there were no losers. We left the car park changed. We had shared a bonding experience that people spend tens of thousands of dollars trying to recreate in team-building exercises, and it was all achieved by something as simple as giving some kids a new pair of shoes. The magic that comes from giving without expectation is something I often talk about. Knowing that I can create opportunities like this time and time again is what gets me out of bed every morning.

I later learnt from Khun Thew that many of the kids wouldn't wear the shoes they had chosen that day in the car park at Surat

Thani. For weeks they would instead carry them around with them, stuffed into the pockets of their pants or jackets. They dared not wear the shoes in case they damaged them or got them dirty. The harsh lessons life had taught them up to this point were hard to see past.

Khun Thew rode with us to send a message to the kids at Yasothon: that just because they have an illness, just because they face challenges, doesn't mean they can't achieve amazing things. The message she sent to the kids wasn't lost on any of us fortunate enough to share the journey with her.

A few days after finishing the first ride, it was time for Nic, Dad and me to return to Bangkok to meet the second group of riders. Dad had joined us on the bikes in 2011, and was sporting injuries from a fall, but Nic and I both felt remarkably well and were keen to begin the second ride. Kels and Jack had flown into Bangkok, whilst Lachie had elected to stay in Sydney working in a new job since finishing school only weeks before. I had missed having the kids on the first ride, especially as it had previously been something that we'd done together. I was looking forward to riding with them again.

This ride had its own dynamic and was a different experience from all the rides we'd done before, but completing the journey for the second time back to back did take its toll. Nic, Dad and I were starting to feel physically and mentally tired. Being somewhere new every day and changing hotels night after night for a month will wear you out at any time, but throw in the bike riding and by the end, we were ready to rest.

Finishing the bike ride can bring with it a new sense of power, ability and accomplishment. Riding on average of one hundred kilometres a day for eight days is no mean feat, particularly in the heat of Thailand. Riding sixteen hundred kilometres over a couple of weeks in similar conditions was very significant for me. Apparently, too, somewhere along the ride I had picked up a new ability: one that entitled me to officiate at a wedding. You might think that is an unusual skill to result from a bike ride and normally you would be right, but for whatever reason this wasn't the case on this bike ride!

Halfway through the 2010 ride, Andrew Mostyn, one of the riders who had become a close friend, pulled me aside and laid out his plans to conduct a surprise wedding with his partner Gabe, who was waiting in Khao Lak for the end of the ride. He asked me to give Gabe away and of course it was a stunning night, with a wedding on the beach as the sun set into the ocean and the kids from the orphanage lined up on the beach, forming a guard of honour for the wedding party.

At the end of the 2011 ride we had a marriage proposal that was accepted, but there was still more to come.

Nong, the staff member from the orphanage at Baan Tharn Namchai who rode with us in 2010, had found love and happiness. After the loss of her husband, as well as her son Pop, aged ten, and her daughter Pin, aged only eighteen months, in the tsunami, she was now rebuilding her life. I felt very humbled to be invited to marry her and Nid in a traditional Thai ceremony on the beach at Khao Lak. Unlike the wedding of 2010, where I wore my best wedding board shorts and new T-shirt, Nong's wedding was to be a little more formal, and that included wearing traditional Thai clothes.

The romance of the wedding started to slip for me when my hotel room was filled with between three and five Thai ladies and lady boys whose job was to dress Nic, Kelsey, Jack and myself in the clothes. They took hours and clearly hadn't dressed anyone in the gear we were meant to be wearing, as they seemed to have no idea how to arrange all the fabric in the outfits. None of them spoke any English and the limited Thai I had was of no use to us. Jack and I were trying to figure out how to dress ourselves. We tried the pants on both ways round, so at one stage they were right, we just couldn't tell when! One of the ladies would come to help us and then disappear out of the room, to be replaced by someone else whose depth of knowledge was no greater.

There came a point when Jack and I were wearing most of the items from the bag of clothes and we just wanted to get on with things. But we had one more decision to make, and ladies across the globe will understand the significance of this decision: what shoes should we wear? I could wear my bike-riding cleats or double plugger thongs – but that was it, there were no other choices!

Nic and Kels finally emerged from the bathroom after a bevy of Thai ladies had transformed them into pictures of beauty. After sixteen hundred kilometres on the bike Nic's legs and butt looked more like a Russian shotputter's than a Thai princess's, but she and Kels both looked ready for a wedding, and were also sporting their best pair of wedding thongs.

Our limousine awaited at the front of our villa to convey us to the beach. Well, it was a golf cart driven by a man in a nice shirt, but it did its job perfectly. On the way to the beach where the ceremony was to be held I was briefed by the wedding planner as to my duties and how I was supposed to run the ceremony. Going by the get-up we were wearing I had realised that I had a part to play in the wedding, but I hadn't really appreciated until that point that I was going to be running it! All of a sudden our golf cart was speeding way too fast to the beach, and I was about to get out and lead a wedding ceremony in front of a couple of hundred people with very little idea of what to do.

However, the anxiety and nervousness that I was feeling left me when I stepped under the cabana and Nong was led up to me. Instantly the last six years flashed through my head like a supercharged presentation, filled with images: some that I had seen and some that I imagined. I thought about the horror that Nong must have felt on 26 December 2004, as she returned to her village of Baan Nam Khem on her motorbike to be faced with a wall of water that had consumed her home, her family and all that she knew. I imagined her searching desperately through the ruins for the bodies of her children, her mother and her husband. I could visualise her walking through the temple at Wat Yan Yao amongst the thousands of decomposing bodies hoping to find her children, yet praying that she wouldn't discover them lying on the ground amongst the dead. I could picture the grief in her as she identified first the body of her eighteen-month-old daughter Pin and then weeks later that of her husband and her ten-year-old son Pop. I pictured Nong alone with nothing but a broken heart, no children to love and no husband with whom to share the grief of her loss. Comfort wasn't found in the community, because over half of the inhabitants of Baan Nam Khem had died as well. This was a community that was broken, and Nong was in the middle of it. She was without a home and without any idea of how she could smile again one day.

But on 26 January 2011, her wedding day, she wasn't just smiling, she was beaming. She was glowing and she was radiant. Dressed in a slim-fitting, off-the-shoulder cream dress, she looked stunning. I, on the other hand, still not sure whether I had my pants on back-to-front or not, couldn't have looked and felt more awkward. Luckily there was a hand behind me and a whisper in my ear to lead me through the ceremony. The only person who looked as out of place as I felt was Nid, Nong's new husband. Nong knew so many of us. She had ridden the entire bike ride in our company the previous year, and many of her fellow riders had returned to Thailand. She understood why all the women in the crowd were crying and wanting to hug her; that is what women do at weddings. Poor

Nid probably felt a bit overwhelmed, but at least he knew which way round to put his pants on. I caught his eye and winked at him, and at that point the universal language between men kicked in and that wink said, *Hang in there, brother, this will all be over soon*. A sense of calmness came over us both, and with that the crowd parted and our golf cart whisked us away.

The transformation of Nong continued and in February, only weeks after the wedding, we learnt that she was pregnant with her third child.

Chapter 32

Tragedy Hits Japan

It's the feeling of carving fresh tracks in deep powder snow at two-thirty in the afternoon that for me is one of the most appealing things about snowboarding in Japan. But I could list dozens of reasons why I love Japan so much. It was a relatively new discovery for me when I first headed there at the start of the 2009/2010 ski season with Nic. Each year in July we take the kids to Wanaka in New Zealand for eight days on the snow, and it's one of the highlights of my year. It's such a healthy pursuit, and the kids love boarding and skiing and racing us down the slopes. But this first trip to Japan had awakened me to the delights that exist in the north of this country. If you love being on the snow, then Japan is the place to go. The snow is metres deep, it is dry and the softest powder you can imagine. If you love the freshest sashimi on the planet or tiny little sake bars, then head to the ski fields of Japan. But it gets better.

The Japanese people working, skiing and living in the area are the friendliest and most polite people on earth and, wait for it, there are no queues at the end of your run to get back onto the chairlift. This is partly because at four in the afternoon the ski field is lit up, and you have another four hours of boarding under lights each day.

Nic and I returned to Japan in March of 2011, as our holiday and time alone after the two bike rides. It was a chance to recharge our batteries and reconnect with one another. We both felt exhausted and were suffering from people fatigue after the bike rides of 2011. It wasn't so much riding sixteen hundred kilometres that had sapped our energy, it was getting up and holding the space as the tour leaders day after day that had worn us both down a little. No, I'll be honest, it wore us down a lot. Japan was just Nic and me. However, the days weren't spent lying around with a good book – we were usually on the mountain around 9 am and I would push out the final run around 7 pm and then be home in time to head out for dinner.

After a fantastic few days, we left Sapporo and flew back into Tokyo for a connecting flight to Sydney. Sitting in the Qantas lounge waiting for the flight I read on the internet that a 7.2 magnitude earthquake had hit Japan that Wednesday afternoon whilst we were in the air. There were no reports of major damage or loss of life. Japan was used to and prepared for such earthquakes. We boarded our flight and flew overnight, arriving in Sydney at 7.30 am. I went straight to a conference in Sydney where I was to speak at 10 am. I presented twice that Thursday and made it home at around 5 pm. I unpacked my luggage from the Japan trip and repacked for Fiji, as I was flying out the following day – Friday 11 March – to speak at a conference over there.

Getting off the plane in Fiji I was first through customs and straight into a waiting car and off to the hotel. My phone then started to beep with message after message after message. The number of messages was unusual given it was only a four-hour flight to Fiji from Sydney. The messages were mostly from friends concerned for Nic and me as they knew we had been in Japan, and there had been the earthquake and now the tsunami. I had been on the flight to Fiji whilst this had occurred so I arrived in Fiji thinking they were talking about the 7.2 magnitude earthquake from Wednesday, not the devastating earthquake that had hit only hours earlier. I responded to the messages of concern saying there was little damage after the earthquake and life was continuing as normal in Japan; nothing really to worry about.

After checking in to my hotel I had a series of meetings with the client and hotel management, and then, turning on my television, I found out what had happened. I spent hours glued to the screen watching the live reports out of Japan. Having been so heavily involved in the aftermath of the tsunami of 2004, the footage I was witnessing brought back a lot of memories and raised a number of emotional responses in me. In Thailand I'd seen the aftermath of the tsunami, and here I was watching it unfold right in front of me. I could hardly believe that I'd been in the country only two days earlier. I felt devastated for the people of Japan, knowing that thousands would die, despite the low numbers of deaths being reported at that early stage. I felt sad and reflective for the kids in Thailand, and wondered how they would feel hearing the news coming out of Japan.

I recall sitting on the end of my bed watching the footage, and listening to the newsreaders reporting that three people had been confirmed dead. It was just like hearing the information that first came out of Thailand: that there had been a tidal wave and there might be some injuries. I wondered how big the disaster in Japan would grow to be, and how many lives would be lost.

Now, of course, we know that tens of thousands of lives were lost, and quickly the deadly effect of the tsunami was overshadowed by the breakdown of safety measures at the Fukushima nuclear power plant. Within days the humanitarian crisis had been pushed off the front page and replaced with the fear of the radiation fallout.

We tend to measure the magnitude of disasters in the number of people who have died, but from a disaster recovery point of view the measure is how many survivors have been affected. How many children are now without parents, how many families are without homes, how many hospitals have been shut down and how will the necessities of life reach the survivors?

My life at the time of the 2004 tsunami was focused on identifying the dead. I wasn't in a disaster recovery position; we were there to send people home, we were there to provide answers to families. But since leaving the police at the beginning of 2009, my field of vision has changed. Hands has certainly not positioned itself as a disaster recovery agency. The scope of our work is not to be there in the early days of a crisis, but to provide long-term support to the communities we engage with. First it was the kids from the tsunami who had been left without homes and families in Thailand, and then the kids from Yasothon came into the fold. Now the question we were asking ourselves was whether there was a role for Hands in Japan.

Within weeks of 11 March, the day that life changed for so many in Japan, I had received a number of phone calls and emails from ex-pat Australians living in Japan seeking advice, support and assistance. Talking through the challenges and opportunities that they saw, I was surprised at how much I now knew about working in the disaster recovery space, without previously realising it. When this ex-pat community of Australians and Kiwis wanted to offer up their now empty ski accommodation to those left homeless, I cautioned them about taking people out of their communities and moving them several hundred kilometres away. What would become of the Japanese people when winter rolled around again and the ski accommodation was required for paying foreigners coming to Japan to ski? Was it the best thing to take people away from their communities and away from loved ones who had died and in many instances were still missing? I wasn't suggesting there was necessarily one right direction to take, but consideration of what would happen in six and twelve months' time needed to be factored in.

As I was engaging more and more with people via the phone or email, that feeling in my stomach returned: I felt just as I had when watching the events unfold in the summer of 2004. I knew I could contribute and make a difference. I needed to travel to the region.

This time there wasn't the same sense of urgency that I'd had in 2004. My role, if indeed there was to be one, would be different. It wasn't going to be about identifying bodies; that chapter of my life was closed. Any work that I might do would focus on supporting the victims who had survived. I was mindful that things took time; Hands hadn't been formed until ten months after the Boxing Day tsunami, and the first orphanage wasn't opened until August 2006.

After due consideration I made the decision to head to Japan. I would return to a country that I have developed a strong affection for, but this time without a snowboard and without the sense of adventure that past trips have held for me. In support of a Japanese-based charity that I have been talking with, I would visit the region of Sendai and the Miyagi Prefecture to better understand the scope of the disaster and opportunities that might exist for us to help. The information that I have received indicates that the humanitarian crisis is far worse than is being reported, and in spite of the strength of the Japanese economy, many victims will suffer long after the event if history repeats experiences from other disasters in the country.

It is hard to know what the scope might be for Hands to assist in Japan. Without going to visit the devastated regions I would remain ignorant of those who are in desperate need, and ignorant of the scale of loss and destruction. I could choose to make excuses as to why I shouldn't go or why Hands should not get involved. I could point out that Japan has the third strongest economy in the world and suggest that it is up to other people to assist. I could also suggest that our work is in Thailand alone. But if I had made any such excuses after returning from Thailand, how very different would the lives of many of the children there be right now. Without exaggeration, children would have died but for the involvement of the Hands Across the Water team.

There are many reasons not to go to Japan and get involved in any recovery work over there. Nic and I discussed at length the impact it would have on us and our relationship if I was to lead a project from the ground up, in another foreign country. What impact would this have on me, on my capacity to be a father and a partner, and what of the financial impact it would have if I were to take this on? As with all the work I do with Hands in Thailand, I would fund the trip myself, and forgo my speaking work to undertake this response. There would be the need to raise new money, to fund whatever we might choose to do, in addition to what we have in place in Thailand.

There are countless reasons and excuses not to do it.

But there is a chance that we can make a difference to the lives of some kids who find themselves in a similar position to those living at Baan Tharn Namchai. That is reason enough to go and get a better understanding of the situation.

Nic and I were out at a restaurant discussing this very decision over dinner. One of the statements she made stays with me more than any other: *You do realise that once you get on that plane to Japan you have made the decision to help. It's no longer if, but how.*

Chapter 33

The Kids, Six Years On

Gill and I first made the commitment to do something for the kids and the community of Baan Tharn Namchai in October of 2005. Several years later we are seeing what happens when you make a long-term commitment.

Nam is one of the older kids who came to live in the tent with Khun Rotjana in those very early days. Her story is one of those that are hard to get your head around. At the age of four Nam lost her mother and father, both of whom were killed in a car accident. Her older sister, who herself was only twelve years old, became Nam's carer. Her older sister moved her to the village of Baan Nam Khem to be near relatives.

On 26 December 2004, Nam was in the forest west of Khao Lak, kilometres away from the coastline and the wall of water that would claim the eight remaining members of her family in the village of Baan Nam Khem. She returned home to find everything, and everyone, gone.

For the second time in this girl's young life she had to deal with the loss of her family. It is hard to comprehend.

She was taken to live with an aunt, but life for her was not happy. Many in the community believed she brought bad luck with her because so many around her had died yet she had survived. The man who lived with Nam's aunt was accustomed to beating Nam for the woes of his life. The final beating was so bad that doctors believed Nam would lose her hearing permanently.

Nam displays the resilience of so many of the kids in the orphanage. She is one of the leading students at her school, constantly receiving top marks; she is an accomplished Thai dancer and excels at sport. Nam has shown that, despite unfathomable setbacks, given the opportunity these kids will exceed all expectations. It is just about ensuring they have the resources they need. They have the determination, the commitment and the desire to achieve; we are simply creating the pipeline for them.

The pipeline for Nam has extended out of Baan Tharn Namchai and even out of Thailand. In the middle of 2010 she commenced a two-year scholarship at a school in the US through partners of the Duang Prateep Foundation.

Perhaps it is because of the loss these children have endured that they seem to understand and appreciate the opportunities that come their way, more so than many kids in Australia who live a life of abundance. We don't have to do anything magical for them to excel; it seems that keeping them safe, nourished and loved is all that is required.

In September 2009 I made a fleeting visit to the orphanage at Baan Tharn Namchai – I was on the ground for just six and a half hours before flying back to Australia – where Khun Rotjana introduced me to Ohn, one of the most recent children to come to the orphanage. She was so incredibly shy that making eye contact was a real challenge and her hands remained tucked up inside her shirt.

Speaking in Thai, Khun Rotjana asked her to show me her hands. With deep embarrassment she pulled out her hands and held them up for me to see. Several fingers on each hand were fused together. Some of her toes were similarly joined. She had been born like this, and because nothing had ever been done for her she had not been to school or had anything like a normal childhood.

Like many of the children in the area of Baan Nam Khem, Ohn had lost her parents in the tsunami, but somehow she had been missed by the various agencies, both Thai and international, who set out to find and care for the children left alone. For the next couple of years this young girl survived certainly more by good luck and her own tenacity than via the intervention of anyone else. She lived alone at the back of the temple and would collect rubbish off the street, in return for which the monks would ensure she was given sufficient food to survive. The fact that this situation was able to continue for as long as it did reflects that the community of Baan Nam Khem in particular had become so inured to loss and hardship that Ohn's daily struggle no longer seemed out of place.

Once Khun Rotjana learnt of Ohn's struggles the girl was taken into our orphanage, and it was only days later that I met her. I certainly don't profess to have any special knowledge when it comes to orthopedic surgery, but it seemed to me that it must be possible to separate Ohn's fused fingers and toes, and that with physiotherapy she must also be able to learn to hold a pencil.

I sent Khun Rotjana off to the Bangkok Hospital, where she herself had been treated for breast cancer, with the mission to have this young girl's hands rendered useful for the first time in her life. The funding for the operation was not a major consideration; after all, if we couldn't take care of this, what use were we really?

Weeks later I received some photos of a smiling young girl proudly holding her two bandaged hands up to the camera. The operation had turned out to be relatively uncomplicated and now Ohn's fingers were as they should be.

The next time I saw Ohn she was no longer the shy little girl without a voice or a smile. She was just like the other kids, and each day, for the first time in her life, she headed off to school just like everyone else. All Ohn had ever wanted to do was to fit in, and now she did.

Game is a young man who lives at Baan Tharn Namchai and he is a delight in every sense of the word. The compassion and caring he shows to the young children when they fall and scrape their knee is equal to any he shows VIP guests who attend the orphanage. His manners and social graces are impeccable.

Game does not know his mother or father, and at the time of the tsunami he was living with an aunt and uncle. His uncle died in the water that day and things spiralled downwards from then on. A new man quickly came into Game's aunt's life, but it was not a happy relationship. Often Game and his aunt were beaten by this new man. Game was attending school at the time and showed real promise in the grades that he was achieving. However, the new partner believed that Game's time would be better spent in working to bring an income into the house. His aunt was sent to the school to inform them Game would no longer be attending.

The teachers knew that this was a critical point in time for Game. If he was withdrawn from school as a thirteen-year-old, it was unlikely he would ever be able to recommence his studies; he had a promising future, but without education it would likely pass him by.

Game's teachers, who had clearly recognised his ability and commitment, approached Khun Rotjana and asked her to take him into the orphanage. They knew there he could continue his studies and, of equal importance, live in a loving environment free from beatings.

Khun Rotjana needed little convincing and thankfully Game's

aunt also saw this for the opportunity it was. Perhaps driven by fear of her new partner or concern for Game's future, or perhaps both, she readily agreed that Game could move into Baan Tharn Namchai.

Within a loving and supportive environment Game flourished at school. In 2011 he commenced a law degree at Phuket University. During a recent trip to Australia, which was funded by HSBC (who have done away with their golf days and instead invested the same amount of money in giving a number of the kids the chance to travel), Game spoke at a function. In English – he practised his speech all day – he told the gathering that he was able to go to university only because of the opportunities he had received. His desire was to complete his degree and return to Baan Tharn Namchai, where he hoped to work to support the other children.

Champ is another one of the older kids who has been at Baan Tharn Namchai since the early days in the tent. Champ lived with his mother and father, both of whom fished for a living. His mother died in the tsunami and his father was critically injured. He sustained permanent disabling injuries that rendered him incapable of caring for himself, let alone Champ. With no other family in the region, Champ found himself alone at the age of eleven. He found his way to Khun Rotjana and took up residence with her.

Like Game, Champ shows patience and love for the younger children of the orphanage and his personality is infectious.

Champ was given the opportunity to work on a trial basis within the local five-star hotel, with whom we've developed a relationship over the last couple of years, as he had expressed a desire to work in hospitality. Because of his strong work ethic and boundless charm he was soon offered a cadetship at the hotel whilst he completed his studies.

It's our role at Hands to create the opportunities and to call on the relationships we have built, but it's the kids like Nam, Champ and Game who shine when given half a chance.

Chapter 34

The Future for Hands

The future for Hands is one that I almost dare not predict, because our pattern over the last couple of years shows me that anything I might anticipate now will be very different from what actually happens.

The opening of the second orphanage and the purchase of the rubber plantation might have been predictable once I got a little bit serious about what we were doing. Taking on Yasothon, however, was right out of left field. Now, as I prepare to head to Japan, no one on the board will be surprised if or when I return with another project in mind after having toured the tsunami-ravaged area.

Does that mean the board isn't thinking strategically enough, that we're limited in our thinking? I don't believe that for a second. I just keep stepping outside the parameters we've set when I find somewhere new I believe we should be. It's a reflection of the strength of those who sit on the board that we are able to adapt and continue to move fast, making a difference and saving lives. If we had been too stuck in our ways or too slow to move, healthy kids who smile, laugh and sing at Yasothon would now be dead.

Of course I do have to think deeply about what the realistic possibilities are for Hands, and what factors might limit us. If we are clear about the possibilities, and we assess and identify the limiting factors, we can surely work to remove any obstacles that stand in our way. If we move into Japan, our current structure will need to expand, but we can do that. It's just a case of finding more like-minded people who want to change lives and have fun along the way. Growth doesn't mean we need to depart from our operating model or principles; growth for us means ensuring we stay aligned with them.

One thing that is consistent in everything we have done so far is that each time we have expanded we have improved the lives of the kids and broader communities in which we operate. The volunteers who have come looking to make a difference to the lives of the children have in turn had their lives changed. The building of the second orphanage gave kids such as Ohn, who were living in desperate circumstances, a safe home and the chance to return to school. The childcare facility at the community centre at Baan Nam Khem is a safe place for parents to leave their children when they go to work, and the immediate success of our venture into Home Hug at Yasothon could not be more obvious. Those children's bellies are full of food, their tiny little arms and legs now have a bit of meat on them and their eyes sparkle just a little more.

So, without wanting to predict our future for fear of knowing it's bound to change, let me share what I am thinking about right now.

Training centre

'The only thing wrong with poor people is that they don't have any money – which happens to be a curable condition.' So said Bill Strickland, who has built a world-class community centre in one of the poorest neighbourhoods in Pittsburgh, USA. The centre is for single mums, at-risk kids and unemployed steel workers. He found that when you provide world-class facilities, you get world-class results. By providing flowers, sunlight, good food and high expectations, his experience is that you can cure spiritual cancer. If you show people that they are valued, they just might start to value themselves, which has to be the first step in changing behaviour.

Strickland's experiences and observations resonate for the children of Yasothon, more so than the kids of Baan Tharn Namchai. Every morning when the kids leave Home Hug and head to school, they wonder if that will be the day they are forced out of another school because of their HIV status. Each day these kids are told by the community outside of Home Hug that they don't matter, they are worth less than others and don't deserve the same things as everyone else.

In building a world-class centre you attract top-quality teachers, and children will reflect those who teach them. I don't need convincing that if we build a centre commensurate with the best that is available, we will attract the best artists, chefs, musicians and scholars to work with the kids. The kids in turn will become world-class teachers and from what we are experiencing already their desire will be to give back to their own community.

The centre that Strickland has built is a dream I hold close. At the moment it sits outside our capacity, but from the moment I heard the story and saw the pictures I knew that was what I wanted to create for the poor communities in which we work. I know I won't feel as though I have done my job until the vision that sits inside my head exists in bricks and mortar.

Care and housing for the elderly

You take away the strong and you are left with the weak and the vulnerable. Tearing the heart out of a community as the tsunami did leaves highly visible victims such as children, but there are also

an increasing number of victims who don't present until years after
the event, long after everyone has forgotten about it, and those
victims are the elderly.

The generation that would have supported their parents has
been decimated and there is no one left to look after the old and
infirm. This problem will only increase with time. Some older members of the community still live on their own and have the capacity
to care for themselves, but eventually that capacity will diminish
and they will be left alone and vulnerable.

Caring and supporting young children is appealing from a
charity worker's perspective and from a donor's perspective. Children will hopefully go on to live long and fulfilled lives; the elderly,
on the other hand, are almost at the end of their lives – not such an
optimistic or attractive proposition for donors. But if we are really
giving from a humanitarian place in our hearts, shouldn't we do
something about the elderly who suffer? Don't they also deserve to
live, and die, with dignity?

We have already investigated the needs of the elderly in the
Baan Nam Khem area to identify what we can do to help. As childcare centres begin to crop up in the affected areas of Thailand,
so too will care facilities for the elderly, should aid agencies and
charities choose to respond to the need. Because at Hands we are
serious about the whole community, this is an area I feel we should
allocate resources to.

Halving the unemployment rate at Baan Nam Khem

When a community has an unemployment rate of fifty per cent,
social breakdown is almost inevitable. Without gainful employment, and without meaningful work and active minds, people not
only have no income but many also lose their sense of purpose
and identity, which leads to all sorts of destructive and antisocial
behaviours.

Already we have seen thirteen-year-old girls from the broader community becoming mothers. Numerous children live at the orphanage at Baan Tharn Namchai because of domestic violence, often the result of alcohol-fuelled fathers or stepfathers who spend their days drinking rather than working. A community with such high unemployment rates amongst the demographic who would normally be working will see a rise in substance abuse, gambling, criminal and other unacceptable behaviour.

This is not to suggest that the community doesn't have the capacity for work; at this point in time the unemployment rate is due to their lack of relevant skills or the scarcity of opportunities. Those who live in subsistence fishing communities like Baan Nam Khem are deeply affected by the lack of demand for their product. The issue is not necessarily the numbers of fish being caught – providing more nets or boats won't address the problem – it is the lack of demand for their catch. So we can either work on increasing tourism to this area, or provide alternative skills for those who sit idle within the community.

The latter seems to be more within our scope of influence, which is why part of the desired outcome from the community centre we have built is the provision of vocational training. Our hope is that by giving people new skills, we are also giving them new employment opportunities.

Reducing the number of kids living at the orphanage

This strategy might sound like a paradox when you consider the raison d'être of Hands, but it is generally accepted that, all things being equal, children are better placed in a loving home than a loving orphanage.

After the tsunami, the option of being placed with family members just didn't exist for some children – they had no family left. But what we are also finding is that some families see the opportunities provided by our orphanages as being better than they feel they can provide for their own children. Over time our focus should shift from predominantly providing fulltime care to providing services and resources that enable families to be supported by the work that we do, but on the condition they stay together as a family unit.

Reducing the number of kids living at the orphanages is not a goal whereby each quarter we hope to see a reduction in numbers. We know that there are many kids who will find their way to us and that the orphanages at Baan Tharn Namchai or Home Hug are the best places for them when all options are considered. But long-term strategies such as the community centre at Baan Nam Khem will be part of the strategy in building a stronger family unit, allowing them to stay together.

If the stories of the kids who present at Baan Tharn Namchai are anything to go by, it will be some time before we cease to offer fulltime care. And that is okay, we are not on a deadline here – kids aren't and won't be forced out. But it is important for us to review what we are doing, to ensure we are considering alternative options and questioning whose needs we are serving.

Scholarships for the kids

I have outlined the evolution that we have seen for a couple of the older kids who are now moving into their late teens. Nam has travelled to study in the US, Game is heading off to Phuket University to study law, and Champ received a cadetship at a five-star hotel, which served as a springboard for him into the hospitality sector.

Not all the kids will want to go on to further study; some will be just as happy farming the crops that we have at the rubber plantation or fishing the waters of the Andaman Sea, as their fathers and grandfathers did, and that is perfectly okay as well.

The vocation that they choose is not the issue – what is important for me is that they have choice. If we expose the kids to as many opportunities as possible, there is more likelihood that something will resonate deep within them. When they make the choice about what they want to do in their lives, then our role is to create a pathway for them.

Part of creating that pathway is to give the kids opportunities, create choice and then remove any obstacles that might prevent them from pursuing their dreams. To achieve this we will set up funding streams that are dedicated only to the kids' education for the years after high school. The problem for the older kids at Yasothon is not that money can't buy them training; it's that they come from a home that is known to care for HIV children, and they are therefore seen as a risk and turned away irrespective of their HIV status. The answer to this problem at Yasothon is finding alternative education or training providers, and that may require the older kids to relocate to Bangkok. If that is the answer we need to build a specific program for them to ensure that is a safe and successful experience.

Our care and support of the kids doesn't end when they turn eighteen or reach some other milestone in their life. Some of the girls at Yasothon are only starting to deal with the abuse they've suffered and come to terms with the past in their late teens. To force them out of their home would surely condemn them to a life of further struggle and hardship with predictable outcomes. Investing in the kids and their longer term futures is a fundamental part of our commitment to building strong communities.

Integrating the kids of Yasothon

The kids living at Home Hug in Yasothon have lived a life of discrimination, such that it becomes a major consideration in all that they do and how they interact with people outside of the caring environment that is their home. Khun Thew tells of how the level of ignorance and discrimination is just as strong today as it was when she first arrived over twenty-three years ago. The kids are ostracised within their own community to such a degree that it has a significant impact upon their opportunities and development. They are often forced out of school and denied many opportunities for social interaction and advancement.

The fear within the community is that the kids, due to their HIV status, pose a significant risk. You don't need to be a trained health professional to know that this fear is unfounded; HIV is not transmitted between people like a common cold. The lack of support from the local community has without question had an impact upon the life expectancy of the kids. If there were more people there who supported them and cared for them, if they had better access to education and health care, and if there was a greater demonstration of love for them, these children would live longer.

Community education around HIV-AIDS is not something that is new to this part of the world. We don't need to develop it, we don't need to deliver it and we probably don't even need to fund it. But it is not happening in the community. It should be. If we can bring about change on this level, and those from Home Hug are more readily accepted into their own community, it would be a significant and life-changing outcome. So part of this objective is to develop a greater understanding in how we support the kids and create opportunities for their continued education and enrichment of life through meaningful experiences.

There are a couple of steps that will assist us to bring about this transformation. The first is to try to break down the barriers that exist between the kids and what they would like to do in the future. It might mean the older kids undertake training outside of Ubon; it might mean we bring specific training programs to them, or it might mean we work with our corporate partners who provide training opportunities in their workplace, which is exactly the model we have with Torsten at the Le Meridian Hotel in Khao Lak. The second step is to make people aware of the kids, the dreams the kids have, and the opportunities they are denied. As more people become aware of them, and hear what we need to support them, there will be responses such as *My sister's company has an office here in Thailand and are looking to build their corporate social responsibility program, I should connect you.* And through the beauty of connections and networks, opportunities start to open up.

In 2012, one of our two bike rides will leave Nong Khai, outside of Udon Thani in the northeast of Thailand, and ride down the Mekong River on the border of Laos, finishing eight days and eight hundred kilometres later at Home Hug in Yasothon. Part of the reason for choosing to do this ride is to bring another forty to fifty people into the world of the kids at Yasothon. From this bike ride and the people who visit the orphanage, opportunities will arise that aren't even on the radar right now.

Increasing the life expectancy of the kids at Yasothon

When I was first asked to consider supporting the orphanage at Yasothon, I thought I'd best learn something more about HIV and what living with it meant. I was incredibly ignorant about the virus, how it manifested into AIDS and how long a person lived once diagnosed. My last exposure to information about HIV had been in contamination-prevention workshops during my time with the Forensic Services Group.

I turned to the net and learnt that people diagnosed with HIV can expect to live fifty or sixty healthy years beyond infection. It certainly isn't the death sentence it used to be. The proviso is, of course, that the infected person takes their medication religiously; they need to live a healthy lifestyle, which includes a nutritious diet; and clearly they need access to a health system that has the experience and capacity to treat them.

So why historically has the death rate at Home Hug been so high? Our intervention has shown over the first twelve months that the kids needn't die and it doesn't take a lot to prevent that. It would seem that if you live in Sydney, Seattle or Scotland and are HIV positive you have a good chance of living a long and happy life. What is missing in Yasothon, then, that money and resources can't change? The answer seems simple: nothing. Nothing is unique about the kids living at Home Hug that can't and hasn't been turned around with the provision of resources ensuring the kids have access to the medical support and nutrition that they require.

However, the problem is not over and that is why it remains a challenge for Hands moving forward. A search of the latest information on the web about infection rates of HIV will show there is an increase in incidents of infection within at-risk communities. A report from the World Health Organization (WHO) in 2006, titled *Mortality Country Fact Sheet 2006*, reports that the leading cause of death in Thailand, for all ages, was HIV/AIDS at fourteen per cent, which was double the second highest cause of death, identified as heart disease, at seven per cent. A 2010 report by the WHO, titled *HIV/AIDS in the South-East Asia Region*, reports that on a percentage basis to overall population, Thailand has the highest number of adults living with HIV. The 2010 report indicates that in Thailand there are an estimated 610,000 people living with HIV. The Thai government has been a leader in the implementation of education and health care strategies, but the figures reported by the WHO would indicate the problem is not one that can be ignored.

Home Hug will continue to take in babies born with HIV or children infected with the virus as a result of sexual abuse, and not just from within Thailand but also from neighbouring, poorer countries, as has been the case over the last two decades. Organisations such as the WHO and forward-thinking governments and committed non-government bodies will continue to tackle the problem of infection and treatment. Hands will in its small way support Home Hug and those children who have the virus, giving them the best possible chance to live a long and healthy life.

A centre for the mums

During Task Force Yasothon in November of 2010, a twenty-day-old baby arrived with its mother. The mother was HIV positive and the baby also showed markers indicating it may have been born with the virus as well.

The mother had, right up until she'd given birth, prostituted herself as a means of earning an income. There was a high degree of probability that she would return to this source of income, given that she was in Thailand illegally and had extremely limited options. What was also a high probability was that the child would become a full-time member of the orphanage.

Rather than taking the child and leaving the mother to return to her life of prostitution, what if there existed an option for her to stay with her child? My thoughts are that if the mothers were supported long enough to give them the chance to develop skills that offered an alternative to prostitution, we could break the cycle of poverty and disease in some small way for at least a handful of people. And that includes the woman's male clients and their families.

This HIV-infected mother was having sex with two or three men every night in order to earn enough money to care for herself. Anecdotal feedback is that a number of the men will only have sex *without* a condom. How many of these men are contracting the virus and then returning to their own homes and spreading it further?

Creating a centre for the mothers would not be in isolation of other strategies, nor would it be the whole answer to the problem. But perhaps there is sufficient merit in at least trying to do something different from what has been happening at Yasothon for the past twenty-three years.

We began by looking at what support and services the mums who arrive at Home Hug need. Now we have commenced work on a project that will provide an alternative to these mums should they choose to take it up. Our initial step has been to create a means of employment, and at the launch of the program in May of 2011, we had twenty-two women jump on board. The project was commenced with the provision of seed funding that allowed for the small-scale production of high-quality scarves, sarongs and other clothing accessories which are made using traditional methods. Hands will assist in the distribution of the garments and items outside of Yasothon, creating an income for the ladies involved. To build upon this we will work towards providing a more complete care facility that addresses all of their needs.

A similar program creating employment opportunities was tried a number of years ago by Khun Thew for mothers who were HIV positive. The program failed, not because of any production fault or lack of quality, but due to the ignorance and bias of the local community. When it became clear that those making the products were HIV positive, nobody would buy them.

Enhancement of our English language program
For the last couple of years we have been in a joint venture with Victoria University that focuses on the provision of English language programs for the community in Khao Lak.

The strategy has a couple of streams to it. The first revolves around the provision of intensive English language programs for the orphanage staff, who come to Australia to live for three months at a time, immersing themselves in the program. This is complemented by English teachers from Australia who work in schools in the Pang Nga province, assisting the teachers to better deliver English education programs.

In February of 2011, the program was expanded to include

staff from Home Hug, and we had two staff members travel to Australia to undertake English training. The provision of the program here in Australia has the added benefit that their learning and use of English doesn't stop when they walk out of the lesson. For ten to twelve weeks they are immersed in communities in Melbourne and Sydney and their use of English is essential to get them around each day. They are on buses and trams, and shopping for themselves, which accelerates their learning even further.

Sometimes it is not without the minor hiccup. In the most recent program two ladies wanted to visit a beach in Melbourne, as they had come from the landlocked area of Yasothon. They were unsure how to get to the beach or even what the name of the beach was, but exercising their independence they chose to sort it out themselves. Then it seemed their problem was solved. On the side of a bus they saw a picture of a sun-drenched beach with clear blue water, and a young, fit, barely clothed couple strolling hand in hand along the sand. That's where they wanted to head, so on the bus they jumped. After more than an hour, the driver stopped the bus, noticing that these two Thai ladies were still in their seats circling the suburbs of Melbourne. After the ladies explained that they wanted to go to the place pictured on the side of the bus, the driver replied that he too would like to visit Hayman Island off the Queensland coast, but the bus wasn't heading there.

There are many avenues for the expansion of this program and it is one of those medium- to long-term strategies that create increased employment opportunities for the kids and the staff.

Experiential giving

Most of the people who come to Hands do so because they genuinely want to make a difference to others. They grasp the concept of feeding the soul by contributing to the wellbeing of other people.

What I have learnt, though, is that without engagement,

without a real experience, the benefits flowing in both directions can be limited. When we offer an opportunity for people to be involved in more than the contribution of money, their commitment and subsequent rate of return is much greater.

A group that exhibits a real and genuine thirst for this type of experiential giving is our young people. I am frequently engaging with school groups or Gen Ys who really do want to do something. They come with a plan and an executable strategy for raising money, awareness or bringing about change. This makes me very hopeful for the future.

There are a number of things that we do well at Hands; there are a number of things I think we do exceptionally well, and of course there are plenty of things we can improve on. One of the things we do best is offer an experience for those who want to take it. There is a standing invitation to everyone, including you reading this book right now, to come and visit the operations at Khao Lak and Yasothon. You can spend the day with the kids; you can kick a soccer ball; you can paint, sing songs and check out where the kids sleep. They are beautiful homes filled with sunlight, colour and love, just like any home should be.

As a small charity we also have the ability to move with speed, interact with our donors and communicate on a level that becomes extremely hard in a bureaucracy. My personal phone number and email address are on the Hands website; we want to make it easy to connect. A couple of years ago a lady whose husband had heard me speak at a conference was touched by our story and wanted to contribute.

We spoke on the phone and she told me about the fundraiser she wanted to run and that she wanted to fund a particular project. I said to her the staff would love a new fridge and, if there was sufficient money, an airconditioning unit for the sick room. This seemed to fit the bill and be within budget. The fundraiser was run and won and we spoke again. Now, though, the lady was concerned that the money would not go into a fridge and airconditioner but would end up in a big pool and be lost amongst all the other donations. I asked her to trust me and that I would ensure the money would be spent exactly as we had agreed. This conversation occurred on a Monday. We received the money into our bank account on the Tuesday and immediately transferred it to Thailand. The fridge and airconditioner were bought and delivered on the Thursday, and by Friday I was able to send our donor photos of all the kids sitting in front of their new fridge and airconditioner. The lady's response was to ask for a bigger project – she was hooked.

As we grow and expand, our aim is to give our donors the same level of experience this lady had. It's one of our responsibilities when someone entrusts their money to us.

Some of the projects that are mentioned in this chapter will happen quite soon, some are already under way and some might take a little time. There will be competing demands that are put before us as a charity and personally there may well be opportunities or challenges that test my resolve.

In six weeks, six months or two years' time there may be an event that changes the future direction of what we are doing. I could never have predicted the changes that I have been part of since 26 December 2004. But one of the important things I have learnt is that clarity certainly comes with action. The more you do the clearer you become. Sometimes the planning stage is all too comfortable and we can spend too much time thinking and searching for answers without really putting ourselves out there and finding out if our ideas will work or not.

What Hands has created is quite special and has changed and saved lives. Mike Hewson, one of the volunteers to work at Yasothon on both operations in November of 2010 and April of 2011, said to me, 'Each day at work I solve problems; that is my job. But when I am at Yasothon, I am solving problems that save lives. The kids and the staff are so appreciative of our efforts, they open their hands and they open their hearts to us.' Mike will tell you that he has taken so much more from his work at Yasothon than he ever could have imagined, and feels indebted to the kids that have given him so much.

We have achieved amazing outcomes at Baan Tharn Namchai and Yasothon, but the skill sets of everyone involved in Hands, from the board to our volunteers aren't remarkable, unique or even that special. The only difference is that we have acted and followed through on a chance or opportunity.

The difference between the many bike riders who join us each January in Thailand and those who come up to me after a conference professing their undying desire and commitment to do the ride only to be never heard from again is action. The ones who join us are inevitably those who follow through on their promises before they let the excuses build up and allow the opportunity to pass.

What turns that voice inside our head from saying *I want to do that, I can do that, I am going to do that*, to *I don't think I can do that, I don't have time, I am not going to do that*? For many I think it is self-doubt and excuses. They package it up with stories to convince themselves or others it's no longer possible. But it's nearly always possible if you believe in yourself and remove the limitations that tell you that unless you get it right the first time you can't have a go. You'll get closer to the one hundred per cent mark by having a crack and achieving an eighty per cent scorecard than doing nothing and missing out altogether.

With this in mind, I know that we at Hands can't limit ourselves based upon current financial statements or a capacity that says something is beyond us. There was no financial position or capacity when I first started Hands; there was nothing. The millions of dollars that have been raised since the formation of Hands grew out of a belief and then a step, followed by another one. After I continued to take steps I found I was off and running.

All we need to do at Hands is keep taking steps. And now, I am not running alone. There is a growing team of dedicated people: board members, supporters, donors and believers, who are taking those steps with me.

Whatever it is you want to do, whatever you want to achieve, start taking steps.

Chapter 35

Reflection

Walking the Kokoda track for ten days you have a lot of time to talk about a whole range of topics. This particular morning I was having a conversation with our guide Aiden. The trek was in 2006 with a group from Police Legacy.

Aiden and I were discussing significant events in our lives and had got to talking about wake-up calls – when something significant happens in your life and your reassess what is really important to you. I told Aiden that I didn't really feel as though I had ever received a wake-up call, despite having been surrounded by death and tragedy for almost all my working life.

Probably the closest I had come was that shocking moment when I uncovered my friend Laurie's body back in Tamworth. That made me re-evaluate my work practices, but it didn't really make me re-evaluate my life.

Everything changed, however, when my doctor informed me I had cancer.

This chapter in my life began with a visit to the doctor to have some skin spots removed. As a card-carrying 'Ranga', let's say I received my share of sunburn growing up. I had consulted a GP earlier about an area of my left calf that was concerning me and had been assured that one innocuous-looking spot was benign. Now all of a sudden the specialist was telling me he needed to take a biopsy. As I lay on the table in his surgery with blood running down my leg from the incision, all I could think of was, *You idiot, why did you let him cut your leg? In a couple of days' time you are flying to Thailand to undertake an eight-hundred-kilometre bike ride.*

The pathology results arrived the day I was leaving for Thailand and the advice from my doctor was that I had early-stage melanoma that would need removing, but it was nothing too dramatic.

My main concern prior to riding was how my leg would react to the repeated stretching of the skin, and of greater concern was avoiding any type of infection from the water and tropical conditions. Luckily, though, the minor surgery on my left leg presented no problems at all during the ride. However, there were a number of times while I was riding when I had time to wonder what the consequences would be if the situation was more serious than it sounded.

After returning unscathed from the ride I knew I had to undergo the procedure; however, timing once again was not perfect. I was scheduled to leave almost immediately for the Canadian ski resort at Whistler for the NARTA conference. The plan was that when not fulfilling my duties as a speaker, I would hit the mountain. This was Whistler, after all, and it was wintertime. As you'd know by now, snow sports are a passion of mine, and if I am not on a ski field at least twice a year, I am not impressed.

Of course Nic was encouraging me to get the procedure done immediately, just as she had encouraged me to seek treatment in the first place. But there was very little chance of me having a large wound on the back of my left calf, right where a boot would rub, just as I was about to visit a snowfield that boasts seriously long ski runs the likes of which we just don't have in the southern hemisphere.

The procedure was put off until I returned from Canada.

When I returned to the specialist he said, 'What are you here for again?' as he fumbled for my chart.

I said, 'Just to have a bit more taken out from where you did the biopsy.' I was hoping the procedure wasn't going to be based upon my instructions!

Then he dropped the clanger: 'Oh yes, that's right. You have the aggressive tumour.'

All I wanted to say to him was, 'Just check that chart again, buddy. I am not the one with an aggressive tumour, that's not what we call it. It's just a little bit extra from the biopsy site.'

This time a larger area was removed and I ended up with thirty stitches in my left leg. The good news was that I could tell Nic I had been right to wait till after we went skiing as that would have buggered the trip.

The pathology would be back in two weeks and I would get the results when I returned to have the stitches out. Nothing really to worry about. And if that's the case, let's change our terminology, shall we? Let's not use the words aggressive and tumour in the same sentence.

A fortnight later, having just arrived in Perth for a couple of days' work, I received a phone call from the surgeon's receptionist whilst I was just about to walk into a meeting.

'Hi Peter, it's Karen from Dr Li's surgery here. We need you to come in to see Dr Li today.'

I followed up with, 'Karen, I have just arrived in Perth and won't be back until Friday night.' It was Wednesday.

Her next line was a beauty. 'We have your pathology results and there is bad news. You need to see the doctor right away.'

'Karen, I am in Perth. I have just arrived. I can't come and see Dr Li today.'

Karen said that Dr Li would call me in about thirty minutes to discuss our options.

'What bloody options? Aren't you listening? I am in Perth.'

I hung up and thought to myself, *Doesn't anyone in that joint know how to deliver a sensitive message?* It reminded me of that cop line about how not to deliver bad news. 'Hello, are you the widow Mrs Jones?' 'No.' 'Well you are now.'

I thought the staff from this surgery had about the same level of tact. 'Aggressive tumour' and 'bad news' might be their language, but it wasn't mine, and I would suggest that's not how ninety-nine per cent of the public wants to receive bad news. Having hung up I went into the meeting as scheduled and despite the phone call was able to continue with business.

When I finally spoke with the doctor fifty-six minutes later, not that I was watching the clock or anything, he advised me that the results from the pathology revealed that I did in fact have a malignant melanoma, the worst type of skin cancer. He was referring me to an oncologist and I needed to be admitted to hospital for surgery as soon as possible.

No one seemed to care that I was in Perth.

After I told him that I would be home on Friday night, which was only two days away, and he asked if I could get home any sooner, my concerns went to a whole new level.

I hung up the phone and although I had been able to carry on with business after the first phone call from the receptionist, this was different. For the first time in a long time I felt vulnerable and scared. I also felt alone as I didn't want to share the news with Nic by phone. I ended the meeting and just returned to my room in the hotel where I was staying. I had no idea of the implications of this latest news, but they certainly felt a whole lot more serious than what I'd been told after the first biopsy in between the Thailand and Canada trips. The thing that concerned me most was the tone and gravity in the doctor's voice, and his sense of urgency as to when I should be admitted to hospital. It was okay for me to be concerned; it was my leg and my health. But for the doctor to be concerned, I didn't like that. He dealt with this stuff all the time, he knew serious and not serious, he knew when to be concerned and when there was nothing to worry about. I didn't want him being concerned about this; that just heightened the anxiety I was now feeling.

The two days that I spent in Perth before I returned to Sydney were filled with questions. I just kept playing out different scenarios in my head. They went from thinking, *If I can wait till just before Easter to have any surgery done that will reduce the impact on work*, through to, *I need to get my affairs in order and how do I tell the kids this news?*

The one thing I wanted to do most was to sit and hold Nic's hands in mine and tell her what was going on. The flight from Perth to Sydney felt longer than ever.

Arriving home on the Friday night I wanted to share the news with Nic, hoping that by sharing it some of the burden would lift as well. I had decided not to let her know any of this by phone as there was little that could be done and I thought all it would do was worry her unnecessarily.

I went straight from the airport to dinner with Nic, her sister and her parents, who were visiting from Brisbane. It was a noisy restaurant and all I wanted to do was get home to have the discussion that I had been planning for a couple of days. Dinner was a pretty raucous event but I was in a more subdued mood and couldn't find it within myself to lift and join in the frivolity. Nic looked at me a number of times and asked if I was okay, and I just kept saying I was tired from the trip. I actually felt sick in my stomach and needed to share with her the knowledge I had now being carrying around for a couple of days.

Nic's parents were staying with us so as soon as we got home I was keen to get to bed and be able to stop pretending I was happy and full of joy, because I wasn't. Lying in bed I finally started talking. I played back for her the conversations I'd had with the receptionist and the doctor, and then explained what the next steps were as I understood them. I used the same words the doctor had used: malignant melanoma; worst type of skin cancer; oncologist; hospital straight away. Nic continued to ask me the same questions in different ways in the hope I could shed more light on the situation. I couldn't; I needed to see the doctor. Nic was asking me questions that I probably should have asked the doctor on Wednesday afternoon, but perhaps I'd been in shock, or I'd just assumed he would have given me all the information he had.

When I saw my doctor the following day, he offered me some reassurance in relation to the depth of the cancer. He explained that the severity of the type of cancer I had was measured in depth, and beyond about one and a half millimetres, the cancer can spread into your lymph nodes, and then it can be really serious. Mine had not yet reached that depth, but being given a referral to an oncologist is never good news.

I was referred to Professor John Thompson at the Royal Prince Alfred Hospital in Sydney. The professor is a delightful man who clearly understands the significance of a cancer diagnosis for his patients. He took the time to explain that although I did have the worst type of skin cancer, I was at the better end of the scale. He expanded on what the doctor had told me about depth and said that because we'd caught it when we had, the odds were well in my favour for a full recovery. I heard that last part and thought, *You mean there is a chance that a full recovery isn't going to be on the cards?*

Surgery went ahead a few days later, and what had been a skin irregularity the size of a fingernail turned into an incision that covered two-thirds of my leg between my knee and ankle, and which would require over one hundred stitches and staples to bind together.

I'm happy to say I recovered in time for the family ski trip to New Zealand in the middle of the year and continue to be cancer-free. I have two check-ups annually, but no ongoing issues.

The entire experience did bring a few things into perspective. This episode started with a visit to the doctor in early January of 2009. In between the first visit for a check-up and the biopsy results I had left the police, and with that I'd jettisoned my dependable income. If the outcome of my cancer had been different and I was forced to take significant time off work, the police would have continued to pay me as I had copious amounts of sick leave built up over twenty years of service. However, having left the police I was on my own, and with no income protection insurance, how would I have paid the bills and mortgage if I'd been sick? I remain very happy with my decision to leave the police and the security of a government career. I just wish I had taken out insurance a little sooner; it's the price I pay for not focusing too much on compliance.

More importantly, though, the experience gave me an opportunity to reflect on what I was doing now and what I planned to do moving forward. Was I happy with things? Taking the time to engage in some naval gazing and ponder the world for a wee second, I found that I was happy with where things were at. I was in a loving relationship with Nic, I was creating and sharing some fantastic experiences with Lachie, Kels and Jack, and I was building some good karma if I needed to cash that in anytime soon with the work I was doing with Hands.

For a brief moment in time I thought about the range of possible implications of my cancer, and leading up to the first couple of check-ups I again considered my life. Having witnessed Khun Rotjana deal with her breast cancer and Khun Thew's absolute resolve not to let her prognosis of six months to live stand in the way, I hardly thought this episode warranted much air time at all. It's all about perspective.

Chapter 36

One Step Followed
by Another

The journey that started over a quarter of a century ago when I graduated from the NSW Police Academy has been a wild one. Never could I have predicted back then that my life would have taken the path it has, resulting in what I do today.

I have no doubt that the pressures I faced as a young constable on the violent streets of Cabramatta gave me the background to deal with the major crime I saw working as a crime scene investigator. And the lessons that I learnt dealing with the complexities of major crime, particularly when working in regional New South Wales when resources were not always close at hand, gave me the ability to step in and step up in times of crisis after the Bali bombings and the Boxing Day tsunami.

The events of 26 December 2004 changed many lives the world over. In the weeks, months and years since the tsunami I have made many life-changing decisions. There have been mistakes, some huge and some hilarious, but you can't change the past, only learn from it.

I feel incredibly fortunate to do what I do each day. I work harder and longer each day than I ever have, but I enjoy what I do more than I ever have. Professionally I am paid to share with organisations my thoughts on leadership, clarity of purpose, building strong teams and how to make it all sustainable. More and more these days I am returning to organisations and conferences that I have previously spoken at and giving them an update on Hands, our growth and the lives that have been saved. I get paid to talk about something that I am passionate about and in turn the stories inspire people to have the courage to bring change to their own lives, to pursue their own dreams.

Those dreams might be on a business level or a personal level. Some of those dreams we will talk about and others we won't. The reason we don't talk about some of them is the fear of what others will say. They will say we are too young, too old, went to the wrong school or are not smart enough. For me, the key to achieving our dreams is to not let other people impose their limitations on us. It really is about focusing on the results and not the excuses. There will always be someone who will tell you why it can't be done. They see that as their job – to hold you back.

Don't let them.

To be travelling the world sharing stories and raising money for Hands came right out of left field. Speaking in Canada one week, New Zealand the next, and Barcelona after that still feels surreal to me. Spending time working in the Kingdom of Saudi Arabia in the middle of 2010, providing advice to a number of Middle Eastern countries on disaster management planning, is something that even twelve months beforehand I wouldn't have been able to see myself doing.

To have raised over four million Australian dollars in the first five years was something I wouldn't have dreamt possible when Gill and I first started Hands. To be making a real and sustainable difference in a community such as Khao Lak inspires me beyond belief.

I love what I do. I love sharing the story of what we've done and what we are creating. I love the opportunity to move some people, rattle others and challenge the thinking of even more.

People talk about a work-life balance.

The very statement implies that work is not part of, or is separate from, your life, and somehow when you stop working you start living. Sadly, for some people that might be true. I spend too much of my time working for it not to be part of my life, for it not to be a source of energy and enjoyment.

The balance, in my opinion, seems to be a little off if you spend the majority of your waking hours in a job you don't enjoy, or spend four weeks a year on holidays trying to escape from the place you spend the other forty-eight weeks.

Such a big part of life is about choice. We all have the choice to do something each day that energises us rather than fills us with regrets. Once you identify the choice, you need the courage to grasp the opportunity. I guess that is why so many stay where it is safe, because they see risk in following their dreams. To my mind, the risk of letting those dreams go is by far greater.

Is there a downside to all the life I lead? The fact that I am so often away from my family is, without question, the only downside. As the kids live the majority of their week with their mum, who does a fantastic job, I hope that the time we spend together is invaluable quality time. But I am sure this is what every parent would like to think, no matter how much time they spend with their kids. I hope that the opportunities such as the bike ride and our annual ski trips, where we ski and snowboard from the first lift of the day till the last, make up a little for my not being around as much as other dads.

I also like to think that they value the work I do. The question of how the kids feel about all of this was answered for me during their first trip to the orphanage back in 2007. When we left the orphanage we were driving back to Phuket and I asked the three of them what they thought of the experience.

Lachie said to me, 'Dad, I understand now why you do what you do.'

Through her school, Kelsey had raised some money to donate to the orphanage. I'd changed it into Thai baht for her and she'd presented it to Khun Rotjana. Kels's comment about her experience was, 'Dad, when I gave them the money it made me feel funny in the tummy, in a good way.'

Jack's observation was, 'They don't have much, do they?'

'No, mate, they don't,' I replied.

He then followed with, 'They sleep on the floor. We should be happy for what we have, shouldn't we?'

I felt as though I had done my job as a dad – for that day at least!

There's no doubt the kids would like their dad around more. However, to do what I do I have to travel and having a clarity of purpose enables me to do it without regret. My lifestyle and the choices I make are not ones that all will judge as right or enviable by any stretch. I don't ask others for approval or understanding, just knowledge that I believe in what I am doing.

I balance the time away from my family knowing that each day I do something related to my work or Hands it has a measurable outcome. When I speak on stage I am not only sharing stories and experiences which I hope add value to those who are present but I am bringing awareness to the kids that we support. Some will do something with that new-found awareness. Some will join the bike ride and raise money, some will travel to one of our renovation projects and others might just tell their friends and families about Hands. But whatever happens there has been change. Even if those sitting in the audience choose to do nothing more with what they have heard, there has still been change because they now have an increased awareness about something they might have known little about. But when someone decides to take action, it means we can continue to bring change to the lives of the kids and communities that we support.

Each of the kids who live at Baan Tharn Namchai has opportunities that didn't exist for them five years ago and some will have opportunities that wouldn't have come to them but for the events on 26 December 2004. We can't change what happened on that day, but we have the ability to change what happens next for them. We can't give them back their parents, brothers and sisters and we don't try. But each day I do something that I hope makes the next day better than the last for these kids. Seeing children such as Game, who now has the opportunity to follow his dream and exercise his ability and potential by studying law at university, is an example of the long-term change that is the result of our commitment.

The experiences of the kids at Home Hug in Yasothon are just as tragic as those at Baan Tharn Namchai, and some would say they are of greater tragedy because of what being associated with HIV-AIDS has meant to their lives. The tsunami that claimed the lives of so many was a natural event, but the sexual abuse and rape of children is a hideous act of depravity.

When I first arrived at the orphanage at Yasothon, I struggled to comprehend some of the stories that were relayed to me. How was it that in a country such as Thailand children could be forced to forage for their food in nearby bushland, catching rats and lizards for their dinner because their economic situation forced them to choose between medicine to combat the virus that had invaded their body and food? In whatever direction your moral compass might point you, what was occurring at Home Hug just shouldn't be allowed to happen. It seemed so easy to turn things around, and so that's what we did.

Khun Thew recently spent a week with my family in our home

in Sydney. I walked into the lounge room early one morning and she was sitting staring out into the bushland that backs onto the rear of our house, watching and listening to the kookaburras singing their merry song. I explained that the kookaburra is my favourite bird and we say it is laughing when it makes the sound that we could hear.

We sat together on the lounge that morning with the sun streaming in through the windows, and for a couple of hours we talked whilst the remainder of the house slept. In a slow and soothing voice she told me more of her story, and of how we had given her a reason to live and to be strong. She said that what we had done had made the children strong; we had stopped them dying. No longer was it a choice between food or medicine, now they could have both.

Khun Thew said that prior to my visit in March of 2010, she was preparing to die. Weeks before she had buried the bodies of three children in one day. Fairness doesn't come into life and death; if it did, children wouldn't die so young. But was it fair that Khun Thew should live her life like this, and as she approached what she believed was the end of her life, should this be her final memory? Khun Thew knew that without any change on the horizon for their circumstances, the children in her care would continue to die, despite her best attempts, and this knowledge had taken its toll. She had finally lost all hope. After burying the three children, she sat on a chair at the orphanage, wrapped in blankets to protect her body, which was withered from the cancer. She had lost the strength to go on, she had lost hope and she had lost her will to fight for life. Her service to the children had kept her alive for many years, but now it was no longer enough to keep her going. She told me that she sat on the chair, alone, and closed her eyes, prepared never to open them again. She was now ready to die.

Sitting on the lounge in my home listening to this story I was wiping tears from my face as they rolled down my cheeks. She reached out, took my arm and started to give me a gentle massage that felt so healing. She explained that sitting on the chair at Home Hug, this was what she felt, sixteen tiny pairs of hands were massaging her arms, shoulders and neck. She opened her eyes and there standing in front of her were the rest of the children, crying just as I was now. Tears were running down their faces as they willed their mother to live.

She came close, but it was not Khun Thew's time. I saw the strength return to her body over that first year after I met her. From having surrendered her fight for life and walking with the aid of a crutch to riding eight hundred kilometres on a bike, it has been an amazing transformation. She is indeed one amazing lady.

In what can only be a cruel and strange coincidence, both Khun Thew and Khun Rotjana have faced a serious and very real fight for life. Both have come as close as you'd ever want to come to finishing their time on this planet, but both have come out the other side. Neither lives without continuing health challenges, but both attribute their survival to the intervention of Hands and the very real hope we have given them as individuals and the children they so lovingly care for and support.

I am filled with optimism and hope for what we can achieve in the future, and this grows with a resounding conviction. It all started with a couple of steps, not knowing the direction or path I would take. But I'm running, and just like Forrest Gump, I feel like running for quite a while yet.

Epilogue

I haven't been to war, but I feel as though I have now been to a war zone.

It wasn't the damage to the buildings, or the sight of cars that had been lifted off the street and deposited on the second floor of an office block; and as horrifying as the victims' stories were, they weren't what left me speechless either.

It was the scale of the destruction of the Japanese earthquake and tsunami that I struggled to comprehend. I stood atop mountains looking down into cities that simply no longer existed. It wasn't as though these cities had been merely damaged or even destroyed; they just didn't exist anymore. The evidence of their previous occupation was the concrete floor slabs that remained. The rest of the buildings were to be found up to ten kilometres away in any direction you might turn.

The Japanese had prepared for the events of 11 March 2011. They had built sea walls standing ten metres above the high-tide mark to protect their cities. At school the kids undertook monthly evacuation drills knowing that the earthquake would come one day. No one expected the almost inconceivable size of the wall of water that would follow.

I was staggered by the tsunami in Thailand in December 2004, and that deadly wall of water had reached the height of ten metres. In Japan they can only wish that ten metres was as high as it got. I heard accounts from survivors who had stood on the roof of a four-storey building and had water wash over the roof. There were estimates of the water exceeding heights of thirty metres in places. And as I stood on the side of a hill well above the destruction, I witnessed scarring to tree trunks so high up it defied logic that water could have come so high.

Travelling through the Iwate and Miyagi prefectures of north-eastern Japan, I met many families who had survived the seemingly unsurvivable, and they recounted to me their near-death experiences. Sitting on the tatami floor mats in the home of one couple, the wife explained how she had lost her parents and brother, their bodies yet to be recovered, and the husband had lost his mother, but he was thankful he had recovered her body.

The stories of sacrifice, of choosing who would live and who would die, were chillingly familiar to those I had heard in Thailand. One Japanese lady recounted her story of running from the water with her mother and her daughter. It was obvious to the two older ladies, the two mothers, that the chances of these three generations surviving was slim, and the risk of trying was that all three might in fact die. As the realisation of the dire situation become clear to the grandmother, she struck at her daughter's arm, which was pulling her through the water, breaking the grip and giving her daughter and her granddaughter a better chance of survival. The grandmother was quickly washed away to her death.

The journey that I made into Japan was very different from the one I made to Thailand. I wasn't there to identify bodies; that chapter of my life was closed. I was travelling through these devastated areas with my eldest son Lachie and the managing director of a large Japanese NGO. I had come to see if we could help, if there was a need. It was no surprise that there was, and is, a need for help; it's just different from the scenario we faced in Thailand. The Japanese government will take care of the infrastructure and they will do it well. Mending the souls and broken hearts will be a different challenge, and that may well be beyond the government's ability.

The similarities to the events of Thailand weren't limited to what I saw and heard. Just as my marriage unravelled during my time in Thailand in 2005, I found my relationship with Nic had come to an end as well. I didn't return homeless as I did from Thailand; this time it was just to an empty home.

With tears running down her face the wife of Mr Hata San said in a voice just above a whisper, 'I have lost my parents and my brother, I don't know if I will ever find their bodies, I should be thankful for my life.'

Despite our own challenges and troubles, we should all rejoice in what we have and look for the next opportunity to laugh.

Acknowledgements

One of the things that comes from writing a book such as this is the time you take to reflect upon that part of your life you're writing about. Without such a project, never would I have spent time thinking so much about the past.

The twenty-two and a half years I had in the NSW Police Force, starting off in uniform but quickly moving into the forensic area, presented many opportunities to work with gifted and dedicated men and women who turned up each day to do the best they could. The police force offers a wide range of challenges and opportunities on a daily basis. I also got to work with people who would leave an impression on the way I wanted to conduct myself. Former Commissioner Ken Moroney and Assistant Commissioner Peter Walsh were both leaders who took the time to invest in those they worked with. Both understood the importance of being present as a leader and spending time with the troops on the ground.

Dr Tony Raymond was the Director of the Forensic Services Group and then the Director of NIFS, and I had the opportunity to work with Tony on both occasions. Not before or since have I

301

worked with anyone who had the work ethic, integrity or absolute conviction for their job as Tony. Working with Tony at NIFS I got to know him as a man and not just a workhorse, and that was a greater pleasure.

Working with both Julian Slater and Karl Kent from the Australian Federal Police in Bali and then Thailand was a great pleasure. I left both operations as a better leader from working with them and Karl showed me that you can laugh at work and still achieve.

To Gill Williams, my mate from the UK who introduced me to Khun Rotjana and the beautiful kids of Baan Tharn Namchai. You showed the way, Gilly, and I just picked up the ball.

It's always easy to jump aboard a cause when there's momentum. To the board members of Hands who have been there from the start and showed such commitment and unwavering support, it means so much on a personal level that I know you believe in me and I feel your support every day. Scott Stein, Kay Spencer, Willie Moulden and Lyle Van Leeuwen, thank you. Hands is only what it is because of your commitment.

Matt Church, thank you, mate, for your Thought Leadership back in 2005, helping me believe that there was value in what I had to say and then continuing to support me each time I wavered.

Khru Prateep Unsongtham Hata, you're an inspirational leader whose grace and fight for those less fortunate has been a lifetime vocation, and your passion today, over thirty years on, is amazing and often beyond belief. I walk behind you in your footsteps eager to emulate not just what you have done but also how you have done it.

Khun Rotjana Phraesrithong, in spite of your own health challenges each day you fight for a better life for the children and broader community of Khao Lak. I believe I am a better father to my children from the way you care for the seventy-eight children at Baan Tharn Namchai.

Khun Suthasinee Noiin (or Khun Thew), your eagerness to

learn, to take on challenges and to do what you can to further improve the lives of children that few others care about, and to have done so for three decades, is hard to fathom. To remain so stoic in the face of personal hardship beggars belief. I have learnt from you that courage has a level I had not previously witnessed. Without question I am a better person for having met you.

Writing a book of quality, which I hope you find this is, is not the work of an author in isolation. There is a team, and, like any good production and just like the Hands team, the team that has helped pull this book together is made up of many people. To those who read one or all the chapters along the way and provided their feedback, your comments have been invaluable. Allan Matthews from Perth, if others had the belief in me that you did right from day one, this book would have been out years earlier, but then we would have missed some of the great stories.

Sophie Hamley, my literary agent, thank you for taking me on, knowing immediately the best publisher to go to and working with me to knock more than a few of the rough edges off along the way. Julia Stiles, my editor, you took the book from a factual account of events to a story filled with emotion, but I have to mention your continual questions of 'But how did you feel?' – I am a man and you have asked me to explore my feelings just way too much during this project! And to my publisher Alex Craig and senior editor Brianne Collins at Pan Macmillan, thank you both for your support, firstly in believing there was a book and then getting it to where it is. But I have to ask: why do you ladies focus so much on feelings?

This book covers the last twenty-five years of my life and for the first twenty I had Nicole, my ex-wife, by my side. Thank you for your support in all those years, your continued encouragement now but most of all for the way you care for and love our three beautiful children, Lachlan, Kelsey and Jack. They are the gorgeous human beings they are because of your presence.

Lachie, Kels and Jack, you guys have missed out on plenty, but I hope the journey we have made is one about which you can say that at least Dad had a crack, and we did have fun along the way.

To Nicole Perry, thank you for your unquestioning support and giving me the freedom to be who I am. You bring beauty, intelligence and a wicked sense of humour to my every day and that makes life an absolute ball. Thank you, beautiful lady, for joining me and the kids in Sydney, and then on the ski fields in New Zealand when you couldn't ski and were petrified of heights and still jumped on the chairlift. Thank you for joining me on the first, second, third . . . bike rides, when you previously didn't ride a bike, and thank you equally for sitting on the lounge with me watching footy, when you don't like footy.

And finally to the kids of Thailand in Baan Tharn Namchai and Home Hug, thank you for opening your hearts and homes to all of us at Hands.

ALSO AVAILABLE FROM PAN MACMILLAN

Tammie Matson
Elephant Dance

It's the middle of the night in the Namibian desert when Tammie Matson wakes to find two bull elephants standing just inches from her head. Totally vulnerable in her tiny tent, she promises the night: 'If you just let me survive tonight I will give up Africa. I'll give it all up. Just don't let them stand on me.'

It's not a promise she will easily keep. At 29, Tammie has spent half her life in Africa working as a conservationist. Africa – with its big skies and extraordinary wildlife – is her first love, and Tammie has just landed her dream gig researching human-elephant conflict.

But as her thirties approach, Tammie is conscious that Africa has left little room for pursuit of dreams that are becoming increasingly important: a partner, kids, a house . . . With her visa running out and close to broke, it seems like Africa may just force Tammie to give it up after all.

On returning to Australia, Tammie unexpectedly lands a job at the World Wide Fund for Nature in Sydney. There she meets Andy, a charismatic Brit, and Africa suddenly has a rival. But she's not ready to give up on the elephants yet . . .

From the magic of Bushmanland in Namibia to the civil strife of Assam, India, *Elephant Dance* takes us to the heart of a quest for elephants to live peacefully in a world with too many people and too little space.

Passionate, funny, and wise, *Elephant Dance* is also a young woman's story of self-discovery, love and the courage it takes to follow a calling, especially when life has other plans.

Dr Catherine Hamlin with John Little
The Hospital by the River

Gynaecologists Catherine and Reg Hamlin left Australia in 1959 on a
short contract to establish a midwifery school in Ethiopia. Almost 50
years later, Catherine is still there, running one of the most outstanding
medical programs in the world. Through this work, thousands of women
have been able to resume a normal existence after living as outcasts.
The Hamlins dedicated their lives to women suffering the catastrophic
effects of obstructed labour – a problem easily dealt with in the developed
world by assisted delivery or caesarean section, but disastrous without
medical intervention. The awful injuries that such labour produces are
called fistulae, and until the Hamlins began their work in Ethiopia, fistula
sufferers were neglected and forgotten – a vast group of women facing a
lifetime of incapacity and degradation.

Catherine and Reg have successfully operated on almost 30,000 women,
and the Addis Ababa Fistula Hospital, the hospital they opened in 1975,
has become a major teaching institution for surgeons from all over
Ethiopia, Africa and the developing world. Since Reg's death, Catherine
has continued their work. As well as being made a companion of the
Order of Australia, being awarded the ANZAC Peace Prize and the
coveted Gold Medal from the Royal College of Surgeons, Catherine was
nominated for the Nobel Peace Prize in 1999.

The Hospital by the River is Catherine's story. Set against the vivid
backdrop of Ethiopia, it is a moving and utterly compelling account of an
extraordinary life.